SHAKESPEARE UNRAVELLED

Court plays: the 1623 deception

SHAKESPEARE UNRAVELLED

Court plays: the 1623 deception

A practical analysis of the First Folio of 1623,
attributed to William Shakespeare

PAULINE AND MICHAEL BLACK

ISBN: 978-0-9935612-0-7

Printed and Bound in Great Britain by
CPI Books (UK) Croydon CR0 4YY

This book is dedicated to Mr and Mrs A. E. Griffiths without whose encouragement and generous support we would not have been able to produce this investigation

AUTHORS' NOTE

This is a hitherto undeveloped argument for the multiple authorship of the plays in the First Folio of 1623 resulting largely from the original literary patronage of Mary Herbert, Countess of Pembroke, nee Sidney and some of her close relatives and descendants.

The Countess and her brother Philip had decades earlier gathered a group of contemporary poets and playwrights at her country seat of Wilton aiming to develop English to rival Italian poetry. Literary patronage was then continued by her sons William and Philip, Earls of Pembroke and Montgomery respectively and her brother Robert, Earl of Leicester.

In 1620 the Herbert family staunchly Protestant and humanist in their philosophy and fearing the resurgence of Catholicism (by the marriage of Prince Charles to a Spanish Infanta) were able through these plays to secure an outstanding national literary heritage.

Fulfilling their duty as patrons by protecting living writers and editors from domestic press control, and impending Catholic repression, the volume was published using the alias of the scribe, theatre-sharer, popular playhouse play-dealer and businessman William Shakespeare. Deceased seven years earlier Shakespeare had published popular theatre play-texts under his own name several years before he left London in 1610.

The Lancastrian history plays are key here, since they help to confirm the "approved" version of history that kept Queen Elizabeth I on the throne; the overthrow of Richard III and the seizure of his crown are rendered legitimate in these plays peopled by Herbert-Sidney ancestors.

Candidates for involvement in the multiple authorship theory, supported by scholarly analysis of language and style include: Fletcher, Peele, Marlowe, Kyd, Middleton, Daniel, Massinger, Anthony Bacon and Fulke Greville with editing by Ben Jonson and John Florio. The Italian plays are likely to have been introduced into England by Michelangelo Florio in the mid-sixteenth century. These have been identified by academics as collaborative writers while some contribution to the First Folio may have been made also by aristocrats.

The authors put forward strong arguments against accepting William Shakespeare as the author of any of the thirty-six plays attributed to him and seek to dispel the notion that the First Folio plays were intended for the uneducated masses: instead they were written by leading writers and performed for the court. Abridged, memorial versions were adapted for the outdoor popular stage.

LIST OF ILLUSTRATIONS

Our thanks are due to the National Portrait Gallery for permission to reproduce illustrations 4, 5, 6, and 10: to Getty Images for illustrations 1, 2, 8, 9, 11, 12 and Custard Design for design and illustrations and Geoff Fisher for typesetting and book design.

CONTENTS

Appendices

INTRODUCTION

IN the literary firmament of the Jacobean age two publications shine especially brightly. The 1611 King James' Bible and the First Folio of 1623. These two remarkable endeavours each signified the work of many hands, yet there exists a unity pervading both of these works which overcomes any awareness of multiple authorship. The new translation of the Holy scriptures, seven years in composition and derived from the Greek, Latin, Hebrew and Aramaic of the many earlier texts, followed the Hampton Court Conference of 1604. This convention was the early attempt by James I to reconcile the divisive Biblical disputation which then existed between the Christian Puritan faction favouring the Geneva Bible and the Bishop's Bible accepted by the Anglican Church.

As was to follow with the First Folio publication a decade later, the newly authorised Bible was to shape the English language with its dramatic vocabulary, beauty of phrasing, striking metaphor and not least its revealing insights into human behaviour. Yet, surprisingly this monumental work is frequently read and quoted without any realisation that more than forty ecclesiastical scholars were party to its eventual production. These academics were formed into six committees supervised by other theologians, who themselves reported finally to two senior Bishops. The resulting literary masterpiece is a testament to the participation of many learned minds in its construction.

The First Folio, while not on the same scale as the Bible – although without question is itself a towering achievement – owed the creation of the thirty six dramatic works to the many writers, translators and editors who flourished under an array of patrons from the mid-sixteenth century up to 1620.

Taking this longer perspective of the volume's gestation also serves to highlight the religious and political influences that were continuously at play throughout many generations in England preceding 1620. A continuous backdrop of competing views concerning faith, royal absolutism and the nation's governance accompanied the exceptional upsurge in patronage and poetic creativity that occurred during the Elizabethan age and the two decades which followed. These factors, as well as the personal concerns of patrons, all had a bearing on the motivation of the writers and their benefactors who were to create the First Folio publication.

The period in history that preceded 1623, from the latter part of Elizabeth's reign to the first decades of James' rule, marked the end of the Middle Ages and the beginnings of the modern world. An England united with Scotland in 1603, in principle, that had embarked upon a journey which embraced Parliamentary government, economic advance and imperialist foreign policy; an England of religious tolerance and scientific progress.

These changes were accompanied by a remarkable flowering of literary activity created by writers and dramatists, aristocrats and courtiers. Despite the marked advances in England's enlightenment in this era its writers by no means enjoyed freedom of expression and publication. A climate of severe censorship was ever-present during the progress and production of the First Folio. This climate of creative inhibition was to have a distinct bearing upon the volume's public presentation in 1623 and offers the most convincing explanation of the false authorship.

The underlying leitmotif which marked the entirety of intellectual and cultural expression in England throughout this period of history is the intense religious conflict between a small independent Protestant state and a powerful Roman Catholic adversary. Catholics considered Queen Elizabeth a wicked apostate, a bastard, a tyrant who should be removed from her position – by force, if necessary. Hence the attempt by the Spanish Armada in 1588, and again in 1596 and 1597 to conquer England. The Catholic duty was to 'rescue' England from heresy and damnation; if not by invasion then by internal subversion.

In contrast, Protestants in England, influenced by the teaching of Luther, Calvin and other Continental theologians, described the Pope and Catholicism generally as the "Anti-Christ." The characteristics of the opposing faith were portrayed as the worship of idols and other false images. Adding fuel to the flames of this conflict of faith was the commercial rivalry between the two major adversaries in the New World, England and Spain. This was exacerbated further by England's encouragement of piracy on the high seas, mainly targeted at Spanish merchant ships.

By the latter decades of the sixteenth century England had become the bedrock of European Protestantism, apart from the five years of "Bloody" Mary's reign. The Reformed faith held sway in the country despite external threats, internal sedition and even attempted regicide inspired by the Catholic foe. During the reign of Mary I, the many executions, banishment for some and the loss of lands and position for others made an indelible mark upon the Protestant aristocracy, well after her demise.

During the reigns of both Elizabeth and James there was a continuous outpouring of polemical, anti-Catholic writings in religious tracts and commentaries, while many plays celebrated the 'true' Protestant faith and England's legitimate monarchy. Each successive generation was conscious of the Catholic threat: the excesses of the Marian upheaval and dark thoughts of Protestant martyrdom never left public consciousness. A copy of Foxe's *Book of Martyrs* was placed in every Church as a reminder of the past. By the end of the second decade of the seventeenth century dread of the Spanish Catholics had reached another peak of apprehension. This in turn affected the 'official' authorship of the 1623 First Folio.

There existed a conviction by the leaders of the Protestant cause that the Pope, in league with a powerful Spain, were intent upon reviving the old religion and Papal powers. This was an eventuality that threatened the English monarchy, the Anglican Church and the power of the Protestant noble families. Not only the position and property of the English hierarchy was at risk: there was every likelihood that at least some nobles would also lose their lives if England was subsumed by Spain.

Following the Dissolution of the Monasteries, Church lands and property awarded to the king's supporters enriched leading noble families such as the Sidneys, Dudleys and Herberts. It was this group who were to head the Protestant movement for many generations that followed, also becoming the principal patrons of major English poets and playwrights. Descendants of these Lancastrian supporting noblemen continued the tradition of patronage given in earlier times by their forbears to writers such as Chaucer, Gower, Lydgate and other literary figures who presaged English humanism.

Elizabeth I inherited a depleted treasury and in the early part of her reign it was apparent that the breadth of studies and scholastic strength of Oxford and Cambridge Universities (England's intellectual treasury) had lagged behind their Continental counterparts. The challenge was to revive them to their former positions as respected centres of learning encompassing Italian Renaissance humanism and the study of Classical and Modern languages. The task was shouldered by Protestant patrons, none more so than Robert Dudley, Earl of Leicester, Chancellor of Oxford. It was a civic duty he shared with Sir William Cecil, statesman and Chancellor of Cambridge.

England's ensuing academic and literary renaissance, coloured by a distinctive Italian influence, had reached a high point by the turn of the sixteenth century. During the next two decades a host of playwrights, almost entirely university educated, had created a wealth of dramatic works: a number of them still admired and performed to the present day.

This exceptional creative output was unmatched in Europe yet it faced possible oblivion in the face of censorship imposed by a foreign power: a conquering Spain with its alien religion and strict opposition to freedom of expression.

It was incumbent upon the leading Protestant patrons, the Sidney and Herbert family, to preserve their family and Humanistic heritage as well as honour their obligation to protect living writers and editors from the wrath of the threatened Inquisition.

The false authorship of the deceased William Shakespeare, provided protection for writers and editors albeit misleading the many generations that followed. The publication achieved its objective: survival. The extended Sidney-Herbert contribution to literary history lived forever in the pages of the First Folio.

In summary this book explores how and why the First Folio came to be published. It is not yet another exposé of the William Shakespeare deception although that wishful claim is rejected in the light of the contemporary evidence presented here. More positively than hitherto the analysis sets out a number of significant facets of the First Folio authorship puzzle usually overlooked. Together these contributory elements explain how the dramatic works reached their final form in the 1623 publication attributed to William Shakespeare.

The authors propose that many First Folio plays originated decades before that date, as early as 1550, written by well- educated authors for performance at court or noble houses played predominately by Boy actor troupes. These complex and often intellectually challenging dramas were not popular entertainment for the masses but fashioned for the Elizabethan and Jacobean intelligentsia.

For publication, the works of many playwrights were selected by Mary Sidney, Countess of Pembroke and her like-minded sons William Herbert, third earl of Pembroke, Philip Herbert, first Earl of Montgomery. Final editing and re-writing is credited to their literary friends who shared similar ambition for a cultured national language: principally by literary figures Sir Fulke Greville and John Florio. Other writers may also have made a contribution to the eighteen plays previously unpublished before 1623.

PART ONE

WILLIAM SHAKESPEARE/SHAKSPER

A literary colossus? Historical evidence is conspicuous by its absence

Poor poet Ape, that would be thought our chief,
Whose works are e'en the frippery of wit,
From brocage* is so bold a thief,
As we, the robbed, leave rage, and pity it,
At first he made low shifts, would pick and glean,
Buy the reversion of old plays; now grown
To a little wealth, and credit in the scene,
He takes up all, makes each man's wit his own
Ben Jonson

(This passage means: Poor imitation of a poet who would like to be known as our leader, who gleaned scraps from pawnbroking pledges. Perhaps buying the rights to old plays, then, becoming richer, acquired other texts boldly claiming them as his own compositions. When challenged the imposter shrugs off the accusation saying the ignorant audience cares not who wrote the work. The suffering authors, 'we the robbed' forbear rage and merely pity the deception. While the ignorant cannot understand the difference, the educated and discerning will recognise the inadequacies of a play made of borrowings instead of the complete work.)

*Brocage: a treaty of a broker or agent (by selling)

THE paramount myth to be questioned in this investigation is the assumption that the First Folio collection of 1623 is from the pen of William Shakespeare of Stratford-upon-Avon. All of the evidence about Shakespeare points overwhelmingly to this not being so. In truth, the name of actor-businessman and money lender William Shakspere, as spelled in his will, has been altered to Shakespeare occasionally Shake-spere and used as a pseudonym. A falsehood.

There are six surviving signatures written by Shakespeare himself, and these are all attached to legal documents. The six signatures appear on four documents: a deposition in the Bellott v. Mountjoy legal case, dated May 11th 1612; the purchase of a house in Blackfriars, London, dated March 10th 1613; the mortgage of the same house, dated March 11th 1613 and his Last Will and Testament, which contains three signatures, one on each page, dated March 25th 1616.

The signatures appear as follows: '*Willm Shakp*', '*William Shaksper*', '*Wm Shakspe*', '*William Shakespeare*', '*Willm Shakespeare*' and '*By me William Shak-speare*'.

In the public records the Stratford family in question had used the spelling Shaksper and not Shakespeare for several generations, as Professor A.J. Pointon has researched in great detail in *The Man who was Never Shakespeare*. While inconsistent spellings of a name were not uncommon at the time in question, this particular confusion (that may well have been a deliberate deceit) sets the tone for the many inconsistencies concerning the unparalleled acclaim given to William Shakespeare as the greatest writer of all time. For the purpose of this investigation the spelling 'Shakespeare' has been adopted to avoid confusion.

Shakespeare was recorded in his time as an actor, money-lender and landowner, but not as a writer. The first appearance of the name 'William Shakespeare' was not recorded until the dedication of the long poem *Venus and Adonis* at its publication in 1593, when Shakespeare was aged twenty-nine. There was no evidence of any written work of any kind composed by Shakespeare before this date, neither in Stratford-upon-Avon nor in London.

The amount of information that exists about William Shakespeare demonstrates that he did not have the education and intellectual capability for such a huge and stylistically varied literary output. William Shakespeare's parents were illiterate, as were his own children. This was a provincial family engaged in trade without any cultural interests.

Moreover, evidence about Shakespeare's life, as distinct from the attribution of his name to many literary works, points to a man of commerce operating within the world of popular theatre, usury and property speculation. There are some one hundred and fifty salient facts known about the Shakespeare family, none of which supports the claim of William Shakespeare to be a writer. There are seventy facts that have survived concerning William Shakespeare, the man, yet once again none of these indicate a life of writing for the stage or indeed for any other artistic purpose.

Because books were so valuable it was standard practice at the time to put the name of the owner, or their book-plate, inside their volumes. There is no record that Shakespeare owned or even appeared to have used books. Yet it is claimed that he referred to many books in order to write the plays attributed to him. There is only one letter sent to him that we know of: a request for a loan from *"our kinsman-William Shakespeare"* by a Stratford worthy, and that letter was never sent.

Shakespeare, from a humble, unsophisticated background did not associate with the highly educated, and usually multi-lingual, English court society: his vastly greater superiors. Any conversation emanating from a courtier would have been the issuing of orders to an inferior. Yet, of the thirty-seven plays said to be written by William Shakespeare, no less than thirty-four have Kings, Emperors, Princes and Dukes as main characters. A class with which the writer would not have had the slightest familiarity. Added to which, the author or authors of the First Folio works enjoyed specialist knowledge of English law, falconry, the court of Navarre and a familiarity with aristocratic pastimes such as the Tilting Yard, Royal Tennis and the Riding School: all activities totally remote from the son of a provincial leather seller.

The literary sources of the First Folio plays are mostly to be found in classical literature as well as Italian and French Renaissance works. Such knowledge implies an exceptional degree of learning never found in the character and known life of William Shakespeare. The vocabulary employed in the First Folio is immense, certainly over 15,000 (some scholars claim over 20,000) words which again could not have been known by Shakespeare. This is an unbelievable range of expression for someone who, at best, received the level of education granted to the son of a Guild member. This tuition would not have included Greek or modern languages. It is especially striking that William Shakespeare's vocabulary, used in the First Folio and the two long poems, was at least four or five times that of the leading writers of the age and far greater than any other author in history by a wide margin.

It is significant, too, that there was no contemporary mention of the death of William Shakespeare by any of the literary patrons or men of letters in London. There was no eulogy concerning William Shakespeare's death written by his fellow poets though that was the normal form for writers of distinction. The poet Ben Jonson wrote some 350 epigrams and elegies, some of which were in memory of contemporary poets but not a single one is addressed to William Shakespeare. Despite the huge praise heaped upon Shakespeare by Jonson in the 1623 publication in contradiction, Jonson recorded no thoughts about the Bard's death in 1616. It seems the demise of William Shakespeare was not mentioned in correspondence by educated society at the time.

Ben Jonson's *Discoveries* (Published in 1641 six years after his death) advises the reading of the five 'best' English authors and he names: Philip Sidney, John Donne, John Gower, Geoffrey Chaucer and Edmund Spenser, but not Shakespeare. In *Wits Miserie* of 1596 Thomas Lodge, the playwright, singled out '*Divine Wits*' as John Lyly, Edmund Spenser, Samuel Daniel, Michael Drayton and Thomas Nashe, but once again Shakespeare is not included despite having works attributed to him by this date.

The scholar Henry Peacham named the seven greatest deceased writers of the Elizabethan era in his 1622 book *The Complete Gentleman*. The authors listed were: Edmund Spenser, Samuel Daniel, Sir Philip Sidney, Edward Dyer, Lord Buckhurst, Lord Paget and Edward de Vere, Earl of Oxford. The book, however, did not include William Shakespeare as a writer even though many of the plays and poems attributed to him by that date had been published.

The poet of distinction Michael Drayton in his *Poets and Poetry* wrote approvingly of many poets and these included: Chaucer, Gower, Howard, Earl of Surrey, Wyatt, Gascoigne, Churchyard, Spenser, Sidney, Marlowe and Nashe but of Shakespeare only a comic verse is used and with reference to the stage:

> *And be it said of thee,*
> *Shakespeare, thou hadst as smooth a comic vein*
> *Fitting the sock, and in thy natural brain*
> *as strong conception, and as clear a rage,*
> *As any one that trafficked with the stage.*

Again it seems astonishing that William Shakespeare was never appointed Poet Laureate despite his supposedly outstanding contribution to England's literary life. In other relevant records Shakespeare is oddly absent.

A valuable record of the playwrights of the late Elizabethan and early Jacobean eras exists in the 'Diary' of the stage impresario Philip Henslowe. Yet of the more than a dozen playwrights commissioned by him and recorded in the pages of the diary William Shakespeare is never mentioned, either in receipt of a writing fee or having been commissioned to write for the stage.

Following Shakespeare's death in 1616 there was no documentation discovered of any books, manuscripts or notes relating to the great Shakespeare's literary life at Stratford-upon-Avon or in London. Equally there was, even more surprisingly, no comment made about William Shakespeare by the educated Dr John Hall, a local physician and Shakespeare's son-in-law.

Dr Hall wrote about those of his patients who had made some contribution to literature notably Michael Drayton, the Warwickshire playwright, but Hall never mentioned his father-in-law supposedly the literary giant of the age and domiciled, late in life, in Stratford. Dr John Hall taught his wife, the daughter of the great writer, to read.

Traditional literary history of the Bard romanticises that a figure of national stature lived in Stratford-upon-Avon, but it seems this was not the case. Local records indicate that respect was afforded to William Shakespeare as a landowner and businessman. No records whatsoever exist supporting literary fame or even some modicum of artistic standing in the town.

This lack of public comment in London and Stratford, or any formal appreciation of the author William Shakespeare by the leading poets and patrons of the age, appears quite inexplicable. Equally remarkable is that at the height of his supposedly great powers of composition, Shakespeare was not called upon by royalty, or was himself prompted, to pen a sonnet upon major national occasions despite being an obvious choice as a leading writer.

The death of Queen Elizabeth, the accession of King James I, the marriage of Princess Elizabeth, the tragic death of Prince Henry were all memorable events that stirred the nation. Where was the poetic remembrance of these figures captured in verse by William Shakespeare? There were none at all. Moreover, the famed poet was not interred in Westminster Abbey alongside other literary giants of the age, such as Edmund Spenser. It appears that William Shakespeare was not venerated for his literary art in any way by his contemporaries other than by second-hand comments and these were mostly derogatory.

On the contrary, there is substantial extant evidence of Shakespeare as a businessman, money-lender, property dealer and landowner as well as holding a share in a theatre. How this man known for commercial dealing came to acquire the mantle of literary genius is a question which has beset investigators for centuries.

Nonetheless, while William Shakespeare: the outstanding playwright is a hugely doubtful assumption it would not be illogical to accept that as a boy, Shakespeare did receive sufficient education at the local grammar school to become a scribe, or copier, and was thus able to provide a valuable service within the world of popular theatre. Charles Hamilton, graphologist, suggests that, having studied Shakespeare's existing six signatures, the handwriting in chancery script clearly shows that Shakespeare had obtained the writing skill indicative of a scribe.

Further evidence for Shakespeare as a scribe is to be found in the Northumberland Manuscript folder, discovered in 1867 in Northumberland House, London. This was a collection of various writings of the statesman Sir Francis Bacon, who is recorded as employing copyists in his scriptorium at Twickenham Park. Only the cover and list of contents have survived time and a fire, but the cover of the folder carries different styles of signature of the Shakespeare name with fancy doodles that may indicate 'time-wasting' by an employee awaiting instructions from his employer.

Shakespeare fits the role of a person responsible for copying the work of playwrights and also 'cobbling together' memorial versions of works performed at court or in noble houses by the playing company of which he was a member. Later these versions would be staged in a simple, short form for the popular theatre. The street-wise scribe was also in a good position to acquire existing plays in return for unredeemed loans, other texts from the effects of deceased writers and by being in possession, as the book-holder, of surplus scripts held by the play-group.

These works genuinely 'owned' by William Shakespeare could then, not unfairly, be sold to printers. At the time playwright collaboration was commonplace and copyright virtually non-existent. The legal ownership of written work only existed for members of the Stationers' Guild. The printers and publishers of the Stationers' Company were protected by their powerful trade body that was itself an instrument of control for the state.

Considering afresh the motive for the gathering of the works in the First Folio demands a more believable explanation than that provided by John Heminge and Henry Condell in the First Folio introduction. These were the two unlearned stage 'players' who had seemingly the 'foresight' to collect Shakespeare's three-dozen plays over a period of more than twenty years.

The assertion of the two players rests on the probability that they had access to all of these original and apparently 'unblotted' manuscripts as they describe them. Added to which, a number of the plays that were not published until 1623 are thought by some scholars to have been written, wholly or in part, after Shakespeare's death seven years earlier. Furthermore, Heminge and Condell had no right to sell plays performed by, and the property of, *The King's Men*. This is an account of the plays derivation that is highly improbable.

John Heminge and Henry Condell knew perfectly well that William Shakespeare had retired to Stratford seven years before his death, so it was simply untrue, as they state in their explanation, that the great writer had no time to revise his works. Conversely, it appears that during his many years in retirement the great writer had no interest either in revising or publishing any of his remarkable range of dramatic works but instead extended his property portfolio and speculated in grain.

The claim by these two relatively impecunious retired stage actors of initiating the First Folio is clearly unconvincing. These old actors would have been in no position to fund or organise such an expensive publication and, unbelievably, obtain dedicatees bearing the status of two premier earls of England. The tone of their address to William, 3rd Earl of Pembroke, and Philip, 1st Earl of Montgomery and boon companion of King James, does not ring true: the wording is far too familiar for people of their lowly rank.

The frontispiece of the First Folio has occasioned much doubt regarding its authenticity as a true portrait of the claimed author. Confusion also exists regarding the skilful engraver Martin Droeshout, an English engraver of Flemish descent and a Protestant migrant.

Martin Droeshout was the originator of several title pages of superior skill than shown by the Shakespeare engraving. The Shakespeare portrait has many clumsy features, notably the position of the head floating above the too-small body, the two asymmetrical armholes and the narrowness of the doublet on the right-hand side. It is unclear on what this artificial interpretation of a real person was based. It seems this engraving cannot be a portrait of William Shakespeare, who died seven years prior to publication, since as far as we know there would be no likeness to follow.

While the engraver's work does demonstrate a low level of competence, as a title page it certainly lacks the draughtsmanship of the elder Martin Droeshout. It is likely to be an apprentice piece of a make-believe figure by his namesake and nephew, another Martin Droeshout.

Much is made of the glowing description of the First Folio author by Ben Jonson, but equally the encomium can be interpreted as a satirical commentary upon William Shakespeare's skill as a plagiarist and acquirer of literary work. Certainly Jonson rarely referred to Shakespeare elsewhere in his lifetime of observations about fellow poets and when he did it was with scant respect.

A careful reading of Ben Jonson's eulogy in the First Folio reveals another Shakespeare: a figure that is ridiculed by exaggeration. The claimed author is portrayed with simply preposterous hyperbole that is in-keeping with the mischievous wit of Jonson. The tribute is intended to expose the comic, fraudulent *soul of the age* for those able to decipher the writer's real message. Unfortunately this witty yet mocking tribute has been taken at face-value by most readers over the years and consolidates the Shakespeare myth.

Ben Jonson, Poet Laureate, leading comic playwright and writer of masques was not deceived, but no doubt was commissioned to play his key part in this fraud. It must be remembered that Jonson did know William Shakespeare, who had performed a small acting part in one of Jonson's productions: itself strange behaviour for the outstanding writer of the age!

In Jonson's play *Every Man Out of His Humour*, the buffoonish and boastful character of 'Sogliardo' is, to many literary observers and analysts, a reference to the upstart actor William Shakespeare. The play mocks the pretentious actor's acquisition of a coat of arms that echoes Shakespeare's possession of the same dignity. Significantly, in his application for the arms Shakespeare describes himself as an actor and not as a playwright. Why not? A writer would have a higher social standing with a better claim to the honour.

Ben Jonson, who carefully guarded his own work, joined in the disapproval of literary theft and fulminated against this activity in his *Poor poet Ape* diatribe. Many believe his target was William Shakespeare:

...From brocage [pawnbroking] is so bold a thief,
As we, the robbed, leave rage, and pity it,
At first he made low shifts, would pick and glean,
Buy the reversion of old plays; now grown
To a little wealth, and credit in the scene,
He takes up all, makes each man's wit his own...
He marks not whose t'was first; and after times
May judge it to be his as well as ours...

Jonson's anger is echoed in the posthumous *Groats-worth of Wit* by the poet Robert Greene in 1592 that also appears to identify Shakespeare as a culprit:

... for there is an upstart crow, beautified with our feathers, that with his tiger's heart wrapt in a player's hide, supposes he is as well able to bombast out a blank-verse as the best of you: and being an absolute Johannes factotum, is in his own conceit the only Shakescene in a country...

As stated earlier, collaborative composition by playwrights was acceptable, but stealing verse was certainly not. Thomas Heywood, a prolific playwright of the late Elizabethan and early Jacobean era, published several texts that corrected pirated versions of his work.

A measure of Shakespeare's wealth, in contrast to other playwrights, is that in 1597 he bought the second-largest house in Stratford, New Place. This purchase was followed by a succession of investments in property, tithes and goods, as well as advancing personal loans. It may well be that this entrepreneurial son of Stratford profited as well from interests associated with the popular stage, such as animal-baiting pits and brothels.

Money lending, too, was commonplace in the purlieus of the open-air theatre. In this age there were no banking facilities so the collection of cash from drink, food and entrance fees provided the wherewithal for loans details of which are recorded in the Diary of Phillip Henslowe.

The extant records we have of William Shakespeare's money-making activities is in stark contrast to the lack of evidence that confirms a writing career of any sort. The commercial success of William Shakespeare in property, money lending and the theatre was exceptional and unmatched by any other contemporary writer. It was certainly not equalled by Ben Jonson or Samuel Daniel, both of them Poet Laureates with notable royal and aristocratic patrons.

There were huge commercial opportunities in and around the world of entertainment. Philip Henslowe, the leading impresario of the age, and his son-in-law Edward Alleyn, an actor and part theatre owner, profited from commercial interests other than the popular theatre in which they were engaged. Alleyn in particular became an extremely wealthy man, purchased land in south London and founded Dulwich College.

Around 1623, seven years after Shakespeare's death – a death that was unacknowledged in London by the literary and theatre world – a monument incorporating his bust was erected in his memory on the north wall of Holy Trinity Church, Stratford. The accompanying plaque compares him to brave Nestor, the mythical counsellor of the *Iliad*, the philosopher Socrates and the Roman poet Virgil Maro. Inscribed on a stone slab covering his grave in the chancel of the Church, presumably the original, is a banal doggerel curse against moving his bones, which has no literary merit or any particular significance for a poet: least of all for the supposedly towering writer of his age, if not for all time. William Shakespeare left no memorable poetry to grace his tomb!

Shakespeare's monument shows him holding a quill pen and paper which are dubious and these visual literary references have been proved to be a later alteration. In the illustration of the monument in William Dugdale's *Antiquities of Warwickshire* of 1656, the figure is shown holding a sack and not a quill pen or paper. The sack may represent the wealth of wool, corn or a bag of money that would be more appropriate for Shakespeare the propertied landowner.

The later idolatry surrounding the 'Bard' such as his Stratford-upon-Avon birthplace and Anne Hathaway's cottage, both lost in the past, and the monument are testaments to wishful thinking. The myth of the grand writer has been used to create a visitor attraction in Stratford-upon-Avon – now one of the world's major tourist centres.

In summary, there is trustworthy evidence of Shakespeare being associated with, and deriving wealth, from participation in the world of popular theatre. There is on the other hand no reliable, first-hand evidence of Shakespeare as a writer. The substantiation of claimed authorship rests solely upon his name being associated with published texts, which he may have obtained by acquisition or by trading. There is no corroboration that these works were written by himself. On the contrary, the life of William Shakespeare was defined by its commercial nature and regularly characterised by money-lending and shrewd property investment. Life's lessons learned from John Shakespeare, his father.

Shaksper's family and Stratford-upon-Avon

There is no evidence of literacy in relation to William Shakespeare's ancestors, siblings or children and equally there is no direct evidence that he or his brothers were able to attend school. If, as is claimed, Shakespeare was taught at the local King's New School and had shown himself to be a bright pupil, it is most likely that he would have been selected for a career in the Church. In this explanation of the derivation of the First Folio however, William Shakespeare's basic education and literacy has been given the benefit of the doubt.

Little is known about Mary Arden, Shakespeare's mother. Although she came from a landowning farming family in the area, Mary was nevertheless illiterate, and she in fact signed her name with a cross. Mary did bring to the marriage around 1557 the legacy of a property in Wilmcote, namely 'Asbyes' in the parish of Aston Cantlow. This property was later used by Mary's husband John as collateral for a loan and in time it became the subject of litigation.

More is known however of Shakespeare's father John, who came to Stratford-upon-Avon from his father's smallholding in nearby Snitterfield in 1551, aged 21. John Shaksper (original spelling used) was also illiterate, as demonstrated by his trade Guild mark, a pair of compasses, used in place of a signature. Despite a lack of formal education John Shaksper acquired property in Stratford-upon-Avon at an early stage of his life. After leaving farm work he enjoyed the respectable occupation of 'leatherseller' (a glover and 'wittawar', someone who worked with white leather) and of necessity, he was a member of the relevant Trade Guild, the Worshipful Company of Leathersellers.

John Shaksper was active in local administration in Stratford during the early part of his life, and was successively a Constable, Burgess, Chamberlain, Alderman and Bailiff, with the title of Master by the age of thirty-seven. Literacy was not a requirement for civic office at the time.

It is known that John Shaksper occupied a property in 1552 as he was fined one shilling for amassing a dunghill outside his house in Henley Street. A later survey, in 1590, shows that John Shaksper also rented another property in Henley Street. Records show that he later purchased or rented further properties in Stratford, and he also appears as a tenant of Ingon Meadow in the parish of Hampton Lucy.

This local worthy also demonstrated a willful contravention of the existing laws of the time, which forbade usury and dealing in the products of another Guild trade. Over many years it was John Shaksper's illegal trading in wool and in money-lending that came to be recorded. Usury was regarded as *"a vice most odious and detestable,"* and severe penalties were levied from those caught in such practices including possible imprisonment. Usury was a term that often indicated money-lending at an extortionate rate of interest: more than ten per cent.

Records show that attempts made to serve writs upon John Shaksper were likely to have been as a result of these serious transgressions and personal debt. For more than two decades from 1576, John was confined to his house and unable to attend Church, Civic council meetings or fully engage in his leather-making trade.

As an example of his law-breaking, John Shaksper, in 1570, was fined for breaching the usury laws by making loans of £80 and £100 to Walter Musshem, and charging £20 interest for each sum.

In 1572 John Shaksper bought 200 tods (5,600lbs) of wool in Westminster, London. The total expenditure on this wool was £210: an enormous sum when the rent for the year on one house in Henley Street in 1590, was sixpence per annum. This large wool purchase by John Shaksper was clearly a grossly illegal action by a member of the Leathersellers' Company.

John Shaksper showed his readiness for litigation by an action in 1572, recorded against John Luther for debt: one of his numerous encounters with the law. In the same year John Shaksper and Richard Quiney went together to London to put the town's case against the Earl of Warwick over a local grievance. While in London John Shaksper successfully fought in the Court of Pleas for the recovery of a £50 debt owed to him by a fellow glover from Banbury.

In 1573 Walter Musshem and John Shaksper were sued for debt by Henry Higford and in that year John Shaksper again faced accusations of illegal wool dealing. It was in 1576, as noted, when Shaksper senior had to withdraw from public life for fear of being arrested for debt and thereafter was confined to his house. Shaksper senior never returned to his municipal duties. John's son William, then aged twelve, could have assisted his mother and father with the external affairs of the Leathersellers' craft.

Since his father was unable to leave his house it is likely that the young William Shakespeare, if he had been at the local school, would have left his studies in order to help earn the family's living: there is no record of William Shakespeare completing his studies even assuming he attended New King's School. This domestic contribution would possibly involve choosing animals to be slaughtered for their hides, or selecting the skins, taking them to the tanners and preparing them for his father to make gloves, then selling the gloves at market. During this period Shakespeare would have been apprenticed to his father at the Leatherseller Wittawar craft. In those days it was the usual practice for sons to follow in their father's occupation.

In 1578 John Shaksper borrowed £40 from Edmund Lambert on the security of the property in Wilmcote, on the condition that in 1580 he would repay the money. John did not do so, and instead brought an action in the Court of Chancery in 1589 against Edmund Lambert's son John. Shaksper claimed that the deceased Lambert senior had agreed to buy the land outright for £20 but the money had never been paid.

In 1580 John Shaksper was fined for non-appearance in court and in 1592 Shaksper failed to attend Church *"for feare of processe for debtte."* Towards the end of his life in 1599, John Shaksper brought an action against John Walford for debt. Shakespeare's father died in 1601.

Assessing Shaksper's character it is noteworthy that there were recorded sixty-seven entries in legal cases where John Shaksper's name appeared on one side or the other, as plaintiff or defendant.

A realistic view of John Shaksper's life shows that he was an unevenly successful and propertied businessman, but one who also sailed close to the legal wind, to a degree that involved very serious law-breaking. Shaksper senior, the dealer in goods and property was clearly prone to litigation, was over-ambitious and exhibited risk-taking to the detriment of good citizenship. In short, the example shown to William Shakespeare by his father was that of a 'wheeler-dealer.'

Perhaps unsurprisingly no evidence has ever been found that John Shaksper had any interest in academic learning or culture. There was no such verification present of such concerns in the home: no trace of music, art or literary enquiry has ever been uncovered. There was no cultural inheritance bequeathed to John's and Mary's offspring, but, no doubt, a commercial awareness was passed down.

John Shaksper's son William was born in 1564, baptised 26 April of that year and raised in Stratford–upon-Avon. Although no attendance records for the period survive, most biographers agree that Shakespeare may well have been educated at the King's New School in Stratford. King's was a free school chartered in 1553 and situated about a quarter of a mile from the boy's home.

Schools such as King's were set up by the Trade Guilds and, as the son of a Guild member, William was entitled to a free education. This first local grammar school became the King's New School in 1568. Such educational institutions varied in teaching standards during the Elizabethan era, but the curriculum was dictated by law throughout England. This provincial school would have provided an education in Latin grammar and some knowledge of the Classics. The quality of education at King's is unknown but the highest level of teaching was obtained at schools situated in the major English cities rather than in the minor rural towns such as Stratford-upon-Avon.

John Shaksper's financial predicament in the 1580s may have influenced William's choice of bride in 1582. It appears from a contemporary document that William Shakespeare, then aged eighteen, married Anne Hathaway of Stratford, aged twenty-six, for a dowry of ten marks. This was an unusual difference in age for the bridal couple if it is presumed to be a romantic union.

A further marriage document has been discovered that consisted of a bond for £40 lodged by two Stratford farmers, Fulke Sandells and John Richardson. This record indemnified the Bishop against any impediment or obstruction that William Shakespeare on the one part, and Anne Hathway of Stratford in the Diocese of Worcester as 'maiden', might *"lawfully solemnize matrimony together and in the same afterwards remain and continue like man and wife."*

The purpose of this protection for the Bishop is not clear but there is the possibility that Shakespeare was previously betrothed to another woman and there was a change of mind in relation to that marriage.

John Shaksper's influence upon his son's choice of bride, which included a dowry, reflects the prevailing belief of the time that children were to obey the matrimonial wishes of their parents. The dowry and financial prospects normally played a significant role in the decision of whom to marry and this union appears to be a commercial arrangement. Anne Hathaway's pregnancy may have been another factor in this marriage according to the speedy timing of the banns.

Six months after her marriage to William Shakespeare, Anne gave birth to a daughter, Susanna, who was baptised on 26th May 1583. Almost two years later she had twins, son Hamnet and daughter Judith, both baptised on 2nd February 1585. Aged eleven, Hamnet died of unknown causes and was buried on 11th August 1596. As it took three to four days to travel from London to Stratford at the time it is unlikely that William Shakespeare attended the funeral, as he was by then in London.

There are few historical traces of William Shakespeare prior to his being mentioned as part of the London theatre scene in 1592: ten years after his hasty marriage. However, even this reference to Shakespeare has been questioned by several scholars who believe that the well-known comment by the playwright Robert Greene refers, in fact, to Edward Alleyn, a leading actor of the time.

Shakespeare in London

It is impossible to know exactly when William Shakspeare left his family in Stratford-upon-Avon for London and it may have been when a brother was old enough to assume his duties regarding his father's trade. Any major journey at that time was subject to the *Act of Vagabonds* of 1572. Shakespeare would have needed a license to travel from Stratford to London as it was a criminal offence to travel in England without this authorisation.

Although the records of the Worshipful Company of Leathersellers were destroyed in the Great Fire of London, it can be safely assumed that John Shaksper was a member of the Guild and that William, as his son, was also accepted into the company as a member. The Leathersellers' Hall was sited near Silver Street where Shakespeare later lodged.

One explanation of this move may be that The Worshipful Company of Leathersellers may have sent Shakespeare to their headquarters in London as a replacement scrivener after the City's population was decimated by the frequency of the plague. If this were the case then the Company would have provided him with the required license.

An alternative account of Shakespeare's move to London indicates that he may have attached himself to the Queen's Men troupe of players when they visited Stratford in 1586–7. It is recorded that one of the company's actors was killed in a brawl in Stratford at the time. If so, Shakespeare would have been a very useful addition to the company, inasmuch as the young man – presumed to have been at school – could read and write. There is the possibility that Shakespeare carried out the function of a 'scrivener' or 'book holder', who had the task of writing individual parts from a complete script. This explanation is less credible for the young man's journey as it is unlikely that the troupe could have obtained a license in time for the written permission which allowed William Shakespeare to travel.

Charles Hamilton, a leading graphologist, in his book, *In Search of Shakespeare: Study of the Poet's Life and Handwriting* has researched Shakespeare's will and ascertains that this document is in Shakespeare's own handwriting – the conventional scrivener's script. It is in the same hand as the alterations on the 'Northumberland' manuscript discussed later.

Likely to have been influenced by his commercially-minded, litigious father, William Shakespeare would have been well equipped to spend his life dealing in valuable commodities such as play scripts as well as the even more profitable money lending and property dealing business and, some believe, brothel-keeping, often an adjunct to the popular theatre. Shakespeare had acquired, by his domestic upbringing, useful skills for a provincial newcomer operating among the cut and thrust of competing London playgroups and the popular theatre.

The first definite record of William Shakespeare's name in London is in 1593, on the publication of the poem *Venus and Adonis,* which carried Shakespeare's dedication to the Earl of Southampton. In 1595, Shakespeare, then aged thirty, is named as receiving payment from the Treasurer of the Chamber for performing in plays in the company of fellow actors William Kempe and Richard Burbage.

Shakespeare was employed as an actor for some years as well as a scribe. In the 1616 edition of Ben Jonson's *Works,* Shakespeare is named in the cast lists for *Every Man In His Humour* in 1598 and *Sejanus, His Fall* in 1603. The absence of his name from the 1605 cast list for Jonson's *Volpone* is taken by some scholars as a sign that his acting career was nearing its end by that time.

The First Folio of 1623, however, lists Shakespeare as one of *"the Principal Actors in all these Plays"* although if this assertion is true we cannot know for certain what roles he played. In 1610, John Davies of Hereford wrote that *"good Will"* played *"kingly"* roles.

Mr William Shakespeare's name again appeared in 1594 on the dedication of the poem *Rape of Lucrece*, which is also addressed to the Earl of Southampton. The inference accepted over the years has been that both *Venus and Adonis* and *Rape of Lucrece*, point to Shakespeare's authorship despite their very marked differences in both content and poetic style.

However, this claim of true authorship has been a matter of dispute for a very long time. Significantly, no evidence has ever been found of any composition by the actor-businessman William Shakespeare prior to these two dedications. Furthermore, centuries of research that would justify Shakespeare as a writer have not uncovered any reliable corroboration. Most tellingly of all, there is no reference to Shakespeare as an author by any other contemporary writer.

In an exchange of satirical writings published during 1597-8, and commenting on the 'Shakespeare' poems *Venus and Adonis* and *The Rape of Lucrece* published a few years earlier (1593-4), the poets Joseph Hall and John Marston indicated that 'William Shakespeare' was a mask for the real author of the poems and pointedly revealed the true writer.

Hall attacked the love poetry of the Shakespeare poems whilst Marston defended it. In doing so they identified the author of the poems as a member of the Bacon family. They begin their exchange of satires by referring to a certain poet as *Labeo*. In Hall's second book of *Certain Satires* he reproves Labeo for the licentious tone of his work and implies that Labeo was writing in conjunction with someone else:

> *For shame write better Labeo, or write none,*
> *Or better write, or Labeo write alone.*

In Satire 1 of his fourth book of Satires, Hall links Labeo with *Venus and Adonis*, satirising Labeo for his use of 'But' and 'Oh' with which he began his stanzas.

Hall goes on to imply that Labeo is writing under another person's name (i.e. Shakespeare's name):

> *Labeo is whip't and laughs me in the face.*
> *Why? for I smite and hide the galled place,*
> *Gird but the Cynicks Helmet on his head,*
> *Cares he for Talus or his flayle of lead?*
> *Long as the craftie Cuttle lieth sure*
> *In the black cloud of his thick vomiture;*
> *Who list complaine of wronged faith or fame*
> *When hee may shift it on to another's name?*

The following year John Marston joined the game in his *Metamorphosis of Pygmalion's Image*, confirming that Labeo was the author Shakespeare:

> *So Labeo did complaine his loue was stone, Obdurate, flinty, so relentless none; Yet Lynceus knows, that in the end of this He wrought as strange a metamorphosis. Ends not my poem thus surprising ill? Come, come, Augustus, crowne my laureat quill.*

The first two lines of this passage allude to lines 200 and 201 of *Venus and Adonis*:

> *"Art thou obdurate, flintie, hard as steele? / Nay more than flint, for stone at raine relenteth,"*

whilst in the remaining lines Marston compares the metamorphosis of Pygmalion, as described in his own work, to that of Adonis, as described in *Venus and Adonis*.

So, here are both Hall and Marston referring to the concealed author as Labeo. Marston himself was no stranger to the use of pseudonyms and masks, for he had hidden himself under the pseudonym of W. Kinsayder for both his poems, *The Metamorphosis of Pygmalion's Image* and *The Scourge of Villainie.*

But why choose 'Labeo' as a pseudonym for the author of the poems? It is a pointed allusion, in fact, to Antistius Labeo, who was a celebrated lawyer in the time of the Roman Emperor Augustus, and lost favour with the Emperor for having opposed his views.

After further exchanges, Marston finally identifies Labeo decisively. In his *Certain Satires, Book 1* another covert allusion to an author who *"presumst as if thou wert unseene."* In *Satire 4*, Marston defends various authors whom Hall had attacked and, without actually naming him, refers to Labeo and identifies him in the following line:

> *What, not mediocria firma from thy spite?*
> [i.e., has not even *mediocria firma* escaped thy spite?]

This Latin phrase, *'mediocria firma'* is the motto of the Bacon family, used by Anthony and Francis Bacon. Since both Francis and Anthony had trained as lawyers and both were poets, there can be no reasonable doubt: Marston was referring to either Anthony or Francis Bacon, who he believed to be the author of the poems *The Rape of Lucrece* and *Venus and Adonis.*

The sonnets of 1609

The sonnet collection attributed to William Shakespeare is composed of 154 poems in sonnet form, which deal with such themes as the passage of time, love, beauty and mortality. It was first published in a 1609 quarto entitled *SHAKE-SPEARES SONNETS: Never before imprinted* (although sonnets 138 and 144 had previously been published *The Passionate Pilgrim*). The quarto ends with *A Lover's Complaint*, a narrative poem of 47 seven-line stanzas written in rhyme royal.

The first 17 poems, traditionally called the procreation sonnets, are addressed to a young man, urging him to marry and have children in order to immortalise his beauty by passing it on to the next generation. In the first ten sonnets the poet has not met the recipient of the poem.

Other sonnets express the speaker's love for a young man. They brood upon loneliness, death, and the transience of life; seem to criticise the young man for preferring a rival poet; express ambiguous feelings for the speaker's mistress; and pun on the poet's name. The final two sonnets are allegorical treatments of Greek epigrams referring to the *little love-god* Cupid. The sonnets include a dedication to one *"Mr. W.H."*. The identity of this person remained a mystery and has provoked much speculation over the years. The dedication reads:

TO.THE.ONLIE.BEGETTER.OF.
THESE.INSUING.SONNETS.
Mr. W. H. ALL.HAPPINESSE.
AND.THAT.ETERNITIE.
PROMISED.
BY.
OUR.EVER-LIVING.POET.
WISHETH.
THE.WELL-WISHING.
ADVENTURER.IN.
SETTING.
FORTH.
T.T.

Nigel Hawkes' article in *The Times* of 31st December 1997 reported an analysis by the retired physicist John Rollet. It was of the dedication publisher Thomas Thorpe had provided on the title page of the sonnets collection. Through counting the letters of the whole piece, John Rollet found that there were 144 characters, a suspiciously round figure and wondered if the odd words concealed a message that was hidden by a cipher, since codes were widely used in Elizabethan times. This analysis suggested the idea to him of laying out the letters in blocks of twelve lines, of twelve letters each, to form a square (or, for example, eight arranged in a rectangle of nine rows, each of sixteen letters. The name 'Henry' appears running diagonally downwards, and when the letters are arranged as a block of eight by eighteen, the name 'Wriothesley' can be teased out although it is broken up into three sections, 'Wr', 'ioth', and 'esley'. Rollet calculates the odds of the word 'Henry' appearing by chance at 1,192 to one and the section 'esley' appearing by chance at 1,056 to one. This appears to confirm the generally accepted view that sonnets were dedicated to Henry, Earl of Southampton (Wriothesly).

Thomas Thorpe's publication of the sonnets in 1609 was met with literary silence. In its original form it was not reprinted, and did not excite comment until a reference was made in the poet John Suckling's work, written around 1640.

As the 1609 sonnets are very personal, the recipient of the sonnets or the author may have wished and been able to suppress the publication. Scholars suggest that unlike Richard Field's strongly edited *Venus and Adonis*, it was not well redacted and printed – inasmuch the original contains many errors. The most notable of which are the two pairs of parentheses enclosing blank space and inserted on consecutive lines at the end of the twelve line sonnet, 126. It constitutes a mistake, and it was concluded by the publisher, printer or other that a couplet was missing from the poem, rather than the fact that it was a twelve line coda or envoi to the first series of sonnets.

A further error is the repeat of the couplet of sonnet 36 at the end of sonnet 96, exemplifying another one of the many mistakes throughout the publication.

The author or authors of *Shakes-peares sonnets* did not own the copyright, as only a Guild member of the Stationers' Company owned the rights of a work when it had been entered into the register and printed. The register also states *Tho. Thorpe. Entred for his copie under the handes of Master Wilson and master Lownes Wardenes a booke called Shakespeares sonnettes vjd.*

If it may be assumed that the printed book was suppressed, as only thirteen copies survived and there was no immediate second edition.

A Lover's Complaint

The work entitled both *A Lover's Complaint* and *The Lover's Complaint* is a narrative poem printed as an appendix to the original edition of the 1609 sonnets, published by Thomas Thorpe.

The authorship of this poem is another matter of critical debate. The poem consists of forty-seven seven-line stanzas written in rhyme royal, a metre and structure identical to that of George Peele's poem *The Rape of Lucrece* authorship credibly established by Professor Brian Vickers.

The Lover's Complaint contains many words and forms that are not to be found in the First Folio, including several archaisms and Latinisms; it is sometimes regarded as rhythmically and structurally awkward.

Some critics have a high regard for the poem's quality – Edmund Malone called it beautiful – and saw thematic parallels to situations in *All's Well That Ends Well* and *Measure for Measure*. John Mackinnon Robertson published a study in 1917 claiming that George Chapman was the writer of the poem, as well as the originator of *Timon of Athens*.

In Professor Brian Vickers' 2007 monograph, *Shakespeare, A Lover's Complaint*, he attributes the *Complaint* to John Davies of Hereford. Brian Vickers details arguments for the non-Shakespearean nature of the poem and lists numerous verbal parallels between the *Complaint* and the known works of John Davies.

An article by Marina Tarlinskaja *Who Did NOT Write A Lover's Complaint?* in *Shakespeare Yearbook 15, 2005*, argues that the author of *A Lover's Complaint* was neither Shakespeare nor John Davies, but a still-anonymous early Elizabethan poet and apparently a follower of Edmund Spenser.

Coat of Arms

From 1596, there is a reference to a shield and crest, drawing from the first of two rough drafts of a Coat of Arms grant to Shakespeare, registered in the College of Arms. The phrase *"Non Sanz Droict"* ("Not Without Right") is written on both documents and appears to be a motto. However in 1602, Peter Brooke, the York Herald, accused Sir William Dethick, the Garter King-of-Arms of elevating base persons to the gentry.

Brooke drew up a list of 23 persons whom he claimed were not entitled to bear arms: number four on the list was Shakespeare. Brooke included a sketch of the Shakespeare arms, captioned *"Shakespear ye Player by Garter."* This is the same coat-of-arms that appears on the poet's tomb in Stratford. As stated earlier it is relevant that in his application for a Coat of Arms, William Shakespeare is listed as an actor rather than the more respected position of an acknowledged poet and playwright.

The humorous motto of Ben Jonson's stage character Sogliardo *Not Without Mustard* is thought to be a satirical comment on the pretensions of William Shakespeare to claim a higher rank in society than to which he was entitled.

Another mention of William Shakespeare in London is connected to the theatre owner Francis Langley's feud with William Gardiner, a Justice of the Peace and property speculator with a long history of criminal activity. In 1596 Langley sought court protection against Gardiner and his stepson, William Wayte. In turn Wayte sought the same protection against Francis Langley, William Shakespeare, Dorothy Soer and Ann Lee. The two women named are without a courtesy title indicating they are considered to be of low character.

In 1597, William Shakespeare bought the second-largest house in Stratford, New Place, and in 1605 he also invested in a share of the parish tithes in Stratford. These purchases indicate that Shakespeare's property ownership, investments and position as a theatre 'sharer' had made him an extremely wealthy man. It has been estimated by A. J. Pointon in his exhaustive work, *The Man who was Never Shakespeare* that the businessman earned today's monetary equivalent of £200,000 annually.

Edward Alleyn, an actor and part theatre owner, and Philip Henslowe, the leading impresario of the age, also profited from commercial interests other than the popular theatre in which they were engaged; albeit some of these activities were illegal. It is generally accepted that animal-baiting pits and brothels were often associated with the popular open-air playhouses, while money-lending was commonplace.

By 1597 it appears that William Shakespeare was leading a financially successful career in London. The relative newcomer was known to be an actor and part owner of a theatre and was also likely to have been the scribe of a playing company called the Lord Chamberlain's Men, later known as the King's Men.

By 1602, Shakespeare was the owner of three houses in Stratford and 107 acres of tenanted farmland north of that town – three years earlier he paid £440 for a share in the area's tithe lands. These are less the actions of an actor-playwright and much more likely to be the behaviour of an enterprising landowner.

By 1604, Shakespeare had moved to an area north of St Paul's Cathedral where he lived in the house of a French Huguenot called Christopher Mountjoy, a maker of ladies' wigs and other headgear. The timber-framed house illustrated in the map, known as the *Agas* map, was shown to be two stories, although it may have been a three-storied building. This dwelling housed the shop on the ground floor, below that was a storeroom and situated at the top of the house a workroom with the best natural light. In a plan of 1520, the frontage appears to be approximately fourteen feet and possibly seventeen feet in depth, and it is unlikely to have changed by 1604.

Accommodation required for the inhabitants were the Mountjoy family of three, a live-in apprentice, a servant and William Shakspeare. Charles Nicholls in his book, *The Lodger, Shakespeare on Silver Street* calculates that there may have been nine adults in the house at one time. There was scarcely room for the library the poet it is said he must have had for play sources and other references to French and Italian translations!

William Shakespeare was most probably trained in leathercraft like his father, and this may have had a bearing on his choice of residence in London. Some wigs were made with a leather base at this time and the young man's skills would be useful. The Worshipful Company of Leathersellers had its headquarters in London at St Helen's Place, Bishopsgate, where Shakespeare, living nearby, could have worked as a scribe. There was a street leather market in Leadenhall Street also close by Shakespeare's lodgings.

In 1612, William Shakespeare was called as a witness in a court case concerning the marriage settlement of Christopher Mountjoy's daughter Mary. In the legal documents of this case, Shakespeare is referred to as Mr Shakespeare *of Stratford-upon-Avon in the county of Warwickshire, gent."* This indicates that by the date of the Mountjoy litigation Shakespeare was a respected person known to come from Stratford and was not directly concerned with any trade. Again it is noticeable that there is no reference of Mr Shakespeare as a writer or poet, despite the majority of his work having been published by this date.

After the death of Queen Elizabeth in 1603, the Chamberlain's Company, of which Shakspeare was a member, was awarded a royal patent by the new King, James I, and changed its name to the King's Men. Previously, in 1599, a partnership of company members or sharers, including Shakespeare, built their own theatre – entitled the Globe – on the south bank of the Thames. It was for open-air daylight performances only. In 1608, the company sharers also took over the Blackfriars indoor theatre.

Quartos which were later to appear as long plays in the First Folio were published at this time; some were of an inferior quality and are now known as the 'bad' quartos. Scholars suggest these scripts may have been compiled from shorthand notes, illicitly taken during performances, or even recorded from the memories of the actors.

As a scribe, William Shakespeare would have had the opportunity and skill to obtain such copies and gain financial benefit for himself – and perhaps fellow players – by selling these scripts to printers. Such action also presented the opportunity for Shakespeare to assume their authorship.

Shakespeare died on 23rd April 1616, and was survived by his wife and two daughters. A daughter Susanna was married in 1607 to John Hall, a physician and diarist – the man who taught her to read; a duty neglected by her supposedly famous poet father. Daughter Judith had married Thomas Quiney, a vintner, two months before Shakespeare's death. In his will, Shakespeare left the bulk of his large estate to his elder daughter Susanna. The terms instructed that she pass it down intact to *"the first son of her body."*

The Quineys had three children, all of whom died without marrying. The Halls had one child, Elizabeth, who married twice but died without children in 1670, thus ending Shakespeare's direct line.

William Shakespeare's will scarcely mentions his wife, Anne, who was probably automatically entitled to one third of his estate. The businessman did make a point, however, of leaving her *"my second best bed"* – a bequest that has led to much speculation. Some scholars see the bequest as an insult to Anne, whereas others believe that the second-best bed would have been the matrimonial bed and therefore an item of status.

Other Shakespeare authorship contradictions

The preceding summary of the facts which exist about the life and character of William Shakespeare denies the romanticised figure worshipped as the world's greatest ever dramatist and poet. Over centuries of investigation nothing has been found that supports Shakespeare's claim except his name printed on the early First Folio texts and later published works. But we know that play ownership was a questionable area when legal copyright for authors did not exist. Yet the conviction about this imaginary literary giant persists. Why has this assertion supported by such questionable evidence led to a largely unquestioned acceptance of the unmatched brilliance of William Shakespeare?

Those academics and critics who have built the imposing Shakespeare-The Bard edifice may well have been motivated by the human desire for a super-hero. After all a desire especially welcomed is the natural "genius" rising to great achievement from humble beginnings. Or maybe it is the immense pride of England's literary St George: the country's internationally acclaimed poet surpassing all others. Perhaps, more mundanely, Shakespearean devotees have not sought to uncover, impartially, the contrary evidence surrounding playwrighting during the later decades of the sixteenth century. Nor explored the existence of plays during this period which relate to a number of works in the First Folio. Such writings, resting in the shadows, that could not possibly have been composed by William Shakespeare.

It is time to unravel a number of suppositions held by present and earlier scholars that support the Shakespeare legend.

1. The timescale for the composition of the plays is not confined to Shakespeare's working life span.

According to E. K. Chambers some of the plays in the First Folio were variations of or improved early plays performed before Queen Elizabeth's court such as *Titus Gisippus* played by Paul's Boys at court in 1577. To this could be added an early performance of *Romeo and Juliet* in 1561 shortly after the departure from the country of Michelangelo Florio, possibly the playwright, in 1554, *A History of Ferrar* is perhaps an early version of *Comedy of Errors*, played at court in 1583. A play called *Wit and Will* another *A Marriage between Wit and Wisdom* were both played at court and may be early versions of *Measure for Measure*.

2. How to explain the Italian play settings.

The plays *Romeo and Juliet, The Merchant of Venice, Much Ado About Nothing,* part of *Othello, The Winter's Tale, Cymbeline Taming of the Shrew, Two Gentlemen of Verona* and *All's Well That Ends Well* all have whole or part settings in Italy with such accurate detail of specific locations that an Italian writer or collaborator must have been involved. Michelangelo Florio and son John are candidates (see chapter 10 *The Early Italian Plays*). William Shakespeare is not known to have ever travelled abroad.

3. There is no evidence that William Shakespeare was a constant member of either the Lord Chamberlain's Men or the King's Men.

It is claimed that William Shakespeare was associated with four playing companies but the evidence does not confirm this view. Some historians have assumed, mistakenly, that when a playing company performed a version of a play later attributed to Shakespeare this implied that Shakespeare was a member of, and wrote for, that troupe. In fact there is no proof of William Shakespeare being a member of the Admiral's Men or Lord Strange's Men as is often asserted There are records of his association with one touring troupe: the Lord Chamberlain's Men, originally Lord Hunsdon's Men, who in 1603 became the King's Men.

There are three records of payment to playgroups with William Shakespeare as a member. The first in 1595 to servants of the Lord Chamberlain, another in 1603 in the letters patent creating the King's Men and in 1604 Shakespeare was the recipient of red material to be made into ceremonial livery on the occasion of the King James' procession through London.

Hunsdon's strolling players may be traced touring the provinces from around 1564. In 1582 Hunsdon's men were present at court (for two days) and returned to the court in 1595/6, 1596/7 and 1597/8. By then the players were known as the Lord Chamberlain's Men following Hunsdon's promotion in 1595. William Shakespeare is recorded in the company that year as a joint payee with William Kempe, a clown, and Richard Burbage, actor and impresario. These three players are from the group but this is not confirmation of the presence of the whole troupe. The reference to Shakespeare receiving some red cloth in 1604 to make a suit of livery confirms him as a King's servant alongside hundreds of other menials.

A reference to William Shakespeare as an actor appears in the cast list attached to the 1616 folio text of Ben Jonson's *Every Man in his Humour*. It is unclear when this list was written or when it was attached to the play.

4. When Shakespeare was named as author?

Examination of the title pages of the first edition of the quartos related to the First Folio reveal that Shakespeare's name is only included on nine title pages. In later editions of some of these quartos his name appears as the author.

Plays from the First Folio were printed in quarto from 1594 and these appeared in more than seventy editions. Nineteen of the plays were printed before the publication of the First Folio and eighteen of them printed before Shakespeare's death in 1616.

Half of the First Folio works were not printed until 1623 seven years after Shakespeare's death.

The nine first editions of early quartos of version of the plays in the First Folio carry variations of Shakespeare's name, They are *Henry IV Part II* and *A Midsummer Night's Dream, The Merchant of Venice, Much Ado About Nothing* printed in 1600 and *The Merry Wives of Windsor* quarto printed in 1602. The first quarto of *Hamlet* of 1603 and *King Lear* quarto of 1608, *Troilus and Cressida* quarto of 1609 and *Othello* a first quarto of 1622.

The quarto published after 1623, *The Taming of a Shrew* of 1631 was also attributed to William Shakespeare.

5. The "Bad Quartos" or early versions of popular playhouse texts

The description "bad quarto" refers to the poor early texts of a number of the 1623 First Folio plays. These examples differ considerably from the final text. One credible explanation for the "bad quartos" is that they were memorial reconstructions by players who took minor roles or who were present at rehearsals and were re-written by the company scribe. An alternative account is that a playwright adapted a court play in terms of its length character and action to suit a popular audience.

There are, for example, three markedly different versions of *Hamlet*, two of *King Lear, Henry V, Romeo and Juliet*, and *The Taming of the Shrew*

A relatively recent interpretation of these early plays by Laurie Maguire of the Department of English at the University of Ottawa concludes that virtually all the bad quartos appear to be accurate renditions of original texts. and "*merit our attention as valid texts in their own right*".

It is relevant to note that an early and crude text exists of Christopher Marlowe's *Massacre of Paris* this appears to be a memorial reconstruction produced by the players and intended for the popular stage. Similarly the extant text of 1598 the second quarto of *Richard 111* and the 1603 first quarto of *Hamlet* are in the same category.

6. Seventeen plays in the First Folio have no connection to William Shakespeare apart from the title page of 1623.

These famous plays, surprisingly, not published previously are:

All's Well that Ends Well, Anthony and Cleopatra, As You Like It, The Comedy of Errors, Coriolanus, Cymbeline, Henry V1 part 1, Henry V111, Julius Caesar, King John, Macbeth, Measure for Measure, The Tempest, Timon of Athens, Twelfth Night, The Two Gentlemen of Verona, and *The Winter's Tale.*

7. The Rose theatre and Shakespeare

Several plays performed at the Rose theatre and noted in Henslowe's Diary bear similar titles to First Folio plays: *titus & ondronicus, tittus, titus & ondronicous, andronicous (Titus Andronicus), Sesar, Seasar, (Julius Caesar), Harey vj, Harey 6, (Henry V1), Harey the V, Hary the V, Harye the V (Henry V), Kinge Leare, (King Lear), Hamlet V .*

These titles do not prove that the like-named First Folio plays were performed at the Rose. There are various reasons why full-length plays, as appear in the First Folio, were not suited to the popular playhouse and these are listed in the next chapter.

8. The strolling players at court... and the plays performed at court.

It is claimed that Shakespeare took part in royal performance with the King's Men. It is evident that the touring playing troupes were present at Elizabeth's court, mostly at Christmas, and these visits coincided with a performance of a play usually of a Classical nature. While it has long been presumed that the strolling players presented and acted in these productions that assumption may be questioned.

The strolling players may have entertained the court with their habitual fare such as acrobatics, swordplay, comedy tricks and jigs before or after a classical play production and formal dinner. The serious acting having been performed principally by the boy troupe: skilled actors and vocalists. The lively repertoire of the entertainers would have been ideal for the amusement of those foreign dignitaries at court not sufficiently conversant with English to follow a sophisticated play text. Some players from the visiting travelling troupe may have taken comic roles such as the comedian Richard Tarlton, Queen Elizabeth's favourite. There were also minor and non-speaking parts to be filled by players.

The boy choristers and the strolling players may have mounted their entertainment in different venues within the palace.

There were several Elizabethan boy troupes and when they became adults the young men joined the acting companies of King James and his family. *All of the foregoing points raise questions that challenge Shakespearean authorship.*

PART TWO

THE FIRST FOLIO
OF 1623

Geoffrey Chaucer 1343-1400

*Poet and father of English literature
received patronage from Lancastrian kings and
noble families*

CHAPTER ONE

The development of the English language and
Lancastrian patronage

PRINTED in 1623, the First Folio publication marks a turning point in the impressive development of the English language from earlier times. This volume represented a collection of dramatic poetry that was the culmination of the endeavours by many scholars, translators, teachers and aristocratic men and women of letters for more than a century. These were leaders of English society, intent on preserving English literature and culture.

Infused with a like-minded motivation these contributors strove to create their ideal: a superior English language. This was an ambition that envisaged an English literature which matched or even surpassed the 16th century Italian and French languages in its ability to articulate poetic feelings and impart intellectual thought. The challenge for them, especially the Protestant patrons, was to harness a subtle, expressive and learned vernacular in order to further develop England's literary output of the preceding centuries, while also communicating the revolutionary thinking of humanism. Following the Norman Conquest and the absolute domination of England, both physically and culturally, by the French invaders, the Norman kings and high-ranking noblemen transmitted their own language to the English people. Achieved through several generations, this imported tongue was to have a strong influence upon the extensive English vocabulary, which expanded almost exponentially in the centuries which followed.

In the 11th and 12th centuries noblemen of lower rank, merchants and officials were often bi-lingual, while Church affairs and law were conducted mostly in Latin. The Anglo-Saxon vernacular was the language spoken by the uneducated masses, with strong regional variations in vocabulary, emphasis and even meaning throughout England.

It was more than one hundred and fifty years before a distinctively written English re-appeared after the Norman invasion; having absorbed the Norman French in the intervening decades, English literate society also had a new awareness of nationhood. This sensibility created a new respectability – even pride – for the expanded English language and

Anglo-Norman declined in usage. While written English came into usage during the 13th century it was to be another fifty years before the native language became accepted as a medium suitable for the expression of a literary culture. In the meantime standard French retained its status of a formal language of prestige and was especially useful in diplomacy where its favour has continued to modern times. From the 1380s English replaced French as the language taught in schools.

It was during the last four decades of the 14th century when recognisable authors and works of English literature began to appear. Of particular note was William Langland's allegory, *Pier's Plowman,* which attacked Government and Church abuse in alliterative verse. The narrative poem appeared in three different texts between 1362 and 1398.

By the end of that century John Gower, Geoffrey Chaucer and Thomas Hoccleve had made their mark; these early writers, heirs to the classical tradition, were all notable recipients of Lancastrian royal and aristocratic patronage.

Born in 1330, John Gower was a well-read gentleman, possibly a clerk, who wrote in Latin and French and only composed in English later in life. A moralistic poet and Chaucer's contemporary, Gower wrote *Vox Clamantis,* a poem stirred by the Peasants' Rising of 1381. Later Gower was to write his *Confessio Amantis* in 1583/4 at the behest of King Richard II: an immense composition of 40,000 lines that included some hundred tales.

Gower was also an admirer of Henry of Lancaster, the son of John of Gaunt: known as Bolingbroke and later to become Henry IV, and his regard was reciprocated. The effigy on Gower's tomb wears a collar inscribed with 'SS' and bearing the Swan badge of the Bohun family, which was used by Henry of Lancaster. It was recorded in 1593 that a collar bearing the device of a chained swan between two portcullises was presented to the poet. The first printed edition of the *Confessio Amantis* is dated 1390; in at least in some copies this volume contains a secondary dedication to Henry of Grosmont, 1st Duke of Lancaster, 4th Earl of Leicester and Lancaster, KG and also Earl of Derby. Lancaster's daughter Blanche married John of Gaunt and her inheritance made him the richest nobleman in England. The tomb of Gower carries the inscription: *This is the tomb of John Gower (d. 1408), Poet Laureate to Richard II and to Henry IV.*

A friend and admirer of Chaucer, John Gower helped to establish the standard literary language of England. His poem *Confessio Amantis* is the central source for the play *Pericles,* which is based upon the Greek story of *Apolonius of Tyre* : "Ancient Gower" is the Chorus who introduces the play.

Pericles was included in the second folio, published in 1632. A character called Gower is present as an officer in *Henry IV part II* and *in Henry V,* and is perhaps included as an acknowledgement of this illustrious figure.

The works of Geoffrey Chaucer, considered the most highly regarded English poet of the Middle Ages by successive generations, was seen by his contemporaries as succeeding to the great tradition of the Roman poet Virgil and the Italian Dante, the father of Italian literature who died in 1321. Well travelled on the continent, Chaucer became acquainted with the works of other giants of the Italian language, including Petrach and his disciple Boccaccio, both of them writing in the mid-14th century. Familiar with the Italian and Provençal languages, Chaucer's narrative poems were either greatly influenced by, or largely translated into Middle English from Latin, Italian or French literature.

Chaucer's courtly romance *Troylus and Criseyde,* the story of the ill-fated lovers set during the Trojan wars, is remembered in the First Folio, but Chaucer was also a gifted observer of the everyday life of the ordinary people of his time: they are well represented in his literary output. Chaucer's *Book of the Duchess,* a long poem written around 1369, was dedicated to Blanche of Lancaster, the first wife of John of Gaunt, marking the occasion of her death.

Welcomed at court by several English monarchs, including Edward III, Richard II and Henry IV, Geoffrey Chaucer benefited from other rich patrons including Lionel, Duke of Clarence and John of Gaunt, his brother-in-law by Gaunt's third marriage to his mistress, Katherine Swynford.

Another notable figure who emerged in 15th century English literature is the poet Thomas Hoccleve, whose life overlapped that of Chaucer, a man whose work Hoccleve much admired. Like the elder poet, Hoccleve gained Lancastrian patronage from Henry IV, Henry V and the learned Humphrey of Gloucester, fourth son of King Henry IV. In the writer's *Regement of Princes, 1411,* Hoccleve comments much on Prince Henry's lineage: he was soon to become Henry V and Hoccleve emphasises the rightful claim of the House of Lancaster to England's throne.

The first Bible to be translated into English from the Latin vulgate was produced between 1380-1382 by John Wycliffe and a collaborator, Nicholas of Hereford, another theological scholar. Wycliffe's biblical language, principally of the New Testament, was to become an integral part of English. Wycliffe, opposed to the organised Church and the Papacy, was the main precursor of the Protestant reformation and his followers were known as 'Lollards'.

The Benedictine monk and prolific writer John Lydgate, who translated from the French and wrote poems, fables, allegories and romances, had a great respect for Geoffrey Chaucer's writings, which he emulated. *The Troy-book*, Lydgate's first full-scale work, was commissioned by Henry, Prince of Wales (later Henry V), in 1412 and was completed in 1420. The King's father and Henry VI, in later years, were both patrons of Lydgate, as was Richard de Beauchamp, 13th Earl of Warwick. In 1431 Humphrey, Duke of Gloucester, encouraged John Lydgate to commence writing the epic poem *Fall of Princes,* the 7,000 stanzas were completed in 1438.

Lydgate's principal patron in later years, Humphrey Duke of Gloucester, or 'Good Duke Humphrey', was a soldier, statesman, educator and literary benefactor who was instrumental in bringing Italian scholarship to England, both with the purchase of books and through the scholars themselves. The Duke corresponded with many leading Italian humanists and commissioned translations of Greek classics into Latin. Duke Humphrey is portrayed as a major character in two First Folio plays and his conflict with Cardinal Beaufort is portrayed in *Henry VI, part 1.* Gloucester's disgrace and death following his wife's alleged sorcery is depicted in *Henry VI, part 2* and the Duke also appears as a minor character in *Henry V.*

The 'Good Duke' name lives on in 'Duke Humfrey's Library', part of the Bodleian Library in Oxford. Duke Humphrey was a patron and protector of Oxford, donating more than 280 manuscripts to the University. The possession of such a library at the University did much to stimulate new learning in England, although unfortunately the library lost a number of religious books as a result of the purge of Roman Catholic writings by King Edward VI, as well as in a later fire.

The skill of John Skelton in translating the classics led to him becoming court poet to Henry VII in 1488, and tutor to the Duke of York, afterwards King Henry VIII. In 1498 Skelton took Holy Orders and was appointed a rector in Diss five years later, but in 1512 he occupied a position at court, advising the king on literary matters and church affairs. In 1516 Skelton wrote *Magnificence,* the first English secular morality play – a political satire – and this was followed by other political and clerical satires attacking Cardinal Thomas Wolsey and the new philosophy of humanism.

A prominent patron of the poet and satirist John Skelton was Margaret Beaufort, Countess of Derby, mother of Henry VII. Lady Margaret used her wealth and status to found schools and became patron of both English universities, albeit favouring Cambridge, where she founded colleges as well as making other gifts and bequests. This greatly influential Lancastrian figure also personally translated religious works, including *The Mirror of Gold* from French, which inspired Henry Watson's 1509 prose translation of *The Ship of Fools*. A verse translation of this satire on the follies and vices of mankind was also printed in the same year by Alexander Barclay. The Countess translated Thomas à Kempis into English and gave generous support to Bernard André, the blind court poet, and the early English printers William Caxton, Richard Pynson and Wynkyn de Worde.

Influenced by the emergence of English poets, the rise of Scottish poetry began with the writing of *The Kingis Quair* by James I of Scotland during the early decades of the 15th century, while he was imprisoned in England successively by Henry IV, V and VI. The main poets of the subsequent Scottish movement between 1460 and 1513 were Robert Henryson, William Dunbar and Gavin Douglas. The version of Virgil's *Aeneid* by Douglas is one of the early monuments of Renaissance literary humanism in English.

With the accession of Henry, Earl of Richmond, in 1485, the French language once again became the language of the Court. King Henry's experience of living in France influenced his choice of courtiers and he surrounded himself with men who promoted the Renaissance 'New Learning'. Henry was interested in the political and cultural life of the main Italian states and during his reign the English court became a more interesting and cosmopolitan place than it had hitherto been. Foreign scholars were welcomed, and Henry became a leading patron of English writers and poets.

Henry's interest in the arts was widely recognized, and knowledge of the Classics was regarded as an avenue to royal favour, encouraging others to master the Renaissance learning. Erasmus reported in 1505, that London had eclipsed both Oxford and Cambridge, and had become the country's most important educational centre, where

> there are ... *five or six men who are accurate scholars in both tongues [Greek and Latin], such as I think even Italy itself does not at present possess.*

The philosophy of Renaissance humanism had been introduced into England at the end of the 15th century and the early part of the 1500s by Sir Thomas More and scholar Dr John Colet, despite their Catholic beliefs. More's work *Utopia* has been described as an outstanding work of Humanist moral philosophy. These 'English Erasmians' were joined by the Oxford scholars, most of whom had travelled to Italy to master the new Platonic learning. The teaching and example of Thomas Linacre, Thomas Lupset and William Grocyn spread humanism into English education and, in turn, influenced the nation's poets.

From the second decade of the 16th century the intelligent, well-educated Henry VIII continued the royal tradition of Lancastrian patronage of the arts, but with particular emphasis upon music, lyrical poetry, painting and magnificent architecture. John Skelton was a principal tutor of the young prince and at an early age Henry was complimented by Erasmus and Thomas More as a man of letters. The prince received dedications and presentation volumes from aspiring authors. The king's main library was at Whitehall, but he also possessed a library at Hampton Court and at least two at Greenwich. It is estimated that in all, Henry VIII owned some 1,500 volumes, including numerous printed classical texts, along with manuscripts taken from the monasteries that Henry had dissolved earlier in his reign.

Any literary influence by the young Edward VI during his six-year reign was not marked, but it was during the regency in 1549, two years after his accession, when the Book of Common Prayer was published. This book contained the first complete forms of service for daily and Sunday worship in English. It was an influential precursor of the 1610 St James Bible in its use of poetic phrasing and dramatic vocabulary. The Prayer Book was revised in 1552 shortly before the king's death.

It was during the latter half of Edward's VI's reign when the Italian Michelangelo Florio Corollanza, a Protestant reformer fleeing persecution from the Inquisition, settled in London under the auspices of Sir William Cecil, Archbishop Cranmer and Sir John Cheke, Greek scholar and tutor to Edward VI. Michelangelo Florio became the Italian teacher of Lady Jane Grey, daughter of the 1st Earl of Suffolk, in whose household he resided. He was also tutor to Henry Herbert, 2nd Earl of Pembroke and presumably he was also resident with the Herbert family.

This teaching of Italian to premier English nobility resulted in two manuscripts about Italian grammar, the *Regole de la lingua thoscana*, and the *Institution: de la lingua thoscana*; one dedicated to the Earl of Pembroke and the other to Lady Jane Grey, whose downfall is described in Florio's 1561 *Historia de la vita e de la morte ... Signora Giovanna Graia*, published in 1607. There is conjecture that Michelangelo Florio also taught Princess Elizabeth, since he dedicated his Italian translation of *Agricola*, on the subject of metallurgy, to Queen Elizabeth in 1563.

Following the accession of Mary I in 1553 and the accompanying severe anti-Protestant repression instituted by the new monarch, Michelangelo

Florio fled the country, settling with his wife and son John in Soglio, Switzerland. Upon returning to London during the early 1570s the well-educated John Florio was to follow in his father's footsteps in becoming the outstanding lexicographer and grammarian of his age. John Florio was to effect the introduction of the Italian vocabulary and idiomatic expression into English; the linguist is also likely to have had an editorial role in the production of the First Folio. The remarkable presence of Italy in many forms within a large number of First Folio plays is reviewed in a subsequent chapter.

Mary I was not noted for patronage of the arts, but Nicholas Udall produced entertainments for her court and he also wrote *Rafe Roister Doister*: a favourite play of Elizabeth I in later years.

The next milestone in English poetry was reached by Henry Howard, Earl of Surrey, one of the founders of English Renaissance poetry, an imitator of Petrach and other Italian poets. Surrey toured Europe and Italy, and became one of the early reformers of English metre and style. Surrey was England's first classical poet to translate Virgil into blank verse, then an innovation, and he developed the sonnet form. Thomas Wyatt, a disciple of Surrey, was also greatly influenced by Petrach. An early sonneteer, Wyatt's first poems appeared in *Tottle's Miscellany* in 1557. While Wyatt's poetry reflects classical and Italian models he also admired the work of Chaucer and his vocabulary reflects that of the earlier poet. Wyatt's best-known poems are those that deal with the trials of romantic love, but others poems were scathing, satirical indictments of the hypocrisies and flattery required of courtiers ambitious to advance at Court.

Minor poets were present in England contemporary with and after Surrey and Wyatt, but it was several decades before the memorable verse of Thomas Sackville came to the fore. This humanist and dramatist reverted to the medieval tradition in his work. Sackville conceived the idea of the famous 1563 *Mirrour for Magistrates,* stories of misfortune of great figures in English history written by several poets, founded upon Lydgate's *Fall of Princes*. Sackville is said to be the connecting link between Chaucer and Spenser, whose *Fairie Queen* was influenced in part by the earlier poet.

In 1590 Edmund Spenser, under the patronage of Leicester and Sir Henry Sidney, wrote the romantic epic *Faerie Queen*, an extended hymn of praise to the queen influenced by earlier allegory and the Italian Renaissance, and introduced the Spenserian stanza.

During Sir Philip Sidney's enforced absence from court having offended Elizabeth, the poet wrote *Astrophel and Stella,* the first draft of *The Arcadia* and *The Defence of Poesy*. Other literary influences upon Sidney included his friends and fellow poets, Fulke Greville, Edward Dyer, Edmund Spenser and Gabriel Harvey, founders of the 'Areopagus', a group centred on Wilton House, one of the homes of his sister Mary, Countess of Pembroke. This humanist-minded group endeavoured to classicise English verse. The members exchanged poems in manuscript form, composing poems on set themes and imitating Marsilio Ficino, the humanist renaissance philosopher. The 'Areopagus' referred to the hill near the Acropolis in Athens, where the Athenian Upper Council met. The 'Wilton Circle', greatly influenced by Mary Herbert (nee Sidney), became a prominent meeting point for contemporary poets and flourished despite Sir Philip's early death.

Spenser's *Shephearde's Calender,* dedicated to Philip Sidney, marks the introduction of the classical pastoral into an English context, and is a mode of poetry that assumes an aristocratic audience with a certain kind of attitude to the land and peasants: the pastoral idyll. The explorations of love found in the sonnets and typified in the poetry of Walter Raleigh, alongside other writers of the age, also infers a courtly audience.

Translations of classical poetry also became more widespread. Ovid's *Metamorphoses* was first translated by Arthur Golding in 1567 and Chapman's translations of Homer's *Iliad* 1611 and *Odyssey* (c. 1615) were some of the outstanding translations that followed.

Examples of the influence of classicism on Elizabethan poetry are Gavin Douglas' *Aeneid* and Thomas Campion's metrical experiments. It remained common for poets of the period to write on themes from classical mythology. *Venus and Adonis* and Christopher Marlowe / George Chapman's *Hero and Leander* are examples of this kind of work.

The notably rapid refinement of the English language in the Elizabethan and Jacobean period owed a great deal to the character and attitudes of Queen Elizabeth. The monarch's steadfast patronage of theatre and writers at the highest level is not to be under-rated.

The Queen, a very well-educated monarch, set the artistic standard for the aristocracy and the rest of sophisticated society. Elizabeth's love of music, drama and poetry fostered an atmosphere in which many of England's greatest writers found encouragement and financial patronage. Under Elizabeth's leadership, England experienced the cultural reawakening or renaissance of thought, art and vision which had begun in Italy a century earlier, centred on the re-discovery of Classical texts.

Elizabeth's court was a magnet, attracting the most talented individuals of the age. At the Queen's direction, Oxford and Cambridge universities were reorganized and chartered as centres for learning and scholarly endeavour; they in turn fostered the majority of the country's leading playwrights.

From the beginning of the early Elizabethan age, plays were warmly welcomed at Court and writers were encouraged to create works for the Queen's entertainment. These plays were performed at the Royal palaces of Whitehall, Greenwich, Richmond and Hampton Court, or on her 'progresses' to stately homes where the plays were staged.

Elizabeth favoured plays as a feature of the royal hospitality accorded by her to visiting dignitaries, principally ambassadors and their retinues. From time to time foreign royalty were in the court theatre audience. The well-educated Elizabeth's appreciation of the unfolding drama enabled her, now and then, to translate for the ambassadors present. It was not unknown for the Queen to translate passages of dialogue for the diplomats, occasionally in several foreign languages, during the performance of the play. There is evidence that theatrical entertainment was frequently staged during an interval or after the lengthy state dinners. This arrangement thus provided the opportunity for a discussion of the subject contained in the drama, perhaps a moral dilemma, and the actions taken by the characters.

With the consolidation of Elizabeth's power, a court of culture emerged that was sympathetic to poetry and the arts in general. This environment encouraged the dawn of poetry aimed at, and often set in, an idealised version of the courtly world.

As an illustration of this poetic activity, Elizabeth I translated part of Horace's 'De Arte Poetica', as did scholar Thomas Drant in 1567. This classical epistle is concerned with the language and purpose of drama; the work heavily influenced the court poets and playwrights of the time, particularly the Wilton literary group. In the next generation, Ben Jonson also translated the 'De Arte Poetica' and absorbed its principles of verse construction. Greek drama was another notable influence on university-educated writers during Elizabeth's reign. However, the character of later drama gradually changed to satisfy the grosser appetites of the Jacobean court.

It was the Elizabethan age that fostered the major intensification in the development of English poetry and drama, both in its extent and its much broader sophistication of language. Inspired by the artistic creativity of the European Renaissance, English poets had found a poetic vigour by the turn of the century that inspired the writers who followed them. The succeeding years were to experience a wealth of literary output. By the end of

Elizabeth's reign some two dozen playwrights were producing works for court performance and the London stage.

The monarch's fondness for plays was to be echoed strongly by her royal successor James I, another most able scholar. The 'poet King', together with his family, proved to be an outstanding patron of poets and playwrights; the advance of English poetry and drama continued unabated from 1603.

While Queen Elizabeth provided the royal seal of approval for English writers, enlightened members of the aristocracy played a major role in the literary development that built upon the cultural foundations and literary patronage of their ancestors. As the Florentine Renaissance owed much to the Medici's, a similar debt was incurred by the English literary Renaissance to the Dudley, Sidney and Herbert families. The Earl of Leicester, Robert Dudley, uncle to Sir Philip Sidney and Mary Herbert, later Countess of Pembroke, was a patron of many writers, including Edmund Spenser; this notable poet also enjoyed the patronage of Sir Henry Sidney, father of Philip Sidney.

A symptom of the new values adopted in England was the immense importance which the humanists attached to education, and their deep faith in what it could achieve. Books were credited with an infinite power to teach, whether it was by precept, historical instance or by the feigned images of poetry – depending especially upon the purity of a child's mind.

This reborn view of human behaviour, well-suited to its expression by poetry and drama, was accepted by the leading schoolmasters of Elizabeth's time, who thought that the art of the play was a powerful form of tuition and knowledge of historical events. It is certainly true that the plays in the First Folio have been accepted without question as records of earlier English history for centuries. Modern revisionist historians however, have shown there to be much distortion of the true record.

The educationalists Roger Ashton at Shrewsbury, William Camden at Westminster and Richard Mulcaster at Merchant Taylors, the leading schools of the day, were all advocates of teaching though plays. The poet Edmund Spenser was one of Mulcaster's boys and the playwright Ben Jonson attended Westminster school.

It is interesting to note that among Ashton's pupils were Philip Sidney and Fulke Greville, later Lord Brooke, who entered Shrewsbury school together on the 16th of November 1564 and were to be lifelong companions and fellow poets.

The Earl of Leicester, the great favourite of Queen Elizabeth, is recognised as the outstanding patron of his age, bestowing his benefaction upon a diverse range of writers, artists and musicians. This son of the disgraced Duke of Northumberland who was attainted upon Queen Mary's accession, eventually rose to become an influential courtier and the leader of the Protestant movement in England during the 1570s and 1580s.

Poets and playwrights gained Robert Dudley's patronage, as did religious writers of the Protestant faith. It was said that the majority of religious books, treatises and anti-Catholic polemics produced at this time were dedicated to the earl.

The obligation of the arts and literary patronage in Elizabethan times was not confined to successive earls of Pembroke, for many others played their part. The roll-call of patrons is lengthy: Thomas, 3rd Earl of Sussex and Frances Radclyffe, Countess of Sussex, daughter of William Sidney of Penshurst. Her brother Sir Henry Sidney and his son and daughter Sir Philip Sidney and Mary, Countess of Pembroke; the Countess' uncle Ambrose Dudley, 3rd Earl of Warwick; Sir Walter Raleigh; Sir Thomas and Sir Francis Walsingham and daughter Frances; Edward de Vere Earl of Oxford, Henry Wriothesley, Earl of Southampton. All were major patrons.

To these benefactors should be added the statesmen and Lord Chamberlains, Lord Howard of Effingham, Henry and George Carey, 1st and 2nd Lord Hunsdon, and others of that office including: Sir Edward Hastings, Charles Howard, Earl Effingham; William Brooke, Lord Cobham; Thomas Howard, Earl of Suffolk; Robert Carr, Earl of Somerset; and statesmen William Cecil, Baron Burleigh and Sir Fulke Greville, Baron Brooke.

A number of those listed above would continue their patronage into the Jacobean age when other notable supporters of poets and playwrights were to emerge, such as Robert, 1st Earl of Leicester, William, 3rd Earl of Pembroke; Philip, 1st Earl of Montgomery and their cousin Lucy, Countess of Bedford, and niece Lady Mary Wroth.

It would be remiss in listing principal patrons of the Jacobean age not to include the Royal family, for King James, Queen Anne of Denmark, Prince Henry, Princess Elizabeth and Prince Charles were each patrons of the arts and also bestowed patronage upon their own performing troupes of players. Following in the Lancastrian cultural tradition, the Jacobean royal family were avid followers of plays and masques.

The period from the accession of James I until the 1620s experienced the great efflorescence of English drama and poetry, but it was also a time of heightened anxiety about England's Protestant existence. Challenging the status quo were the twin terrors of the threat from Catholic Spain and internal danger from the seditious Jesuit infiltrators: both intent on destroying English monarchy, the existing establishment and the Protestant Church.

The Catholic faith of Queen Anne and the seeming ambivalence of the King in his acceptance of a Spanish royal marriage for firstly Prince Henry, and after Henry's demise, Prince Charles, led the Protestant aristocracy to fear for their wellbeing, as well as their historical and cultural inheritance.

A Spanish marriage, if it took place, meant that many of the leading noble families, such as the Sidneys, Nevilles and Herberts, were to be dispossessed once again. Their lives would be put in danger, as they had been under Mary I. Certainly, the personal history of leading noblemen and that of the Lancastrian historical narrative would be obliterated. The danger of losing England's cherished Lancastrian royal and noble family history was imminent in these years of diplomatic negotiation and uncertainty about the future. The true record, as perceived by the Protestant rulers, must be preserved for future generations in England.

If the Protestant aristocracy was under threat, then so too were the writers to whom they gave protection and patronage. Much of the First Folio was created within a humanistic view of mankind, which stemmed from the Classical age via the Italian Renaissance. This view would be seen as heretical and blasphemous in the eyes of the Inquisition; severe punishment would surely follow for the offending writers. Throughout English history, censorship with attendant punishment had inhibited freedom of expression, but not as absolutely as under Catholic rule since the formation of the Spanish Inquisition. How much worse was to come under the 'Auto-da-fe' public penance in England?

The English nobleman and patron had a deep respect for the obligation of protection for their writers for it was the poet who, from Classical times, bestowed immortality. It was incumbent upon the patron to save their authors and poets from punishment, or even death. In gathering together the plays in the First Folio, the brothers William, 3rd Earl of Pembroke, and Philip, 1st Earl of Montgomery, and possibly Robert, Earl of Leicester and Fulke Greville succeeded in publishing an English history narrative that confirmed the legality of the Tudors, praised their ancestors and recorded occasions of great significance for this inter-related family for posterity.

It has to be acknowledged that centuries later it is impossible to know precisely which family occasions and events were thought worthy of note, such as a royal visit to their homes, the celebration of marriages, the award of an honour or the valour of an ancestor in battle. What is indisputable is that the large number of characters in the English history chronicles are ancestors of the Herbert-Sidney family group – and their association with other First Folio plays – demonstrate the involvement in the publication of those outstanding patrons: Mary Sidney and her two sons.

The fearful atmosphere of this time prompted an action which protected the living writers and editors associated with the First Folio from retribution by later censoring authorities, who were anticipated to be the conquering Spanish Catholics.

The ensuing subterfuge was to present the long-dead William Shakespeare as author. This figure was the businessman, play-dealer and probable scribe who had first acquired and then put his name to half of the works in the publication. The bold Shakespeare deception was strengthened by the seemingly sincere endorsement of ex-theatre colleagues, Condell and Heminge, and the extravagant praise of writers Ben Jonson, Leonard Digges and either James Mabbe or John Marston. These high-flown tributes are for many thoughtful readers highly questionable and deliberately deceptive, as argued in later chapters.

King James - the 'Poet King'

Known as the 'poet-king', King James I of England had earlier, as James VI of Scotland, brought to his birthplace a literary renaissance that celebrated the poetic heritage of his ancestor, James I of Scotland, as well as the Scottish 'Makars', a group of poets of the 15th and 16th centuries who were compared at the time to England's earlier poets Chaucer, Gower and Lydgate.

Upon reaching maturity, the king had placed poets at the centre of Scottish court activity, and after his accession to the English throne this favoured treatment was repeated at the English court. While in Scotland, the young king had encouraged the group of Scottish poets known as the 'Castalian Band'. James VI was not only the prime motivator and head of this group, which included among others William Fowler and Alexander Montgomerie, James was also a practising member.

The principal literary figure to be directly associated with the group was Sir Robert Aytoun who, in addition to being a lawyer and Ambassador of James VI, joined the English Court in James' entourage and became secretary and court poet to Queen Anne. The French humanist writer du Bartas was another literary and philosophical influence on James. Music also played an important part in Castalian performances; some members of the group are known to have been musicians and many of the works were set as songs.

By the time of his English kingship in 1603, James, being well noted by the educated classes for his scholarship in theology and classical languages, had earned recognition as an author and lover of books. The king's literary absorption was well illustrated by his declaration on a visit to the Bodleian library in 1604, when he announced that if he were not king there would be no greater pleasure than in being chained to the library.

James I had laboured to become a poet and was ambitious to shine in prose, as a theologian, as a critic and sociologist; he was confident in his sanguine moments that he excelled in every field. No one in the presence of Apollo affected more ecstasy or assumed a greater claim to poetic immortality.

Sang King James in his invocations to the Goddis:

> I shall your names eternal ever sing;
> I shall tread down the grass on Parnass hill;
> By making with your names to ring;
> I shall your names from all oblivion bring;
> I lofty Virgil shall to life restore.

James aimed at no less glory than is given by "the perfection of Poesy, whereunto few or none can attain."

The King sought literary recognition in Scotland and later in England. In 1584 he published *Essays of a prentice in the divine Art of Poesie*, sonnets which emulated the French writers. A romance in rime royal called *Phoenix* and versions of his favourite poet, du Bartas, and of Lucan followed. Further publications, including a theological work called *Meditations* in 1588; a prose dialogue on *Demonology* in 1597; and in 1599, a political treatise called *Basilikon Doron*, dedicated to his son Henry.

In 1603, as James I of England, he published *The True Law of Free Monarchies*; in 1604, *A counterblast to Tobacco*; in 1607, *Triplici Nodo Triplex Cuneus,* as well as a number of controversial works of theology. The King's works were collected in 1616 by his chaplain Richard Montague.

In terms of their shared interest in the arts, James was well-partnered by his Queen consort. Anne was deeply interested in a wide range of cultural pursuits and was a sophisticated and significant patron of writers, artists and musicians.

Anne played a central role in the development of the court masque – a notable entertainment form of the early Stuart court – and was a principal patron of the playwrights Samuel Daniel, Robert Aytoun, Ben Jonson and the stage designer Inigo Jones. All were directly involved with the Queen's Lord Chamberlain, Robert Sidney, appointed in 1603 when King James created him Baron Sidney. Sidney was created Viscount de L'Isle two years later, and eventually Earl of Leicester in 1618. Sidney died in 1626 and was immortalised as a patron of poets in Jonson's poem, *To Penshurst*.

The Queen commissioned or encouraged the writing of specific works, and her largesse extended to financially straightened writers. An interest in languages, especially Italian, led Anne to engage an Italian tutor, John Florio, son of the earlier Italian exile Michelangelo Florio Crollalanza, and in 1611 the translator dedicated to her a new version of his Italian-English dictionary, *Queene Anne's New World of Words*.

The Queen, Prince Henry, Princess Elizabeth and Prince Charles had their own companies of players, who performed at court and elsewhere, and the Queen had an additional company of child actors, *The Children of the Revels to the Queen*.

In 1615, Anne successfully mediated with the king, on behalf of poet and dramatist Samuel Daniel, for James to appoint a company of youths to perform comedies and tragedies at Bristol. They were named *The Youths of Her Majesty's Royal Chamber of Bristol*.

The Queen's interest may have been fostered initially by Mary, Countess of Pembroke a member of the court entourage. The court of Queen Anne was composed of like-minded women of notable families and relations of the Sidneys, such as Lucy, Countess of Bedford, Lady Elizabeth, Countess of Rutland, (Sir Philip Sidney's daughter), Susan de Vere, and Lady Mary Wroth. These early feminists were highly-educated women, who were writers themselves and often translators of classical texts. They may have, together with members of the Royal family, played an influential role in the selection of plays that were included in the First Folio, as well as in some instances the individual content of plot and character.

Before his untimely death in 1611, Prince Henry also shared the Stuart royal family's general interest in the arts and writers of stage entertainment. When officially ensconced in St James' Palace, Henry, although primarily concerned with warfare and military matters, developed into a major patron of the arts and commissioned leading continental architects.

Being a collector of paintings, the Prince also sponsored musicians and scientific enquiry, and earned the praise of many authors, including George Chapman, John Davies, Michael Drayton and Henry Peacham. In addition,

Francis Bacon dedicated the second edition of the *Essays* to him. Prince Henry's library commenced with Lord Lumley's book collection, with the acquisition of 3,000 books in 1609. The Prince maintained his scholarly interests until his untimely death.

The Globe, a popular playhouse

A modern excavation of the site in Bankside, London revealed that the external foundations of the original Globe were between 97 and 100 feet in diameter. This building stood until the fire of 1613. The second Globe theatre was opened by 1614 and also used for rehearsals for court productions.

"When the beer took effect, there was a great upturned barrel in the pit, a peculiar receptacle for general use. The smell rises, and then comes the cry "Burn the Juniper!" They burn some in a plate on the stage, and the heavy smoke fills the air."

Taine's *History of English Literature*

CHAPTER TWO

Elizabethan and Jacobean popular entertainment, indoor plays,
Inns of Court theatre

PUBLIC drama existed well before the English Reformation that was encompassed in the performances of the Miracle and Mystery plays. These were two different forms of public entertainment and they were both religious in content. One type was performed by the Trades Guilds: the 'Mysteries', focusing mostly upon the representation of Bible stories presented as tableaux. These differed from the 'Miracle', or 'Saint's', plays, which specifically re-enacted miraculous interventions by the saints into the lives of ordinary people. 'Miracle' dramas were usually written and performed by clergy and members of the Church congregation.

Both types of play were banned following the Church Reformation and the establishment of the Church of England in 1534. It was not thought prudent to encourage gatherings since an assembly in itself was seen to be a danger to the State. Throughout the countryside, where often the old Roman Catholic religion lingered, uncontrolled groups of people provided an opportunity for a priest to give the forbidden Sacrament to villagers and townspeople.

There is evidence nonetheless that some dramas continued to be performed until the early 1540s, particularly the 'Mystery' plays, which had mostly superseded the 'Miracle' plays by this time. The secular entertainers continued to tour the countryside with their 'Mystery' plays as late as 1572, using their cart as a stage. Although often discouraged by the local authorities of the towns and larger villages, performers and audiences frequently ignored such disapproval.

When Elizabeth I came to the throne in 1558, there were few specially designed theatre buildings in England. The general populace would have seen only small groups of itinerant entertainers such as jesters, tumblers, musicians, dancers, jugglers and swordsmen. These early 'players' toured England and performed when permitted, in spaces such as market squares and inn yards. By 1560, crude plays and interludes were also part of the entertainment and it is recorded that the largest inns accommodated touring players at various times during the first half of the 16th century.

Concerns over public health and morality led to legislation forbidding performances within public houses, so it became necessary to provide adjoining bespoke structures, whilst also incorporating the trading tradition of the inn. That is why food and drink, sack and bottled ale, were served during the performances at these public theatres. Forbidden in the City the hostility of the authorities led to several major venues operating beyond the jurisdiction of the City of London.

Two of the earliest open-air theatres in London were active by 1557 and they were followed within a decade by half a dozen more. Another ten open-air theatres were in existence by the turn of the 17th century, beyond the jurisdiction of the City of London authorities, some were converted from old monastery buildings. The public dramas centred upon religious themes were to develop in time to popular shows incorporating scenes of everyday, or historical, subjects but much interspersed with tumbling, swordfights, juggling, songs, repartee, jigs and similar amusements. A mix of turns that had previously engaged the unruly uneducated mass audience on tour. It was within this crude staging in outdoor venues of action and direct entertainment in which the minor actor and entrepreneur William Shakespeare was to operate for two decades.

The early open-air venues, which drew custom from the general populace, could be described in to-day's terms as 'pub-theatre or music-hall'. The stage attractions competed with the popular animal-baiting shows, which often alternated in the same venue. The common audience of the popular theatre was held in contempt by the authorities, as demonstrated by this extract from a letter sent from the Lord Mayor and Aldermen to the Privy Council, July 28th 1597:

> *They are a special cause of corrupting their youth, containing nothing but unchaste matters, lascivious devices, shifts of cozenage, and other lewd and ungodly practices... They are the ordinary places for vagrant persons, masterless men, thieves, horse-stealers, whoremongers, cozeners, coney-catchers, contrivers of treason and other idle and dangerous persons to meet together and to make their matches to the great displeasure of Almighty God and the hurt and annoyance of her Majesty's people' which cannot be prevented nor discovered by the governors of the city for that they are out of the city's jurisdiction... They maintain idleness in such persons as have no vocation, and draw apprentices and other servants from their ordinary work.*

The acting troupes had, of necessity, performed under the patronage of a nobleman since the Poor Law Act of 1572 when without this protection the travelling players would have been punished as vagabonds: whipped, branded and driven from the town. At this time, James Burbage appealed to Robert Dudley, Earl of Leicester, seeking appointment of his troupe of strolling players as the earl's liveried retainers and 'household servants': they thus became the Earl of Leicester's Men. All playing troupes thereafter operated under the patronage of aristocrats or royalty.

As mentioned, the entertainment provided by the early Elizabethan stage was composed of itinerant entertainers such as jugglers, acrobats, dancers, swordsmen, musicians and comics. The nature of the entertainment is illustrated by these examples.

In 1580 Leicester's brother, the Earl of Warwick, reacted sharply to the Lord Mayor of London by a letter when the Mayor blocked Warwick's player from competing for a fencing prize. Public fencing on stage was seemingly most popular.

Research by historian E. K. Chambers has revealed *"The Bath accounts for the year 1588-9 show a payment to the queens men that were tumblers."* and he also states that in the same year of the Queen's Men playing company on a tour of the provinces *"Acrobatic feats still formed a part of their repertory and in these they had the assistance of a Turkish rope-dancer."*

Chambers also states that the leading personality of the Elizabethan stage Richard Tarleton, *"Tarleton's own talent probably ran more to 'jigs' and 'themes' than to legitimate drama."*

Much of what we know today about Elizabethan popular theatre has been gleaned from the Diary of Philip Henslowe, which covers his theatrical activities from 1592 and continues, with several gaps, until 1609.

There are many subjects covered in the document, including indications the actions of an early bank: a list of loans, everyday expenditure, property transactions, together with theatrical performances and payments to play-wrights.

The Diary records loans made to more than a dozen playwrights, namely: Ben Jonson, Christopher Marlowe, Thomas Middleton, Robert Greene, Henry Chettle, George Chapman, Thomas Dekker, John Webster, Anthony Munday, Henry Porter, John Day, John Marston, Thomas Downton and Michael Drayton. Significantly there is no mention of William Shakespeare in Hens-lowe's Diary.

Loans to impecunious playwrights appear to be commonplace and brings into question the ownership of plays at that time, and the subsequent attribution of printed texts. There was no copyright law and therefore no formal arrangement for royalties.

In 1599, Henslowe paid Thomas Dekker and Henry Chettle for a play called *troyllus and cresseda,* which is possibly the fragment of the play in the British Museum (*MS. Add 10449*). According to the historian W. W. Gregg it is not the play in the First Folio.

It is claimed by some Shakespearean scholars that *King Henry V, King Henry VI, Titus Andronicus, Julius Caesar* and *King Lear,* were all staged at Henslowe's Rose theatre in the early 1590s, represent the first texts of the plays in the First Folio. This view is touted by scholars wishing to strengthen the argument that the actor-sharer Shakespeare was also the outstanding playwright of the age and, furthermore, that the works from the First Folio were performed on the popular stage.

This uncertain supposition is largely based on the works having similar titles, namely: *Harey the vj, harey v, titus ondronicus, sesar and King Leare.* Contradicting this assertion are the following facts, mentioned previously in the overview of the First Folio controversy:

Firstly, popular plays were changed daily and this frequent change in subject did not allow the cast to memorise lengthy texts. The popular theatre playing companies performed half a dozen plays a week with minimum rehearsal. The average length of the First Folio play is some 3,000 lines so the claim of authenticity for the Rose productions is incredible.

In their 1623 First Folio published form, *Henry V* has 3,227 lines, *Henry VI* 2,702, *Titus Andronicus* 2,558, *Julius Caesar* 2,636 and *King Lear* 3,499. *Hamlet* has some 4,000 lines and at 1,000 lines spoken per hour the performance would last four hours. Quite an attention span for the groundlings standing in front of the stage!

Secondly, the popular and largely illiterate audience was incapable of appreciating complex language; while thirdly, the noisy ambience of the playhouse was totally unsuited for the delivery of a serious play. The environment of the popular theatre is described in detail in this chapter.

A point worth repeating is that inexplicably, despite the claimed Shakespearean authorship of these five plays there is no reference to the actor-sharer in Henslowe's Diary, either for payment of these particular plays or in any other respect. William Shakespeare is indeed conspicuous by his absence in this account of theatrical life.

Payments recorded were also made, in 1601, to Henslowe's son-in-law Edward Alleyn a leading actor, for the purchase of several plays: *Spanish Figge, The Nut, Massacre of France, French Doctor* and *Vertiger.* The *Massacre of France* may have been a short popular version of Christopher Marlowe's *Massacre at Paris.* These plays were owned by Alleyne's company, the *Admiral's Men* and changed hands when Edward Alleyne joined Henslowe as a partner with responsibility for the theatrical side of the business. It was not uncommon for plays to change hands as commercial transactions.

Because of recurrent outbreaks of the plague in London, public theatre tended to be authorised primarily during winter months. In winter, plagues were less frequent and hence there was less danger of contagion among crowds of citizens. Winter performances created a time problem for apprentices due to the shorter day and the night-time curfew. This comparatively short playing timescale included not only the play but possibly swordplay, dancing the obligatory jig, jesting and other musical entertainment as previously mentioned.

A detailed account exists of a performance of *Julius Caesar* at the Globe by Thomas Platter a Swiss gentleman who visited England in 1599. Platter attended a play called *Julius Caesar* and reported home by letter about his experience. *"On 21 September after lunch about two o'clock, I and my party crossed the water, and there in the house with the thatched roof witnessed an excellent performance of the tragedy of the first Emperor Julius Caesar with a cast of about fifteen people. When the play was over they danced marvellously and gracefully together as their custom is, two dressed as men and two as women."*

In fact the play of the same name in the First Folio lists a cast of over forty characters along with an unspecified number of extras: *"Plebeians, Senators, Guards and Attendants"*. It follows that the Globe staging was a much simpler version of this play, a memorial script suitably dramatised, which was appropriate for the popular stage,or a play of the same name.

Yet it is asserted by some scholars that, despite not being trained actors, a handful of players were able to perform the complex plays listed in the First Folio volume. It must be concluded that a more credible explanation is that much simpler versions of the plays were performed by the smaller troupes.

Major outbreaks of plague caused the ban of public assembly in London in 1563, 1574, 1577, 1578, 1581, 1593, 1603, 1625 and 1636; subsidiary outbreaks led to a restraint on plays in 1580, 1583, 1586, 1587, 1594, 1604 and 1605. It became an established custom to close the London theatres when registered deaths reached forty in any one week. Summertime proved the best period for continued, popular theatre performances, but often it was to coincide with an outbreak of plague

Specific restrictions on hours regarding the popular theatre were laid down by the authorities as this contemporary edict demonstrates:

"the which I praie you the rather to doe for that they have undertaken to me that where heretofore they began not their plaies till towardes fower a clock, they will now begin at two and have done betwene fower and five, and will nott use anie drumes or trumpettes att all for the callinge of peopell together, and shall be contributories to the poor of the parishe."

A passage from the French critic and historian Hippolyte Adolphe Taine's *History of English Literature*, describes the unruly atmosphere of the popular playhouse in the Elizabethan period:

There were already seven theatres in London ... so brisk and universal was the taste for dramatic representations. Great and rude contrivances, awkward in their construction, barbarous in their appointments; but a fervid imagination readily supplied all that they lacked, and hardy bodies endured all inconveniences without difficulty. On a dirty site, on the banks of the Thames, rose the principal theater, The Globe, a sort of hexagonal tower, surrounded by a muddy ditch, on which was hoisted a red flag. The common people could enter as well as the rich; there were sixpenny, two-penny, even penny seats; but they could not see it without money. If it rained (and it often rains in London), the people in the pit, butchers, mercers, bakers, sailors, apprentices, received the streaming rain upon their heads...while waiting for the piece they amuse themselves after their fashion, drink beer, crack nuts, eat fruit, howl, and now and then resort to their fists; they have been known to fall upon the actors and turn the theater upside down. At other times they were dissatisfied and went to the tavern to give the poet a hiding or toss him in a blanket; they were coarse fellows, and there was no month when the cry of 'Clubs' did not call them out of their shops to exercise their brawny arms.

When the beer took effect, there was a great upturned barrel in the pit, a peculiar receptacle for general use. The smell rises, and then comes the cry 'Burn the Juniper!' They burn some in a plate on the stage, and the heavy smoke fills the air. Certainly the folk there assembled could scarcely get disgusted at anything and cannot have had sensitive noses. In the time of Rabelais there was not much cleanliness to speak of. Remember that they were hardly out of the Middle Ages and that in the Middle Ages man lived on a dung hill.

Above them, on the stage, were the spectators able to pay a shilling, the elegant people, the gentlefolk. These were sheltered from the rain, and if they chose to pay an extra shilling, could have a stool, they play cards, smoke, insult the pit, who gave it them back without stinting, and throw apples at them into the bargain. They also gesticulate, swear in Italian French, English; crack aloud jokes in dainty, composite high-coloured words.

With such spectators illusions could be produced without much trouble; there were no preparations or perspectives; few or no movable scenes; their imaginations took all this upon them. A scroll in big letters announced to the public that they were in London or Constantinople, and that was enough to carry the public to the desired place.

History of English Literature, volume ii, 154

There is another revealing description of popular stage drama provided by a contemporary visitor to London in 1599, a Thomas Platter, as shown in Appendix 3. The excerpt from his diary, translated from Basel German, describes the many popular amusements and spectacles to be witnessed in Elizabethan London.

This eyewitness account of a nationalistic themed burlesque by Platter does not portray the experience of witnessing a play of quality nor equate the vulgar, noisy behaviour of the London citizen to an appreciation of fine verse. There is a huge gulf of literary comprehension between the First Folio plays and the fare of the popular theatre that was served to its uneducated audience.

As Taine, historian, remarked...*while waiting for the piece they amuse themselves after their fashion, drink beer, crack nuts, eat fruit, howl, and now and then resort to their fists; they have been known to fall upon the actors and turn the theater upside down.*

A further comment from the writer John Lyly underlines the atmosphere of the public playhouse. Lyly's prologues, written in the 1580s for 'boy' plays at Blackfriars indoor theatre has the poet more than once express the hope that the gentlemanly audience in the halls would react with *"soft smiling, not loude laughing,"* or at worst would be too courteous to hiss. This behaviour was evidently a common reaction elsewhere by London theatre audiences. The comments by playwrights John Lyly, Anthony Munday and others are also included in Appendix 3.

The most prominent feature of the amphitheatres was indeed the physicality of audience responses to the play. The sitters in the galleries matched the reactions of the section standing in the yard. As Gosson said in 1596,

"In publike Theaters, when any notable shew passeth over the stage, the people arise in their seates, & stand upright with delight and eagernesse to view it well."

Stephen Gosson, The Trumpet of Warre, 1598

Applause, too, was delivered with both cheering and clapping. Michael Drayton has a sonnet written in about 1600, which refers to his writing plays for Philip Henslowe at the Rose amphitheatre, sitting in the *"thronged Theater,"* and listening to the *"Showts and Claps at ev'ry little pawse, / When the proud Round on ev'ry side hath rung."*

Marston, Dekker and many other poets used epilogues to appeal for applause at the end of their plays, but it seems that it was not only at the play's end that applause came. Moreover it was not just *"brawny hands"* which delivered the audience's opinion. In 1616, William Fennor brought to the reader's eyes a performance recently given to a royal audience and offered a pained account of his play's original reception at the Fortune indoor theatre:

> *Yet to the multitude it nothing shewed;*
> *They screwed their scurvy jawes and look't awry,*
> *Like hissing snakes adjudging it to die:*
> *When wits of gentry did applaud the same,*
> *With silver shouts of high lowd sounding fame:*
> *Whil'st understanding grounded men contemn'd it.*
> *And wanting wit (like fooles to judge) condemn'd it.*
> *Clapping, or hissing, is the onely meane*
> *That tries and searches out a well writ Sceane,*
> *So it is thought by Ignoramus crew,*
> *But that good wits acknowledge's untrue;*
> *The stinkards oft will hisse without a cause,*
> *And for a baudy jeast will give applause.*
> *Let one but aske the reason why they roare*
> *They'll answere, cause the rest did so before.*

The poet Tatham's verse confirms the suspicion that when an audience was addressed as "Gentlemen," or "Gentles," the poet was likely to ask for less riotous behaviour than he had reason to expect:

> *Here Gentlemen our Anchor's fixt; And wee*
> *(Disdaining Fortunes mutability)*
> *Expect your kinde acceptance; then wee'l sing*
> *(Protected by your smiles our ever-spring;)*
> *As pleasant as if wee had still possest*
> *Our lawfull Portion out of Fortunes brest:*
> *Onely wee would request you to forbeare*

Your wonted custome, banding Tyle, or Peare,
Against our cu'taines, to allure us forth.

It may serve as a rough measure of the changes in audience behaviour developed through the 17th century, if we set Jonson's parody of a gallant at Blackfriars indoor theatre in 1616 against what Clitus-Alexandrinus (the Inns of Court poetaster, Richard Brathwait) wrote about an amphitheatre playhouse in the 1620s. Brathwait's Theophrastan character, 'A Ruffian,' is a belligerent swaggerer who attends plays on his own terms.

> *... To a play they will hazard to go, though with never a rag*
> *of money: where after the second Act, when the Doore is*
> *weakly guarded, they will make forcible entrie; a knock with*
> *a cudgell is the worst; whereat though they grumble, they rest*
> *pacified upon their admittance. Forthwith, by violent assault*
> *and assent, they aspire to the two-pennie roome; where being*
> *furnished with Tinder, Match, and a portion of decayed*
> *Barmoodas, they smoake it most terribly applaud a prophane*
> *jeast unmeasurably, and in the end grow distastefully rude*
> *to all the Companie. At the conclusion of all, they single out*
> *their dainty Doxes, to doze up a fruitlesse day with a*
> *sinnefull evening.*

By the end of the second decade of the 17th century the character of entertainment for the masses remained physical 'shows' that did not meet with the approval of their betters. In his capacity as Lord Chamberlain, the Earl of Pembroke although a great patron of the arts wrote in 1622 to all mayors, JP's and sheriffs:

> *...that there are many and very great disorders and abuses daily committed*
> *by diverse and sundry companies of stage players, tumblers, vaulters,*
> *dancers on the ropes, and also by such as go about with motions and shows,*
> *and other like kind of persons, who, by virtue of their licenses: do abusively*
> *claim to themselves a kind of licentious freedom to travel as well as to show,*
> *play, and exercise in the kingdom.*

These players and their 'shows' were to Pembroke: *...full of scandal and offence both against the Church and state."*

This view of the popular audience is echoed again in the prologue to a play performed at the Globe in about 1640 by James Shirley which indicates the regular fare of that audience

> Gentlemen, I am onely sent to say,
> Our author did not calculate his Play
> For this Meridian, The Bank-side he knows
> Is far more skilful at the ebbes and flowes
> Of water then of Wit. He did not mean
> For the elevation of your Poles this Scene.
> No shews: no frisk, and what you most delight in,
> (Grave understanders) here's no Target fighting
> Upon the Stage, all work for cutlers barrd,
> No Bawd'ry, nor no Ballads, this goes hard.
> The wit is clean , and (what affects you not
> Without impossibilities the plot;
> No Clowns, no squibs, no Divells in't oh now
> You Squirrels that want nuts, what will ye do?
> Pray do not crack the benches, and we may
> Hereafter fit your palats with a Play.
> But you that can contract your selves, and fit
> As you were now in the Black-Friers pit,
> And will not deaf us with lewd noise, of tongues,
> Because we have no heart to break our lungs,
> Will pardon our vast Scene, and not disgrace
> This play, meant for your persons not the place

These statements shown above again belie the claim that the cultured First Folio plays were performed for a popular, mass audience.

The First Folio works compared to plays in the public playhouses

On several occasions, the eye-witness description of the public playhouse performance does not conform to the play of the same name in the First Folio. Two examples recorded are the plays *Richard II* and *Henry IV*.

From the Calendar of State Papers Domestic 1598–1601, 578:

> *Examination of Augustine Philipps, servant of the Lord Chamberlain and one of his players, before Lord Chief Justice Popham and Edward Fenner.*

On Thursday or Friday sevennight, Sir Chas Percy, Sir Jocelyn Percy, Lord Monteagle, and several thers spoke to some players to play the deposing and killing of King Richard II, and promised to give them 40s. More than their ordinary, to do so. Examinate and his fellows had determined to play some other play, holding that King Richard as being so old and so long out of use that they should have a small company at it, but at this request they were content to play it.

Furthermore:

Examination of Sir Gelly Merrick before Lord Chief Justice Popham and Edw. Fenner. On Saturday last was sevennight, dined at Gunter's in company with Lord Monteagle, Sir Chris Blount, Sir Chas. Percy, Ellis Jones, Edw. Bushell, and others, On the motion of Sir Chas. Percy, they went all together to the Globe over the water, where the Lord Chamberlain's men used to and were there somewhat before the play began, Sir Charles telling them that the play would be of Harry the Fourth. Cannot say whether Sir John Danvers was there or not, but he said he would be if he could; thinks it was Sir Chas. Percy who procured that play to be played at that time. The play was of King Henry the Fourth, and of the killing of Richard the Second, and played by the Lord Chamberlain's players.

Calendar of State Papers (Domestic). 1598-1601, 575.

Clearly, this is not a reference to the play of *Henry IV* or *Richard II* as they appear in the First Folio.

This example of part of an early script for the popular theatre by the dramatist Richard Brome from *A Mad Couple Well Matched* aptly indicates the quality of writing:

The rakish gentleman Careless and his servant Wat are penniless, and discussing how to make some money:
Wat: If you could leave her now, and betake your selfe handsomely to other Women, I have thought on a course.
Careless: What, quickly, what ist?
Wat: To set up a Male bawdy house.
Careless: Fy upon't.
Wat: You are handsome, lovely, and I thinke able to do one Man's worke, two or three such Gentlemen more which I know, and can describe to you,

with the wayes I'le finde to bring in custome shall fill your purses—
Car: And empt our bones. I ever had enough of one Mistris Variety would
destroy me. No Gentlemen can be able to hold it out. They are too weake to
make common He whores.
Wat: For a little while Sir, till we have got a stock of rich cloathes; And then
we will put Drey-men, and Wineporters, Cornish Wrastlers & such like into
those cloaths; and make them Country Cavaliers. Have you not seen course
snowt-faire drudges, clapt into bravery, that would doe more bodily service in
a Brothell then twenty Ladies Daughters? They are the Game-beares of a
Bawdy-house, can play ten single courses for a cleane-bred Gentle-womans
one, wee will hire fellowes for groates a peece a day, that shall (without the
additaments of Clary, Cawdle or Cock-broth) get us forty peeces a Man before
Night, or perhaps a hundred by next Morning, out of such shee customers, as
an Aunt of mine shall finde out for us.
Careless: O base Villaine! No I'le never fall so deep below a Gentleman, as to
be Master of a Baudy-house.
Wat: Very good decay'd Gentlemen have done as much.

This example illustrates the point made earlier that the normal fare of the popular theatre was far removed from the complexity and intelligent writing of most of the First Folio texts. The majority of the plays that appear in the First Folio are admired not only for their rich, original use of the English language and memorable characterisation but because of their thoughtful and most often intellectually challenging content.

Drama of this calibre composed by educated writers must have been in the court or in noble houses. As explained crude versions of these intelligent works may well have subsequently found their way into the popular theatre using the same or similar titles.

A distinction should also be made within this classification of 'popular' entertainment, between the enclosed theatre, dealt with in more detail later, attracting a more affluent better-educated audience, and theatre for the ignorant masses, who witnessed shows of mixed stage spectacle antics and coarse verbal humour *(dealt with in more detail later)*. It is not credible that *Hamlet, Coriolanus, Measure for Measure* or even the witty comedies such as *Love's Labour's Lost* would be appreciated or even understood by the audience previously recognised as popular theatregoers.

In several of the First Folio plays there are striking examples of the standing of the popular players in the eyes of intelligent and cultured class. Pre-eminent of these descriptions is that of Hamlet, Prince of Denmark:

Speak the speech, I pray you, as I pronounced it to you, trippingly on the tongue; but if you mouth it as, as many of your players do, I had as lief the town crier spoke my lines.... O! it offends me to the soul to hear a robustious periwig-pated fellow tear a passion to tatters, to very rags, to split the ears of the groundlings, who for the most part are capable of nothing but inexplicable dumb-shows and noise....O! there be players...have so strutted and bellowed that I have thought some of nature's journeymen had made men and not made them well, they imitated humanity so abominably.

Again, in *A Midsummer-Night's Dream* the 'rude mechanicals' led by Quince are mocked for their rendering of *Pyramus and Thisbe* while Bottom is of course the ignorant, yet conceited rustic behaving above his station in life. It is a recurring theme, appearing in the *"Nine Worthies"* pageant in *"Love's Labour's Lost."* It seems likely that the sly, comical characters such as Lancelot Gobbo in the *Merchant of Venice,* or Speed and Launce, the clowns in *Two Gentlemen of Verona,* are comical character parts for the ordinary players who could bring their inn-theatre skills of clowning and other entertainments for the amusement of their social superiors.

Further contemporary descriptions of plays ostensibly from the First Folio, by Dr Simon Forman

Simon Forman, an Elizabethan Apothecary and soothsayer, attended the productions and different versions of named plays ostensibly from the First Folio plays, and his thorough accounts of the performances and the minor details of narratives are at odds with the text in the First Folio. However, they nonetheless give modern readers an impression of what it would be like to be an audience member at the time.

Appendix 3 shows relevant excerpts from Simon Forman's record-books, with some of the spelling modernised.

Three popular open air theatres. The Rose, the Swan and the Globe

The Rose theatre

It was in 1585 that Philip Henslowe obtained a lease on recently reclaimed land from the Thames river amidst the "stinks and stews" of Bankside, an area outside the jurisdiction of the authorities of the City of London, which was noted for brothels, gaming dens and animal baiting. In 1587 an agreement was made for eight years three months between Henslowe and the chef John Cholmley, or Chalmley, for an amphitheatre which was built by the carpenter John Griggs. It was called the Playhouse and later renamed the Rose. The discovery of the building foundations of the Rose in 1989 on Bankside established certain facts regarding its structure. Archaeologists from the Museum of London uncovered the foundations of two thirds of the playhouse ground plan. The Rose comprised a small timber polygon building of lathe and plaster with fourteen slightly irregular sides. The outer measurement diameter was estimated at 72 feet (22 metres) and an inner area of about 47 feet (14 metres) diameter, To modern eyes these measurements are astonishingly small. In effect the Rose interior was slightly less in size than two thirds of a tennis court, at 78 feet (23.78 metres) x 36 feet (10.79 metres). Within this building was a sloping floor of crushed hazelnut shells and mortar leading to a lozenge shaped stage. The audience either stood in front here or could purchase a place to sit or stand in the layered tiered areas surrounding the pit or centre. There was a Tiring house, (a changing area), for the performers and a Lord's room where wealthy patrons could observe the entertainment. The design was based on a bull, bear baiting or cockfighting arena where the audience needed to be close to the action and in the case of cockfighting detect any cheating. As a roofless space the floor became muddy after a heavy downpour and the water gathered at the foot of the stage. Although a rudimentary timber drain was found in the excavation it was probably inadequate for much of the time. There were no lavatories in the popular theatres so an empty upturned beer barrel was placed for the use of the spectators. According to the historian Taine a cry went up periodically of "Burn the Juniper" when a branch of that bush was burned on the stage above the barrel to disguise the smell of urine. Taine's account of audience behaviour is reproduced in this chapter.

It is thought that because the imprint of the stage in the excavation is slightly off centre there may have been a doorway at the side of the stage. There may also have been two levels within the stage area used to enhance the visual effect. Traces of an adjoining building was also revealed in the excavation. This space was probably used for food and drink storage to be sold by grocer Cholmley, licensed to sell provisions, and may additionally used to store props and costumes.

In 1592 Edward Alleyn a leading actor of the time married Philip Henslowe's step-daughter and brought plays from his acting company. Shortly after this time the Rose was extended by approximately six feet which would have increased the space for the audience and probably given the players, and fellow entertainers a larger performing area. The original lease on the land was due to expire in 1593 but historian E.K. Chambers states that Henslowe's lease was due to expire in 1605.

The Rose playhouse gradually fell into disrepair and ceased operating by 1603. The building of the Rose encouraged construction of other amphitheatres on Bankside namely the Swan in 1595 and the Globe in 1599, previously, The Theatre, Shoreditch.

The Swan

Details exist regarding the Swan amphitheatre built in the Manor of Paris Gardens, once the site of Bermondsey Monastery outside the jurisdiction of the City of London, purchased by Francis Langley. The Swan was probably slightly larger than the Rose but archaeologists have been unable to excavate the site in Hopton Street, Bankside to ascertain its size. From the plan described by E. K. Chambers it was a double circle or dodecahedron divided into twelve compartments with a small tiring house or porch. On November 1594 the Lord Mayor wrote to Lord Burleigh that Langley *"intended to erect a new stage or Theater (as they call it) for the exercising of playes vpon Banck side"* A Dutchman, Johannes De Witt, who visited London about 1596 left a description in Latin which describes the Swan as the finest and biggest of the London amphitheatres with a capacity he suggests of 3,000 spectators. The figure of three thousand spectators appears to be well overestimated and would have created a logistical nightmare of crowd control. How could such a number arrive and depart through a single doorway or even two, within an acceptable time of possibly an hour? Furthermore how was it possible to fit in thousands of people in a space of at best 100 feet diameter or slightly over 30 metres. It may be noted that the Albert Hall has a capacity of 5,272 seats and it is 272 feet (83 metres) by 236 feet (72 metres) and 135 feet (41 metres) high to accommodate the three tiers. The Swan theatre was in comparison approximately one third in size. Finally, how were such large numbers assembled quickly upon merely the raising of a flag above the theatre or the sound of a bugle? The accepted signals for announcing a performance. De Witt also drew a sketch of the interior showing the stage and galleries. If the Lord Chamberlain's Men used the Swan for rehearsals for performance at court in 1596 it would be those actors represented in the drawing. The Privy Council was irked by the performance of plays outside their control, such as Bankside, and threatened to close the popular entertainment venues. However the Swan continued to offer various entertainments for Londoners including *"extemporall"* versifying and feats of activity including fencing but was not a very popular venue and only used intermittently until it finally closed in 1632. One description survives of an entertainment seen by a Richard Vennar. The account of the event shows that the Swan stage was fitted with hangings, curtains, chairs and stools capable of scenic effects. Impressions such as the appearance of a throne of blessed souls in heaven, black and damned souls accompanied with fireworks from beneath the stage. The Hope theatre, Bankside, was another building of similar construction to the Swan and it had a removable stage when it accommodated bear baiting. This feature may also have applied to the Rose, Swan and Globe

The Globe - earlier known as The Theatre

The first theatrical enterprise in London was known as The Theatre and built in April 1576 on the initiative of James Burbage in the Liberty of Holywell, Shoreditch adjoining Finsbury Fields, on a lease for twenty years. Burbage was a Joiner as well as a player and found a partner in his brother-in-law John Brayne a successful grocer who had been connected with a speculation at the Red Lion Inn. The partnership proved to be fractious and soon litigious with Burbage accused by Brayne of deceitful behaviour regarding the box-office takings among several other grievances. Burbage's original building estimate of £200 grew to more than £500 funded almost entirely by Brayne who also laboured on the site with his wife but without charge. The Theatre was in use by 1577 and by the following year the partners were engaged in acrimonious litigation which persisted for many years including lawsuits with Brayne's widow after her husband's death in 1597. The theatre was used for "activities" as well as plays and it was constructed mainly of timber and some ironwork and included a tiring house and galleries one of which at least was divided into upper rooms where spectators could sit as well as stand. The Theatre building was octagonal, approximately 36 feet (10 metres) in diameter.

Entrance money was taken by appointed gatherers, or housekeepers, placed in lockable boxes and then shared out. It appears that one penny was charged for admission to the building and another one or two pence more for a gallery place. The players were awarded the entrance fee and the owners the whole or an agreed proportion of the gallery money. At this time typical daily earnings for a soldier was ten pence, a labourer nine pence and a maid seven pence. When the lease was due for renewal a legal dispute and opposition from the Middlesex Justices caused the sharers (shareholders, usually players) to dismantle The Theatre and transport its timbers across the river to Bankside. Here they re-erected it in 1599 and renamed The Theatre as the Globe. Elizabethan timber-framed buildings were constructed from massive upright vertical timbers supported by diagonal timbers pre-cut and numbered to fit together off-site, the wattle and daub walls were added after the frame was erected. It follows therefore that the Globe on the South bank was the same size building as The Theatre from Shoreditch, 36 feet in diameter. Corroboration of the size of The Theatre is to be found in Joseph Quincy Adams' book *Shakespearean Playhouses*. Here a detailed site map shows The Theatre as close in size to that of the Rose Theatre. This site map was based on the lease and on other documents in the possession of the Shakespearean scholar Halliwell Phillipps and others. Quincy Adams was a noted Shakespearean scholar and the first director of the Folger Library in Washington DC. Records indicate that the land occupied by the re-erected Globe extended from Southwark Bridge Road to Porter Street and from Park Street to Gatehouse Square. A small part of the foundations were excavated in 1989 beneath the car park at the rear of Anchor Terrace, numbers 67-70, on Park Street. The partial dig, restricted by the limitations of the site, suggested that the construction of the later Globe of 1614, following a fire, was a polygon of twenty sides. In contradiction to this assumption contemporary engravings of the Globe show six to eight sides while a later engraving of 1629 indicates seven to eight sides. Precise details of the later Globe's dimensions are unknown although it has been suggested that the later rebuilt theatre was a three story open-air structure 100 feet, 30 metres, in diameter: twenty two feet larger in diameter than the length of a tennis court. It is also speculated that the stage was 43 feet (13.1 metres) by 27 feet (8.2) metres. On this stage, half the size of a tennis court, was a trap door to allow the performers to access the stage. Again it is presumed that there was a standing space in front of the stage with an area for "groundlings" or the impecunious who paid a penny admission. For a seat or standing in the galleries surrounding the central area additional payment was required. Norden's Map of London of 1593 shows the theatre later the Globe, as smaller than the nearby Bear Garden.

There may have been doors at the back of the stage to allow access but this is speculative as is the proposal that there may have been tiring house to the rear of the stage.

These assumptions are mostly based on what would have been needed in this theatre in order to perform lengthy plays with extensive casts. In other words to justify the claim that some of the First Folio plays were performed at the Globe during the Elizabethan and Jacobean era before the 1613 rebuild. Regarding this assumption it should be noted that prior to the Globe rebuilding the playing area was smaller, the size of The Theatre and a space unable to mount the First Folio plays of 1623.

After 1594 early plays with similar names as the plays in the First Folio were performed by the Lord Chamberlain's Men, the company owned by the sharers of the Globe theatre.

Records indicate that the Queen's Men rehearsed and possibly performed there too. The Lord Chamberlain's Men possibly continued this tradition until 1603 when they were renamed the King's Men and were directed to use the Globe for rehearsals.

The first Globe theatre was owned by some of the of the actors, or the Sharers, including William Shakespeare. When the Globe was destroyed by fire in 1613 Shakespeare had by then returned to Stratford according to author Diana Price. Shakespeare's name does not appear on documents regarding the Globe after 1610.

Common misconceptions regarding the plays performed at these three theatres.

It has been shown that the central stage area in all of the Bankside theatres was small ranging from slightly larger than half a tennis court to less than two thirds of that size. How many actors could move freely on stage in this area? Three or four? Yet Christopher Marlowe's *Tamburlaine* supposedly played at the Rose lists seven characters, with others, as the first act begins. Henslowe's Diary records performances of plays of similar titles to the plays in the First Folio. It has been accepted by a number of academics that these plays are the same works as the productions named at the Rose. This assertion is untenable and may be challenged on two grounds.

Firstly each of the First Folio plays in question are too long in relation to the playing time available. Secondly the philosophical and sophisticated content of the plays are clearly unsuited for the audience comprising in the Lord Mayor's description, "vagrants, masterless men, thieves, horsedealers, whoremongers, cozenars, ...dangerous and idle men...".

The plays in question performed at various times from 1591 to 1596 are named in Henslowe's Diary as:

> titus & ondronicus, tittus, titus & ondronicous, andronicous (Titus Andronicus), Sesar, Seasar, (Julius Caesar), Harey vj, Harey 6, (Henry V1), Harey the V, Hary the V, Harye the V (Henry V), Kinge Leare, (King Lear), HamletV .

The bad quarto that exists of Henry V is almost certainly the text performed on the popular stage. This would have been a memorial construction of a full length play performed before a sophisticated audience at court, later re-written for the popular stage by the players themselves. The bad quartos that exist of *Romeo and Juliet*, *The Merry Wives of Windsor* and *Hamlet* are also most likely to be the texts performed on the popular stage and varied with each performance in response to audience reaction.

Henslowe's Diary also shows that three plays of similar titles to Christopher Marlowe's plays or short versions of his plays were performed in 1594 *Tamber-came, tambercam, doctor ffostes/fostes /fosstes and the Jewe of malltuse, the Jewe of malta, the Jewe of malta*. It is difficult to envisage the full length play *Tamburlaine* being performed in its entirety on a stage the size of half a tennis court.

Although the play *Tamburlaine* is performed periodically nowadays, the challenges it presents of a large cast and long duration, together with a declamatory style of acting, does not make it a popular play. However if some of the speeches were assembled and shortened for leading actor Edward Alleyn and the two parts of the play condensed to episodes *Tamburlaine* may indeed have been a popular production. The same may be true of *Dr Faustus*. Were the Rose popular productions re-written by Marlowe for a more discerning audience? It is a possibility.

It may be noted that the disparaging remark by Ben Jonson condemned *"the Tamerlanes and Tamer-chams of the late age, which had nothing in them but the scenical strutting and furious vociferation to warrant them to the ignorant gapers."* Is Jonson referring to Christopher Marlowe's play? This seems unlikely. A text survives of a short play attributed to Marlowe is a bloodthirsty work half the length of Marlowe's other plays *The Jew of Malta*, each part of *Tamburlaine* and *Edward II*. This brief work of Marlowe comprises violent action with little characterisation and indifferent verse. This is probably the text for a popular theatre production, either written by Marlowe for the popular audience or adapting an existing, longer work.

The appearance of similar names of plays in contemporary documents and the surviving texts we have of the leading playwrights draws most scholars to assume that they are the same works. But practical considerations dispel this perception. The size of the popular theatre stage and the nature of their audience both militate against this claim.

The supposed performances of First Folio plays at the Swan and the Globe amphitheatres

Plays performed at the Swan

Contrary to the belief of some writers no First Folio plays are recorded in the Swan theatre

Plays performed at the Globe

A play called *Julius Caesar* was performed in 1599 and others of significance were either performed or rehearsed namely, *As You Like It, Hamlet* in 1600-1601, *Measure for Measure, Othello, King Lear,* in 1605 *Macbeth*, in 1606, *Antony and Cleopatra* and *Henry VIII* in 1613. What is open to question is whether these plays were rehearsals of the parts to be played by the company later at court or alternatively were shortened or re-written versions of original texts. Alternatively these short plays were re-written for inclusion in the First Folio.

Plays by Ben Jonson, Thomas Dekker and John Fletcher were performed at the re-built Globe in 1614 indicating that the company was likely to have been better described as actors rather than players or entertainers. The King's Men were directed to rehearse in the new Globe theatre.

The indoor theatre

There is a contrast between the popular theatre of Elizabethan time, described in Henslowe's Diary, and the later Jacobean theatre, both indoor and outdoor. The early Jacobean age theatre companies were using adult actors trained in the boy chorister troupes for a different educated audience.

Admittance to indoor theatre was more expensive than the other types of Elizabethan theatre. Attending a public theatre performance would cost between 1 to 3 pence, but admission to a private, indoor theatre rose to between 2 and 6 pence.

Indoor playhouses were not so much private as exclusive in character, as the higher price of entry prohibited the attendance of most common folk. Everyone in the private theatre audience was given one of the several hundred seats and the price of admission related to the position and comfort of the seat.

The indoor playhouses were lit by candles so that performances could be staged in the evening. The use of such lighting led to the introduction of intervals when the candle wicks had burned down and they needed to be replaced. Much like today, food and drink was served or sold, during these interludes. Music and songs were strongly featured, and the acoustics of indoor theatres lent themselves to this effect. Elaborate scenery was introduced and as the stage was not open to the outdoor elements they could be re-used; for similar reasons actors' costumes tended to be quite sumptuous.

The plays themselves were selected to suit the better-educated indoor audience and the emphasis became more upon the words of the play than on noisy special effects and the crude visual entertainment presented on the popular stage. In the latter part of Elizabeth's reign, as stage drama developed in sophistication, longer plays were performed in smaller indoor theatres, outside the jurisdiction of the City of London such as the Blackfriars theatre, occupying a part of the old, dissolved Blackfriars Priory. Despite the opposition by local residents and various changes of use, Blackfriars became a commercial enterprise as an indoor theatre that catered for the superior classes such as the "gentlemen of the Inns of Court," and the better-off playgoers.

Some historians refer to the Blackfriars theatres as separate entities: the first from 1576 to 1584 and the second from 1600 until the closure of all theatres four decades later. The theatre opened in 1576 through the endeavours of Richard Tarrant, composer and master of the Children of the Windsor Castle: the choirboys entertained the Queen and court on holidays and important occasions. The small theatre was mentioned in 1579 by Stephen Gosson in his anti-stage pamphlet *School of Abuse* stating that *a great many comedies* were performed there.

The Blackfriars theatre was used for some of the most innovative drama of the reigns of Elizabeth and James, encompassing the pastoral euphuism of John Lyly and the satirical plays of Ben Jonson, George Chapman and John Marston.

The trained and maturing chorister-actors who had been associated with the Queen's Chapel or Paul's Boys were young men who had experienced voice coaching and could read music and scripts. Songs and instrumental pieces were a regular and prominent part of performances at the private theatres of the Children's companies. Such staged musical arrangements continued when the choristers joined the fully adult theatres during the transition from the Elizabethan to the Jacobean era.

The Children of the Chapel troupe and choir achieved its greatest eminence during the reign of Elizabeth I, when William Byrd and Thomas Tallis were joint organists of the Chapel. They were a high-powered group with influence and the Master of the Children had the authority to 'press gang' promising boy trebles from provincial choirs for service in the Chapel. There were instances of boys being seized on their way home from the Grammar school.

In January 1576 and January 1577, *The Comedy of Error* and *History of Error* were performed before the Queen by the Chapel Children, and these were possibly early versions of the play in the First Folio.

In 1600, the Children of the Chapel returned to the public stage with regular performances at the Blackfriars. Nathaniel Giles, their Master from 1597 to 1634, became one of the lessees of James Burbage's Blackfriars theatre. It is known that the boys performed at court on 6th January and 22nd February 1601, and in the same year the Chapel Children enjoyed success at the Blackfriars with Ben Jonson's *The Poetaster*.

During the early years of the Stuart reign the Children of the Chapel, specialised in the satirical comedy that appealed to Court wits and a 'Gentle' audience; they were later re-named the Children of the Queen's Revels (1603–5).

They also experienced the downsides of satirical drama, when the play *Eastward Ho* (or *Eastward Hoe*), 1605, attracted official censure and landed two of its authors, Ben Jonson and George Chapman, in gaol. The actors also earned a share of the Crown's disapproval since they lost their royal patent and became simply the Children of the Revels (1605–6).

After another scandal, this one involving *The Isle of Gulls* by John Day, they were known as the Children of the Blackfriars. The Blackfriars company managed to offend the King a third time, in 1608, with regard to their production of George Chapman's two-part play *The Conspiracy and Tragedy of Charles, Duke of Byron*. The double play offended the French Ambassador, whose complaint to King James led to Chapman's work being banned from the stage.

In 1608, the King's Men took over the lease of the Blackfriars theatre, effectively evicting the previous tenants. The children's company moved to the new Whitefriars theatre in 1609, and became, perforce, the Children of the Whitefriars. In the following year however, they regained royal favour due to the influence of Philip Rosseter, lutenist to the Royal household and their new manager: they became once more the Children of the Queen's Revels.

The company performed Jonson's *Epicene* in 1609. In 1611 they acted Nathan Field's *A Woman is a Weathercock*, both at Whitefriars and at court. Field was in the cast of both productions. They played at court four times in 1612–13, performing plays by Francis Beaumont and John Fletcher.

For a time around 1613, the boys' troupe was linked with the Lady Elizabeth's Men. After losing their Whitefriars lease at the end of 1614, they moved to Rosseter's short-lived Porter's Hall theatre (1615). The last play they are known to have acted was Beaumont and Fletcher's *The Scornful Lady*, and the company apparently collapsed around 1616.

The adult companies did not start to use the private hall theatres until after Elizabeth's death, when the mature boy players had been taken on by the earlier playing companies such as the King's Men.

Lesser known to history are the other private theatres existing during the reigns of Elizabeth I and James I. Performances of plays at the private theatre, such as the Cockpit near Drury Lane, may be taken to approximate those at universities, Inns of Court and royal residences – altogether a more refined audience than the rowdy public playhouse. Although noblemen and even ambassadors were known to have visited the open air public playhouse, enjoying the ribald entertainment and other services available, generally the aristocracy viewed plays and masques at court or their town and country houses.

The Cockpit was active from 1616 to around 1665 as a theatre, and after damage in 1617, it was re-named the Phoenix. The original building was an actual cockpit: a staging area for cockfights. Like most earlier theatres, such as The Theatre in Shoreditch and the Globe in Southwark, the location was just outside the jurisdiction of the City of London. The Cockpit was indeed small: on one estimate, 52 feet by 37 feet and circumstantial evidence points to Inigo Jones as its architect.

Queen Anne's Men were at the Cockpit from 1617 to 1619. When the company dissolved upon the death of Anne of Denmark in 1619, their place was taken by Prince Charles' Men from that year until 1622. Lady Elizabeth's Men played the theatre from 1622 to 1624 and perhaps for sporadic periods, as early as 1619 the two companies combined for a time around 1614. From 1625 until 1636 Queen Henrietta's Men were in residence. Henrietta Maria was the French Catholic consort of Charles I.

Other indoor venues catered for the Jacobean playgoer notably the Whitefriars theatre active from 1608 until the 1620's and situated beyond control of the City. Occupied briefly by the King's Revels Children and then the Children of the Queen's Revels the theatre staged plays by leading dramatists Nathan field, Ben Jonson, George Chapman, Robert Danone, John Marston and Beaumont and Fletcher. In 1629 the Whitefriars was replaced by the Salisbury Court built in the grounds of Dorset House by St Brides. The theatre was played by the King's Revels Men, Prince Charles Men and Queen Henrietta's Men (writers?)

Another venture by Philip Henslowe this time in partnership with Philip Meade was the Hope theatre on Bankside between 1613-14. Here was staged Ben Jonson's Bartholomew Fair acted by Lady Elizabeth's Men. This company was joined by Prince Charles Men in 1615. The theatre was of mixed use from its beginning and after 1619 was devoted to bear, bull baiting, prize-fighting, fencing contests and similar public amusements.

Gray's Inn

The Knights Templar Hospitallers leased many of their establishments to London lawyers which were used as hostels, or Inns, by Barristers and Law Students. As time passed so began the Inns of Court and Chancery. This group of buildings evolved into the equivalent of a University which taught, in addition to Law, the Arts, Theology and Medicine. They were even described by Edward Coke in 1602 as *a third University.*

The Inns, besides training for the law, educated the sons of the nobility and country gentry and the Inns retained close contacts with the Court, and so with government and its administration.

In addition to playwrights there were poets among the Inn's members' for it was a time when the writing of verse was considered to be a necessary social accomplishment. The writing for the Gray's Inn Revels of 1594/5 was of such a high standard that a publisher thought it worthy of reprinting the text later. Many of the famous Elizabethan courtiers and statesmen were members of Gray's Inn and it became a fashionable place for wealthy noblemen to send their sons. Representatives of the English aristocracy at Gray's Inn in their early years included William Cecil, Lord Burleigh; Lord Howard of Effingham, Sir Walter Raleigh, Sir Francis Walsingham, Sir Francis Bacon, Anthony Bacon and Henry Wriothesley, third Earl of Southampton.

Gray's Inn became famous for hosting various forms of entertainment including Revels and dancing and even Elizabeth herself was the Grays Inn's Patron. In 1594-5 the famous Christmas festivities featured on Innocents' Day

> a Comedy of Errors [like to Plautus his Menechmus] was played by the players. So that night was begun, and continued to the end, in nothing but Confusion and Error; whereupon, it was ever afterwards called, The Night of Errors.

The following day a mock-trial was held at Grays Inn, in which a pretend sorcerer was arraigned on the charge that *"that he had foisted a Company of base and common Fellows, to make up our Disorders..."* It seems that the Players taking part were not held in any great respect.

This play does not seem to be the same version of *The Comedy of Errors* that was played at court on Innocents' Day ten years later.

The Middle Temple Great Hall

To earn their title, English Barristers were, and still are, required to join one of the four Inns: Gray's Inn, Middle Temple Inn, Lower Temple Inn or Lincoln's Inn. The Middle Temple Great Hall was built between 1562 and 1573, and was used as a venue for Elizabethan plays. The Hall measures 100 feet in length; it has a 60 foot high oak double beam roof and a carved wooden screen.

During the 15th and 16th centuries the Great Hall was used as a venue for lavish entertainment. The festival occasions celebrating Christmas and Candlemas were especially important, and Middle Temple became well known for hosting various forms of entertainment including plays. In 1602, the Chamberlain's Men were invited to perform at the Middle Temple Hall. This was the first recorded performance of *Twelfth Night* at the Great Hall, and it is believed that William Shakespeare, an actor, was included in the cast. John Manningham, who was a member of the Temple, watched the production and wrote the following in his diary:

> *Feb 2 at our feast (Candlemas) we had a play called Twelfth Night or What you will, much like the Comedy of Errors or Menaechmi in plautus... A good practise is it to make the steward beleeve his Lady widdowe was in Love with him by couterfayting a lettre, as from his Lady, in general termes, telling him what shee liked best in him and prescribing his gesture in smiling his apparraile etc. And then when he came to practise, making him beleeve they took im to be mad*

The Middle Temple indoor Playhouse was located outside of the City of London limits, and was suitable for winter and evening productions with an audience capacity of up to 500 people. As a Great Hall in an existing, prestigious building it was well suited as a venue for performance. The area was lit by candlelight and food and drink was served in the intervals.

Music and song were strongly featured since the acoustics of the Middle Temple Halls lent itself to their use. The plays were selected to suit the indoor venues and audience with an emphasis on the words of the performance rather than the noisy special effects of the popular stage.

The Cockpit in Court after an engraving by Mazell in
Pennant's London.

CHAPTER THREE

Ritual and entertainment at Court

COURT theatre, in its broadest understanding, would be found well before the 16th century, when entertainment for the monarch and courtiers would have included musicians, troubadours or bards, dancers, acrobats and clowns. By the latter decades of the 16th century, the strolling players were present to augment the cast of dramatic works and masques played at court, as well as to provide the skills required for lighter entertainment. It was during Elizabeth's reign when the boy players who were trained choristers, first occupied a central role in productions at court. Their presence continued in the Jacobean era when a number of them had become adult.

The Elizabethan court referred both to the various royal palaces, mostly in and around London, and to the body of people who surrounded the monarch. The great hall at Whitehall had been used for coronations and for the housing of Parliament and the Courts of Justice. The day to day activities of the court had been transferred to York Place, a conglomerate of buildings covering many acres from St James Park to the river Thames.

The court was present wherever the Queen happened to be and it was made up of the privileged group who served her Majesty: the members of the Privy Chamber, Royal Household, the Privy Council and lesser courtiers. One estimate suggests that Elizabeth's court included some 1,250 people in attendance. Once a year the Queen would go on a 'progress' to the noblemens' houses but most of the time she resided in one of her great royal palaces. These included Whitehall, reputedly the largest palace in Europe, spanning 23 acres; Hampton Court; Greenwich; Richmond; Westminster; St James; Windsor Castle; and towards the end of her reign, Nonsuch. The latter palace Nonsuch was destroyed later.

Entertainment at court included such pastimes as jousting, dancing, poetry reading, dramatic performances, hunting, riding, banqueting and concerts. In addition to pleasure and recreation, court entertainments provided a means to interact with the Queen and to attract her attention. The intense cultural life of the court also partly explains why the Elizabethan age was noted for its poetry, drama and music, usually centred upon the monarch.

Two comedies were performed before the Queen in December, 1594, at the Royal Palace at Greenwich. The players took the leading position as servants to the Lord Chamberlain, though no record has been found listing the names of the plays in question. It is, however, known that *"The Pleasant Conceited Comedy of Love's Labour's Lost"* was played before her highness in the Christmas holidays on December 26th, 1597. Both in this year and the year after, the Queen watched the *First and Second Parts of King Henry IV*, and it was said she was very pleased by the performances of what was then the two new plays.

The Queen's playing company (the exact troupe is unclear) performed at court in the Christmas holidays of 1598–9. The troupe also played again before her Majesty at Richmond and at Whitehall during the Christmas festivities of the same year

Moreover, the company played before her majesty at Whitehall during the festivities of 1601–2. In December 23, 1599, the State papers reported from the Council Chamber, Richmond Palace, that *"There is no other news than of dancing, plays, and Christmas pies. The Court is the only school of wisdom in the world."*

In connection with the drama, it has not hitherto been observed that in the latter part of her life Queen Elizabeth was often at Nonsuch Palace during the summer months. Elizabeth held court at Nonsuch as early as 1582 until her closing years, and we cannot but suppose that the players frequently performed at this favourite royal mansion, as they did at her other palaces. Eventually the palace came into the possession of Queen Anne of Denmark – a notable patron of drama and court masque.

The last time the company had the honour to perform before the aged Queen Elizabeth was at Richmond Palace on February 2nd, 1603 but her death followed soon after on March 24th of the same year.

While Queen Elizabeth welcomed theatre at court her successor exceeded her enthusiasm as the records demonstrate. Stage companies played before Queen Elizabeth at court on thirty-two occasions in the last ten years of her reign. In the first decade of James' reign there were one hundred and thirty-eight performances at court and rather than ending at Epiphany on January 6th the play acting season was extended.

Within only a few weeks of arriving in London King James I issued a royal warrant setting up his personal official players. These were the King's Men, called previously the Lord Chamberlain's Men, and noting *"as well for the recreation of our lovinge subjectes, as for our Solace and pleasure when wee shall thingke good to see them, during our pleasure."*

Characteristics of the Elizabethan court

Elizabeth maintained a splendid court to project an image of power, but she did not spend money on expensive vanity projects, such as the major building works of Henry VIII. This investment was left to her wealthy courtiers, like Christopher Hatton and William Cecil, Lord Burleigh, who built massive country houses as symbols of status and power. These private houses were often used as surrogate palaces for the Queen and the court on their 'progresses' around the country.

The court revolved around elaborate ceremony and ritual, which reinforced Elizabeth's position as head of state and provided opportunities for courtiers to catch the Queen's eye. While Elizabeth relied on the devotion of her courtiers for advice and protection, they depended on her continued favour for their position and promotion.

Elizabeth's favourites were often in direct competition with each other for her affection and support. It may be said to resemble a wooing; pursuing her favour and royal patronage literally adopted the forms of a courtship ritual. This behaviour often echoed that of a man for his lover in traditional Romance poetry.

Elizabeth had pet names for many of her favourites and they showered her with extravagant compliments, gifts and letters using the language of love. The Lord Chancellor, Christopher Hatton, one of the Queen's most trusted courtiers whom she called 'Lids' and her 'sheep' is a case in point. Hatton built an immense house at Holdenby, the largest in England at the time, in honour of the Queen and wrote to her in language more befitting a lovesick suitor than a government official:

> Would God I were with you but for one hour. My wits are overwrought with thoughts. I find myself amazed. Bear with me, my most dear sweet Lady, Passion overcometh me. I can write no more. Love me, for I love you.

The Lord Chancellor never married so as not to incur the wrath of his beloved Queen, and to keep the courtship ritual alive. Many of Elizabeth's courtiers did not marry and when they did, as with Sir Walter Raleigh and Robert Dudley, Earl of Leicester they found themselves out of favour or even in greater disgrace and in danger of imprisonment..

These entertainments also allowed Elizabeth to both see and be seen. One of her first public appearances after her coronation took place at London in July 1559, with courtiers and citizens in attendance. An elaborate entertainment was held over several days, including a staged military skirmish, a tilt (a form of jousting), a masque, a banquet and fireworks. It seems a good time was had by all, and Elizabeth's behaviour – dignified, confident, gracious and joyful – reassured those present that she was fitted for the role of appealing to and ruling over both court and commoners.

Tilts, in particular, were rituals designed to impress, allowing Elizabeth's favourites to show off their athletic prowess. Henry Lee, one of Elizabeth's favourites, became her first Champion, representing the Queen in tournaments until his retirement in 1590. Lee was responsible for initiating her Accession Day celebrations, one of the grandest events of each year.

New Year's day and gift-giving

An important ritual in the Elizabethan court calendar was the annual practice of giving gifts to the monarch on New Year's day, when the Queen's courtiers and servants gave her presents to show their respect and devotion to keep her favour.

It was on such an occasion on 1st January 1577 that the comedy *The History of Error* was performed by Paul's Boys at Court, having been arranged by her Lord Chamberlain, Thomas Radclyffe, third Earl of Sussex. This was possibly a version of *The Comedy of Errors:* one of the plays in the First Folio.

In the First Folio text the translation of key plot elements are taken from two Roman comedies of Plautus, which observed the classical unities of time and place when actions happen on one day. From the *Menaechmi* of Plautus comes the main premise of mistaken identity between identical twins, plus some of the stock characters such as the comic courtesan. In *Menaechmi* one of the twins is from Epidamnus, which the author changes to Ephesus, and there are many allusions to St Paul's Epistle to the Ephesians included in the work.

The twin servants with the same name are borrowed from the *Amphitryon* of Plautus, as is the scene in Act 3 where a husband is shut out of his house while his wife mistakenly dines with his double. The story of Egeon and Emilia derives from *Apollonius of Tyre*, a play that is also a source for both *Twelfth Night* and *Pericles, Prince of Tyre*.

The later play of the First Folio, *The Comedy of Errors*, contains a topical reference to the wars of succession in France which would imply the original text was rewritten between 1589 and 1595.

William Warner's translation of the *Menaechmi* was entered into the Register of the Stationers' Company, 10th June 1594, and published in 1595. Warner's translation was dedicated to Lord Hunsdon, the patron of the Lord Chamberlain's Men.

Charles Whitworth, in his edition of the play, argues that The Comedy of Errors was written *"in the latter part of 1599"*, however the piece was not published until it appeared in the First Folio of 1623 with additions.

There is the intriguing possibility that the scholarly Frances Radclyffe, a senior Lady of the Bedchamber, may have supplied the translation for the court performance of this play, or that she even co-wrote the original text of an early version of the Elizabethan comedy, a precursor of the later work, *The Comedy of Errors*.

The translation would have been appreciated by the learned Elizabeth, who had delighted in scholarship from her early childhood. As an adult the Queen was fluent in written and spoken Latin, French and Italian, conversant in Greek and much admired for her language skills. It was recorded that Queen Elizabeth translated Latin or Italian dialogue for ambassadors during performances of plays at court.

Frances Radclyffe, Countess of Sussex, was the second wife of Thomas Radclyffe, 3rd Earl of Sussex, Viscount Fitzwalter and the daughter of Sir William Sidney of Penshurst, who was a prominent courtier during the reign of Henry VIII. As such, the Countess was the sister of Sir Henry Sidney and an aunt of the poets Sir Philip Sidney, Mary Sidney, later to be Countess of Pembroke, and Robert Sidney, Earl of Leicester, father of the poet Mary Wroth. Philip Sidney was the father of the poet Elizabeth Sidney.

In July 1572, the Earl of Sussex became the Lord Chamberlain and he was henceforth, until his death in 1583, in the frequent company of Queen Elizabeth, both in her progresses through the country and at court.

In her will, Lady Sussex left the sum of £5,000, together with some plate, to found a new college at Cambridge University, *'to be called the Lady Frances Sidney Sussex College'*. The college was established seven years after her death and the mascot of the college is the blue and gold porcupine copied from the Sidney family coat of arms.

It is also of interest that Sir Richard Ratcliffe, one of Thomas Radclyffe's ancestors, appears in the play *Richard III*.

Choristers as actors at court

An excerpt from *"The Child Actors"* by David Drew-Smythe (from the internet).

> *The extraordinary popularity of the child acting companies during the sixteenth century began in the centres of choral and ecclesiastic service. Windsor, St. Paul's and The Chapel Royal set themselves up as performance*

> *companies, who specifically furnished players and singers to provide*
> *entertainments for royal and noble households. The "founding father" of*
> *these was Sebastian Westcott, from the West Country, who died in 1582*
> *having guided the "Paul's Pigeons" through a period of some thirty years*
> *of successful presentations."*

Westcott is known to have taken groups of St Paul's Boys to put on entertainments for the young Princess Elizabeth at Hatfield House in 1551/2 when Edward VI was still alive, and possibly again in 1554 or in 1557, during the reign of Mary I.

Under Queen Elizabeth, groups of choristers such as those of St. Paul's and the Chapel Royal had freedom to pursue 'the drama'. For many years, Elizabeth gave her preference to Westcott as a provider of entertainments at court, and soon the Paul's Boys were unrivalled in their list of performances. Hampton Court, Whitehall, Richmond and Greenwich were frequently on their arduous itinerary. They were renowned for their sumptuous costumes, their props and the quality of the entertainments provided for them by a long succession of writers. It brought them wealthy patronage. By 1575, Sebastian Westcott was running a popular and successful small private theatre within the precinct of St. Paul's.

Several of the child actors, trained in music and acting, were employed by the Lord Pembroke's Men: Thomas Downton and Richard Jones, were members of the cast at the time of the *Isle of Dogs*, when Robert Shaw and Gabriel Spencer were sent to Marshalsea prison for their presence in the insubordinate production.

Plays at the country house

In contrast to the open-air theatre, household revels in the establishments of noblemen flourished under the patronage of the aristocracy. Here musicians and performers such as singer-actors were household servants and readily available for rehearsal and festive events:

> *A dozen boys and men, trained in music and rhetoric, were constantly*
> *at the disposal of the great households, a fact that enabled patrons to*
> *request elaborate performance specific to an occasion at almost any time,*
> *for which the household would provide sets, costumes, and playing space.*

> Suzanne R. Westfall, *Patrons and Performance.*

Many plays were therefore commissioned from poets by their patrons, including noble families, statesman and other gentry, for the pleasure and instruction of their peers. The household and visiting players were, in turn, responsible for familiarising the household drama on occasion for the population at large.

In the great household revels, minstrels, players and writers interacted and performed with their combined talents at the Christmas festivals of Advent, Twelfth Night, Shrovetide as well as weddings, christenings and other family celebrations. It was normal practice for musicians and poets to be resident in their master' manors and travelling players lodged from time to time. Suzanne R. Westfall writes:

> *Artists became an integral part of the household structure, crucial to the social position of their patron, and patrons became preservers and promoters of culture.*

The painting of a Tudor great household revel *'Sir Henry Unton's Wedding,'* held in the National Portrait Gallery, illustrates the patronage scene well. The painting shows two viol players, a group of musicians and, in disguise, ten boy players (perhaps Chapel Children) and eight adult actors. Also shown, but of lesser importance, are the household retainers. It is assumed that this scene follows a wedding ceremony as a figure in a Cope (an ecclesiastical garment) suggests that an earlier religious ceremony has taken place.

Probably the best known performance of a First Folio play at a country house was that of *As You Like It* was thought to have taken place at the Wilton country seat of Mary Herbert, Countess of Pembroke. The entertainment was provided for James VI on his journey to London in 1603 for his coronation as James I of England.

At the wedding of Sir Thomas Heneage to the widow Mary Wriothesley, Countess of Southampton in May 1595, Queen Elizabeth was presented with *The Taming of the Shrew.*

An entertainment mounted for Queen Anne, *Love's Labour's Lost,* was arranged by the Earl of Southampton and Sir Robert Cecil. The venue is unclear but it seems to have been at one of their residences.

In 1601 it is known that Sir Fulke Greville, statesman and poet, wrote a 'closet' drama, *Antony and Cleopatra:* that is to say, he wrote it for private presentation.

A record exists of *Titus Andronicus* being performed at Exton Hall, Burley-on-the-Hill in Rutland, one of the households of Sir John Harington, 1st Baron Harington of Exton, who was married to Lucy Sidney, daughter of Sir William

Sidney and his wife, Anne Pagenham. Sir John was guardian of King James' daughter Elizabeth. Lucy Russell, Countess of Bedford, a great Jacobean literary patron was his daughter.

There are many instances recorded of plays performed in England's manor houses, but it was the English court that was the principal cultural centre of the nation during the reigns of Elizabeth and James. Members of the court were educated in the classics and were sympathetic to the new perspective of personal morality that had been introduced from the Italian Renaissance.

Evidence that when a play was performed at a nobleman's house the family would have taken part is supported by a reference in R. W. Chambers' book on Sir Thomas More, wherein he states:

> The Revels office and the control of More's next experience was to be more exciting. He must have left St Anthony's (school) about the age of twelve, and was by his father's procurement received into the house of the right reverend, wise, and learned prelate Cardinal Morton; where, though he was young of years, yet would he at Christmas tide suddenly sometimes step in among the players, and never studying for the matter, make a part of his own there presently among them, which made the lookers on more sport than all the players beside.

Court entertainment

It seems in Henry VII's time that the Master of the Revels was a minor official of the household. In Henry VIII's court, however, the post was notably more important and an officer of the Wardrobe was permanently employed to act under the Master of the Revels. With this came the patent given to John Farlyon in 1534 as 'Yeoman of the Revels': a title that may be considered an independent office of the Revels within the general sphere of the Lord Chamberlain.

In 1544 Sir Thomas Cawarden received a patent as Master of the Revels, and thus became the first head of an independent office.

Sir Thomas Benger succeeded Cawarden in 1560, who was followed by Edmund Tylney in 1579. It was the appointment of the latter's nephew, Sir George Buc, as deputy-master with the reversion to the mastership which led to so much resentment on the part of the dramatist, John Lyly, who was himself a candidate. Under Tylney, the functions of the Master of the Revels gradually became extended to a general censorship of the stage, which in 1624 was put directly in the hands of the Lord Chamberlain.

Commissioning of court plays

It was the cosmopolitan world of the court with its attendant aristocracy, statesmen and scholars, centred upon two highly-educated monarchs, which fostered the patronage of poets during the Elizabethan and Jacobean age.

The Lords Chamberlain of the period were usually patrons of writers and, as such, had knowledge of poets and their work. A familiarity with contemporary authors existed alongside their formal duty of supplying suitable plays for court performance and overseeing the staging of such works.

The mechanism of finding new plays, or locating existing texts, for court theatre placed the Lord Chamberlain in a 'catalytic' role. It follows that there would be considerable overlap of patronage, marking celebratory occasions.

In time a number of these plays, which had individual significance for the begetters of the First Folio, were gathered together and became a permanent collection. These plays were not the work of one author, but the testament of many strands of English life, people and ideas that were embodied in the plays.

It is surely impossible in this context to pass lightly over the presence of William Herbert, 3rd Earl of Pembroke to whom, with his brother, the 1623 publication is dedicated. Pembroke, the contemporary holder of the Lord Chamberlain's office, was acknowledged not only for his own literary patronage, but as the embodiment of the contribution made to the development of English poetry and drama during several generations of those great patrons the Sidneys' and Herberts'.

The juxtaposition of plays with notable social and royal court occasions in turn provides an explanation for the employment of writers by the officer responsible for court entertainment.

The Lord Chamberlain's office

For centuries, the office of Lord Chamberlain was central to the sourcing, selection and staging of plays and other entertainment for the court. This was a tradition which continued during the Elizabethan and Jacobean periods. The duties of the Master of the Revels fell under the jurisdiction of the Lord Chamberlain. As censor, the Master was responsible for ensuring court entertainment did not contain material that might be offensive to the reigning monarch.

In the task of fulfilling their role successive Lord Chamberlains, of necessity, came into contact with playwrights to a greater or lesser degree. Some of those holding the office certainly exhibited an affinity as patrons of writers. Henry Carey, Ist Lord Hunsdon and his son George, 2nd Baron Hunsdon were in turn patrons of the Lord Chamberlain's Men and George and Lady Carey were faithful supporters of playwright Thomas Nashe.

There is the likelihood that various Lord Chamberlains played a deliberate part in the choice of playwright for court occasion plays and also used their authority in determining the subject and the broad content of the plays produced for the royal entertainment.

Significantly, versions of twenty two of the plays contained in the First Folio were performed before the courts of Queen Elizabeth, King James and Queen Anne.

The plays given royal production were:

> *The Comedy of Error or History of Error, Titus Andronicus, The Merry Wives of Windsor, King Leir (Lear), Henry V, Twelfth Night, Two Gentlemen of Verona, Love's Labour's Lost, Romeo and Juliet, Richard II, Midsummer Night's Dream, The Merchant of Venice, Othello, Measure for Measure, Macbeth, Coriolanus, Cymbeline, The Tempest, The Winter's Tale, Much Ado About Nothing, Henry VIII and Henry IV Part 1.*

Additionally, three First Folio plays were presented at noble houses (some of which were in the presence of royalty) and these are: *The Taming of a Shrew, As You Like It* and *Anthony and Cleopatra.*

There are only eleven plays, in all, for which there is no note of a performance at the courts of Queen Elizabeth, James I and Queen Anne, or at noble houses. They are: the three parts of *Henry VI* and an additional part of *Henry IV, Troilus and Cressida, Timon of Athens, Richard III, Julius Caesar, Hamlet, King John* and *All's Well That Ends Well.*

A chronology of court performances of works relating to the First Folio, along with a list of the dates of their first performances can be found in Appendix 4.

The preponderance of First Folio plays performed at court compares favourably with the paucity of First folio plays, even in an inferior form, played in the popular theatre.

Court performance: a case study

Dr Hotson's description of a particular performance in the Great Hall at Whitehall of *Twelfth Night* before Queen Elizabeth.

Dr Leslie Hotson in his book *The First Night of Twelfth Night* describes a day of celebration at Whitehall, 6 January 1600/1, when the Muscovite ambassador and Virginio Orsino, Duke of Bracciano, were entertained by four troupes of actors in various rooms in the Palace: they were the Admiral's Men, Derby's Men, the Children of the Chapel and Lord Hunsdon's Men.

Dr Leslie Hotson discovered the following document in the archive:

A full narrative or description of the reception and entertainment of the Muscovite ambassador and of an Italian noblemen the Duke of Brachiana, who were received at the Court of Queen Elizabeth, together with the names of the noblemen in attendance on her majesty at her dining abroad upon Twelfth-day January 6 1601–2.

The manuscript is in two parts: one part contained an original memorandum of Lord Chamberlain Hunsdon:

To confer with my Lord Admirall and the Master of the Revells for takeing order generally with the players to make choyse of play that shal be best furnished with rich apparel, have greate variety and change of Musicke and daunces, and of a Subiect that may be most pleasing to her Maiestie.

And at the foot of the memoranda a note states:

In the Hall, which was richly hanged and degrees [tiers of seats, grandstands] placed rownd about it, was the play after supper.

From the records, Hotson also found a reference to the play performed by the Admiral's Men at the same event. This work was Thomas Dekker's *Phaethon*, which had been performed in 1598, but was re-written for this state occasion. Henry Carey, Lord Hunsdon, addresses an item in the orders issued by the Lord Chamberlain and states that *"The Children of the Chappell to come before the Queene at Dinner with a Caroll"*. This may have been embellished in some way by Nathaniel Giles, the Master of the Children, because the children received five pounds for *"a show with music and special songs"*.

Hotson's "The First Night of Twelfth Night."

Her maiestie dyned in the great chamber and the Duke of
Brachiano dined in the Councell chamber.
The Muskovy Ambassador...was appointed to be ther.

Mary Herbert née Sidney, Countess of Pembroke 1561-1621.

A poet, author and a major literary patron of her age. Mother of William and Philip Herbert to whom the First Folio of 1623 was dedicated. The engraving above shows well the 'swan' motif in the collar of her gown with which Mary Sidney was associated.
The Swan of Avon.

CHAPTER FOUR

Jonson's 'Swan of Avon': conjecture and doubt

... Sweet swan of Avon! what a fight it were
To see thee in our waters yet appeare,
And make those flights upon the bankes of Thames,
That so did take Eliza, and our James!
But stay, I see thee in the Hemisphere
Advanc'd, and made a Constellation there!
Shine forth, thou Starre of Poets, and with rage,
Or influence, chide, or cheere the drooping Stage;
Which, since thy flight fro' hence, hath mourn'd like night,
And despaires day, but for thy Volumes light.

Ben Jonson, First Folio

BEN Jonson's reference to the 'Sweet Swan of Avon' in his verse encomium introduces the plays of the First Folio, but the allusion is a matter of conjecture among those who doubt the authenticity of authorship of the plays. By discounting the traditional view that this phrase refers to Stratford-upon-Avon, an alternative explanation of Jonson's true meaning is required.

The subtle and layered reference to the Swan is best understood by placing Mary Herbert (née Sidney), Countess of Pembroke, within the context of the legendary tale of mythical swans that preserve the best poetical works for posterity and ensure that the authors' names are remembered. Tributaries of the river Avon run through the Wilton estate and also through the town of Salisbury, where Mary Sidney was buried.

Mary Sidney, like her brother Sir Philip, was a notable literary figure who exerted an exceptional influence upon the major poets of the age and who sought to preserve the foremost writings of her time. The praise accorded to the *'Sweet Swan of Avon'* would be a fitting tribute to Mary Sidney, a clear acknowledgement of her patronage and her role in the creation of the First Folio: the compilation of poetical dramas by contemporary and deceased poets.

The Countess, with the support of her brother, Robert Sidney, Lord Chamberlain to Queen Anne, and her son, William, 3rd Earl of Pembroke, is most likely to have brought together the contents of the First Folio.

In Dr Robin P. Williams' book, *Sweet Swan of Avon,* the author researches the connections between Mary Herbert's ancestors and the sources of the plays in the First Folio. Meticulous research by Dr Williams establishes too many associations between the Sidneys' and the plays to be assigned to mere chance.

The following chapter details the immense contribution made to England's literary life in her time by Mary, Countess of Pembroke. Briefly, this highly educated noblewoman was acknowledged for her translations of classical and religious works as well as for her versification of the Psalms.

Mary Sidney also had a considerable influence upon the content of Sir Philip Sidney's *Arcadia* and helped complete her brother's work; later it was published as *The Countess of Pembroke's Arcadia.* Throughout her lifetime she was to provide guidance and encouragement to a host of writers. Wilton, the country seat of the Herberts, and their London home at Barnard's Castle were centres of literary activity where poets and playwrights congregated. What is less well known is that Mary Herbert adopted the swan as her personal emblem. This choice may have been a tribute to her late brother, who was known by his French admirers, such as the poet du Bartas, as a swan. The frontispiece of a translation of *Arcadia* printed in France shows a portrait of Sir Philip Sidney topped with figures of swans.

That the Countess was compared poetically to a swan is acknowledged in Michael Drayton's *Shepherd's Garland:*

> *the lofty subject of a heavenly tale, Thames' fairest swan,*
> *our summer's nightingale.*

In Dr Williams' *Sweet Swan of Avon,* Mary Sidney's affection for her emblem is graphically displayed in a portrait of her at the age of fifty-seven, which shows her wearing a gown with a large lace collar and wrist cuffs decorated with the swan motif, while swans wings connect the bottom of the oval frame.

The Cygnus constellation within the Milky way derives its name from the Latinised Greek word for swan, 'Cygnus'; it contains one of the brightest stars in the sky, with nine main neighbour stars and many lesser. In Greek mythology Cygnus has been identified with legendary swans: in particular, the god Zeus. Several literary works and myths portray the transformation of mortals into swans: a re-birth inferring immortality. Revered in her time, Mary, Countess of Pembroke, was acknowledged to be at the centre of a constellation of Elizabethan and Jacobean poets. A star bestowing her patronage upon many of the leading writers of her age: the *Sweet Swan of Avon*.

A great admirer of Mary Sidney, Fulke Greville, Lord Brooke, may have also been involved in the preparation of the First Folio volume. By his participation, Greville was able to immortalise, in the Lancastrian history plays, the Warwick name and his illustrious ancestors in the annals of English history. Sir Fulke Greville, truly personifying the Renaissance man, was a lawyer, statesman, poet dramatist and patron of the arts, serving for over forty years as a statesman in the service of Queen Elizabeth and King James.

Upon his deathbed Greville was reported as deeming himself *"the master of Shakespeare."* Another, more cryptic comment was made by Greville when he was asked about the disappearance of his play, *'Antony and Cleopatra'* and remarking in reply *"It is in a far better place."* Was this comment a reference to the First Folio? Further evidence has been uncovered by computer research and analysis, detecting the hand of Fulke Greville as a writer or collaborative editor of the First Folio.

It therefore follows that the most convincing explanation for the swan metaphor is that Ben Jonson is indeed honouring Mary Herbert, Countess of Pembroke.

The swan's place in literary mythology

In the *Legends of Charlemagne* there appears Astolpho, a royal but fictional character who, although bewitched, enjoys magical powers during his mythical adventures. At one stage, taken to a river bank, Astolpho is shown an immense number of skeins of different coloured threads. There, three old women, symbolising the Fates, were spinning and winding bundles each with a label of gold, silver or iron. The bundles were then thrown into the river.

Birds then circulated trying, mostly in vain, to snatch the labelled bundles before they sank, but two swans gathered a few of the bundles and dropped them on the far river bank. Then a nymph carried the selected bundles to adorn a sacred column on the bank upon which stood the statue of immortality.

The swans had chosen only the great poets, who thus remain saved from oblivion and preserved forever. Jonson further emphasises his reference of Poets' immortality in the First Folio encomium, where leading poets of the age are listed (some deceased): Chaucer, Spenser, Beaumont, Lyly, Kyd and Marlowe. It is not unreasonable to suppose that these named poets were all contributors, in one way or another, to the First Folio.

"There is no immortality can be given a man on earth like unto plays."
Thomas Nashe, Elizabethan poet 1567-c1601.

(Left) Sir Robert Sidney 1st Earl of Leicester 1563-1626
Statesman and poet-brother of Sir Philip Sidney, Lord Chamberlain to Queen Anne.
(Right) William Herbert 3rd Earl of Pembroke 1580-1630.
Literary patron and Lord Chamberlain.
Dedicatee with brother Philip of the First Folio

CHAPTER FIVE

Sidneys and Herberts: families immortalised in print

T HE English history plays in the First Folio owe their presence in the volume principally because of the desire for the creation of an historical record favourable to certain noble families in the Jacobean age. The accounts of historical events created in dramatic works several decades before 1623, would now be understood as the historical truth by the generations that followed because of their preservation in this landmark publication.

There are movingly poetic passages to be found in most of these plays and several represent skilled stagecraft and powerful characterisation. Other chronicles, however, are of lower literary quality and most unlikely to have been selected as the best dramatic works of the age. The most convincing alternative reason for permanently recording all of the English history plays is, that together, they provide a favourable narrative of national events. Equally important is the acknowledgement of those members of the noble families who played their part in the development of the independent English state of the Protestant monarchs Elizabeth I and James I. The royal line which stemmed from Henry V11.

What does appear most striking upon examination is the exceptional number of members of the Sidney, Herbert and Neville extended family group who appear in these works over a number of generations. The Nevilles, Earls of Warwick, too were the direct ancestors of Fulke Greville, Baron Brooke, the lifelong companion of Philip Sidney and Mary, Countess of Pembroke.

The ten plays in question span a period from 1199 with *King John* up to 1533 at the end of Henry VIII's reign, and together they mark a significant development in the content of English drama. Prior to this, the only well-known historical dramas were *Gorboduc* by Thomas Norton and Thomas Sackville, and the *Famous Victories of Henry V,* which has been attributed to the stage player Richard Tarlton. The ten English history plays in the First Folio therefore developed this new genre of historical drama.

The stimulus of this progression is most likely to have been provided by the

Countess of Pembroke: an explanation examined fully in *Sweet Swan of Avon*, written by the Shakespearean scholar Dr Robin P. Williams.

In her book, Williams notes that Mary Sidney (Herbert) translated Garnier's *Marc Antoine* and inspired the translation of *Cornelie* by Samuel Daniel, who had received her patronage at Wilton, where he was a tutor to her son William: these works were precursors of the English historical plays.

The association of the Countess with a large number of the characters listed in the English history plays has also been revealed by Dr Robin P. Williams, following her extensive detailed genealogical research (see Appendix 5). Mary Sidney's lineage provides a remarkable connection between many generations of her family and the historical figures recorded in the First Folio national dramas.

The historical narrative of several centuries firmly legitimised and then preserved for posterity the royal claim of the usurping Lancastrian line of English monarchs. The two hundred year history of the House of Lancaster resonates through the English history plays in the First Folio. This became a version of history that ensured status, certainty and unquestionable glory to many Jacobean noble families. Not least the Herberts and Sidneys who had flourished under the English crown.

Later examination of the actual events of the reigns described on stage demonstrate that the plays distorted many of the leading characters, Richard III being a prime example, as well as various events and timescales. Nevertheless, for many centuries these plays were accepted as a true historical record. Indeed, until modern times, when revisionist historians examined these fictional accounts, the play's historical interpretations were accepted without question.

The Countess of Pembroke, strongly associated with the creation of the First Folio, was married to Henry Herbert, 2nd Earl of Pembroke, and descended from a long line of Nevilles, stretching back to Ralph Neville, 1st Earl of Westmorland who died in 1425. The seven generations preceding Mary Sidney included the noble families of Dudley, Guildford, Mortimer and Beauchamp as well as Brandon and Blount.

The Herbert name and the Earls of Pembroke also feature as an illustrious line of noblemen and noblewomen, who date back to the thirteenth century. Holders of the title of Pembroke appear in several of the English history plays.

A notable historical figure appearing in *King John* is the famed knight, William Marshall, 1st Earl of Pembroke, a loyal servant of four kings: Henry II, Richard I, John and the infant Henry III. Known as 'the Marshal', the tournament champion was celebrated for his courage and chivalry throughout the Christian world.

An early manuscript celebrates the life of the knight in rhyme; it was commissioned by his son John around 1200, after the death of Marshall. Entitled *Histoire de Guillaume le Marechal* it was written by a French poet and is extant in the Morgan library, New York.

In addition to the famous names listed above, other characters are present who relate to the Sidney/Herbert/Neville family group. The presence of all these characters to such a marked extent has to be explained by more than co-incidence. The only satisfactory reason is that of a deliberate selection in order to affirm the role of these families and thus preserve their worthy historical place within a publication intended to be a written record for future generations.

In Jacobean times, leading descendants of this group of past dignitaries were the Earls of Pembroke and Montgomery, and their wives Mary Talbot, daughter of the Earl of Shrewsbury, married to William Herbert; and Susan de Vere, daughter of the 17th Earl of Oxford, married to Philip Herbert. Their close friend was Fulke Greville, Baron Brooke, who was directly descended from the Neville branch of the Earls of Warwick. The Earls of Pembroke and Montgomery are the brothers named as dedicatees on the title pages of the First Folio, senior peers of the realm.

Marriage alliances during the Elizabethan age (and in earlier times) produced blood-tie relationships between the Sidney, Herbert, Talbot, Grey, Hastings, Neville and Dudley families, as well as more distant relationships that included Berkeley, de Lisle, Willoughby, Mortimer, Despenser, Montague, Montacute, Abergavenny, Percy, de Ros, Stafford, Ratcliffe, Strange, Brandon and Grey. A number of the English history plays emphasize the proximity of these noble families to the Lancastrian kings of England that, in time, would include James I, who was a descendant of a daughter of Henry VII.

There are a significant number of other Sidney/Herbert/Greville related ancestors who appear, or are referred to, in the English history plays, and they include the following:

Eleanor Neville married to Henry Percy; Lady Elizabeth Neville, married to Henry Hotspur; George Neville, 3rd Baron Abergavenny; George Neville, Archbishop of York; William Willoughby, 5th Baron Willoughby; Henry Percy, 1st Earl of Northumberland; Henry Percy, 3rd Earl of Northumberland; Thomas Percy, Earl of Worcester; Lord Thomas Berkeley, 5th Baron Berkeley; William de Ros, 6th Baron de Ros; Edmund Stafford, 5th Earl of Stafford; Henry Stafford, 2nd Duke of Buckingham; Henry Stafford, 3rd Duke of Buckingham; Sir Humphrey Stafford, Earl of Stafford; Humphrey Stafford, Duke of Bedford; Sir Humphrey Stafford, Knight; Sir Richard Ratcliffe; Sir John

Stanley; Sir Thomas Stanley; Lord Thomas Stanley; Sir George Stanley, Lord Strange; Sir John Talbot, 1st Earl of Shrewsbury; Sir Gilbert Talbot, Knight; Sir Ralph Hastings, Sir Richard Brandon; and Sir Thomas Grey.

The Pembrokes

As earls of Pembroke, the Herbert family occupied a distinguished role in English history for several centuries during the late Medieval period. The influence of the Herberts, Sidneys and their related family was also marked throughout Henrician, Elizabethan and Jacobean times and also present during the short reign of Edward VI.

The Pembroke title was obtained by marriage with Isabel de Clare, daughter of Richard de Clare, 2nd Earl of Pembroke, known as 'Strongbow' like his father Gilbert de Clare, 1st Earl of Pembroke, a title created by King Stephen. Holders of the title of the Earl of Pembroke appear in several of the Lancastrian history plays and in *Henry VI, Part III*, as a non-speaking part alongside Lord Stafford.

William Herbert, 1st Earl of Pembroke KG, who died in 1469, known as 'Black William', replaced Jasper 'Tudor' in the Earldom which itself was a new creation of Henry VI. Herbert was the son of William ap Thomas, founder of Raglan Castle, and Gwladys ferch Dafydd Gam, and he was also the grandson of Dafydd Gam, an adherent of King Henry V of England.

Dafydd Gam was the grandson of Hywel Fychan who served at both the famous Battle of Crécy and the Battle of Poitiers. The family's power base developed mainly due to their being loyal supporters of the de Bohun family, who were both earls of Hereford and Lords of Brecon from the 13th century onwards.

The family's traditional loyalty followed the new Lord of Brecon, Henry Bolingbroke, as he gathered support in Wales for the overthrow of Richard II around 1399. It is claimed that Dafydd was previously in service to Henry's father, John of Gaunt, and Gam was certainly being paid the substantial annuity of 40 marks by Henry's estate before Bolingbroke became King Henry IV.

Stories of Gam's exploits at the Battle of Agincourt as part of the King's bodyguard – in which he saved Henry V's life – claim that he was also knighted either posthumously, or as he lay dying by King Henry V. These accounts are not vouched for in contemporary sources and the legend has been discounted by many historians. Some scholars suggest that Dafydd Gam's Welsh comrade, and posthumous son-in-law, Sir William ap Thomas may have been knighted at Agincourt.

Herbert's father had been an ally of Richard of York, and the earl supported the Yorkist cause in the Wars of the Roses. Herbert was rewarded by King Edward IV with the title Lord Herbert of Raglan in 1461, having assumed an English-style surname in place of the Welsh patronymic, and was invested as a Knight of the Garter.

When Herbert replaced the attainted Jasper Tudor as Earl of Pembroke in 1468 he gained the control of both Pembroke Castle and custody of the young Henry, Earl of Richmond, whom he planned to marry to his own daughter. However, Herbert soon fell out with his great rival the Earl of Warwick, 'the Kingmaker', who had turned against the king.

The Earl of Pembroke was executed by the Lancastrians, now led by Warwick, after the Battle of Edgecote Moor near Banbury, but this execution is not referred to in the play *Henry VI, Part III* in which the Earl of Pembroke is bidden by the king *"Go levy men, and prepare for war."*

Jasper 'Tudor', Earl of Pembroke, is portrayed in *Richard III,* in which Sir Walter Herbert, the son of William is mentioned.

Herbert was succeeded by his legitimate son, William, the son of Black William's illegitimate son, Sir Richard Herbert of Ewyas. The earldom was surrendered in 1479 and merged in the crown conferred upon Edward, Prince of Wales. Following the defeat of the House of York, the earldom, and kingdom, were restored to the Tudors with the accession of Henry, Earl of Richmond (King Henry VII). The Pembroke earldom was conferred upon another William Herbert, born in 1506, who married Anne Parr, the Queen's sister, and secondly, Anne Talbot.

Early literary patronage of the Herberts

The Herberts held a centuries old relationship with Welsh poets, including the poems of Lewis Glyn Clothi and Guto'r Glyn in the 15th century, which celebrated the achievements of the Herbert family. When Katherine Talbot, wife of Henry Herbert, second Earl of Pembroke, died in 1575 the poet William Middleton wrote a long elegy in Welsh in her honour.

After the battle of Bosworth, Lewis Clothi addressed a congratulatory poem to Henry VII, whose ascent of the English throne fulfilled Welsh prophecies. A renewed interest in Arthurian legends led Henry VII to call his eldest son Arthur, which probably prompted Edmund Spenser to include the character and legend in his heroic poem *Faerie Queen.*

Sir Philip Sidney, closely related to the Herberts by the marriage of his sister Mary to Henry Herbert, Earl of Pembroke, shows an appreciation of Welsh culture in his *Apologie for Poetrie* written around 1579 commenting:

In Wales the true remnant of the ancient Brittons, as there are good authorities to shewe the long time they had poets which they called Bardes, so through all the conquests of Romaines, Saxons, Danes and Normans, some of whom did seeke to ruine all memory of learning from among them, yet doo their Poets even to this day, last; so as it is not more notable in soone beginning then in long continuing.

Henry Herbert, 2nd Earl of Pembroke KG, was a statesman, the son of William, President of Wales. Henry was married very briefly to Lady Catherine Grey in 1553, a political match arranged by their parents who supported the manoeuvring by Dudley, Duke of Northumberland to place Catherine's sister, the Protestant Lady Jane Grey, on the English throne. The couple had their marriage annulled in 1554 when Queen Mary was crowned, shortly after the failure of the attempted coup. The Herberts were nonetheless able to continue in favour at the new court of Queen Mary I.

Herbert's second wife was Katherine Talbot, daughter of George Talbot, 6th Earl of Shrewsbury, and his wife Gertrude Manners, daughter of Thomas Manners, 1st Earl of Rutland.

Herbert's third wife Mary Sidney was more than twenty years younger than her husband and it was her uncle, Robert Dudley, Earl of Leicester, who had arranged the marriage; a match requiring a £3,000 dowry, of which he advanced half. Another uncle of Mary Sidney was Ambrose Dudley, Earl of Warwick, and her aunt was Katherine Dudley, Countess of Huntingdon

Mary Herbert nee Sidney, Countess of Pembroke, author, literary patron and her notable connection with two First Folio plays.

Mary Herbert, Countess of Pembroke, was one of the first English women to achieve a major reputation for her literary works, including translations, and also for her literary patronage.

Born at Tickenhill, Bewdley in 1561, her mother was Mary, wife of Sir Henry Sidney and daughter of John Dudley, 1st Duke of Northumberland. The well-educated Mary Dudley is known to have written poetry a year after her daughter Mary's birth in 1561. Having nursed Queen Elizabeth I through smallpox Mary Dudley was herself severely disfigured: thereafter she was to lead a secluded life.

After the death of her sister, Ambrosia, in 1576, fifteen year old Mary Sidney, as the only surviving Sidney daughter, was summoned to London by the Queen to be one of her noble attendants. In 1577, the Earl of Leicester, Robert

Dudley, arranged the marriage of his niece to a close ally, Henry Herbert, 2nd Earl of Pembroke, then in his mid-forties.

At seventeen, Mary became the mistress of Wilton House near Salisbury and Baynards Castle in London; there were also other substantial family properties. Mary had four children including William and Philip to whom the First Folio is dedicated. At different times both of these noblemen were patrons of the King's Men acting troupe.

Mary Sidney was highly educated by her tutors, one of whom was an Italian teacher. Like her learned aunt, Lady Jane Grey, she was educated in the reformed humanist tradition. In the 16th century, noblewomen required a good understanding of theological issues and were taught to read original texts. The Countess was later to translate Petrarch's *Triumph of Death* and other European works.

Mary was also schooled in poetry, music, French, the Classics and possibly Hebrew and rhetoric, as well as in needlework and practical medicine. Unusually for the time, Mary had a keen interest in chemistry and set up a chemistry laboratory at Wilton House, run by Sir Walter Raleigh's half-brother.

The Countess was herself a Calvinist theologian and her public persona was pious, virtuous and learned; she was celebrated by the community for her warmth, charm and beauty. In private, it was said, the Countess was witty and (some reported) even flirtatious.

Mary Herbert was a natural cultural catalyst and she had a gift of inspiring creativity in all those around her. Her brother, Philip, wrote much of his *Arcadia* in her presence. Sir Philip Sidney was engaged in preparing a new English version of the *Book of Psalms* when he met his death at Zutphen, during a military campaign against the Spanish in 1586 and had completed forty-three of the 150 *Psalms*.

Mary Herbert took on the task of amplifying and editing his *Arcadia*, which was published as *The Countesse of Pembroke's Arcadia,* one of the most widely read books in England for the next three centuries. The Countess also completed Philip's translation of the *Psalms,* which are sung unaccompanied in Calvinist worship, composing *Psalms 44–150* herself using the 1560 Geneva Bible and commentaries by John Calvin and Theodore Beza.

As a competent theologian, Mary Herbert was unafraid to disagree with Calvin on minor points. A copy of the completed book was presented to the Queen in 1599, and it has since been referred to as *The Sidney Psalms,* or *The Sidneian Psalms.* The work is regarded as an important influence on the development of English poetry in the late 16th and early 17th century.

Mary Herbert was widowed in 1600. Thereafter she played a large part in managing Wilton and the other Pembroke estates on behalf of her son, William, 3rd Earl of Pembroke, who took over her role of literary patronage. After King James visited her at Wilton in 1603, Mary moved, renting a house in London. From 1609 to 1615 she lived at Crosby Hall.

The Countess died of smallpox at her house in Aldersgate Street, London, near the French Protestant Church. in September 1621. After a grand funeral in St Paul's cathedral which celebrated her widely recognised literary achievements Mary's body was buried next to that of the 2nd Earl in Salisbury Cathedral.

The poetic epitaph, which is ascribed to Ben Jonson, but which is more likely to have been written in an earlier form by poets William Browne and Mary Herbert's son William, summarises how the Countess was regarded in her own day

> *Underneath this sable hearse,*
> *Lies the subject of all verse,*
> *Sidney's sister, Pembroke's mother.*
> *Death, ere thou hast slain another*
> *Fair and learned and good as she,*
> *Time shall throw a dart at thee.*

Mary, Countess of Pembroke was regarded as the most gifted female writer of the English Renaissance and upon her death she was praised by many literary figures of the age, including poet Aemilia Lanier. The Countess also influenced the religious writing of the divine and poet George Herbert, the first cousin of her sons.

Mary Sidney's imaginative, lively and warm style is described as filled with 'Sidneian fire', transparency and holy ardour exemplified in the death scenes in her closet drama, *The Tragedy of Antonie* of 1592. This text possibly provided source material for the play *Antony and Cleopatra* of 1607, published in the First Folio, as well as in her poetic masterpiece *The Psalms of David*, which she personally considered to be her memorial.

The Countess' patronage, the completion of her brother's work and not least her own canon of poetry, drama and theology exhibits a significant contribution to the literature of the English Renaissance.

The poet Edmund Spenser wrote the *Ruines of Time* for the Countess of Pembroke *"In praise of the race of the Dudleys."*

It was Herbert's country seat at Wilton where, under the aegis of Sir Philip and Mary Sidney, the endeavour to classicise English verse gained momentum. At Wilton, the 'Areopagus' group of like-minded poets met, whose founders were the Sidneys, Sir Fulke Greville, Edmund Spenser, Edward Dyer and Gabriel Harvey.

Despite the death of Sir Philip Sidney, Wilton House remained the outstanding literary centre in England and now centred upon Mary, Countess of Pembroke. Wilton became known as a *"paradise for poets"* and home to the Wilton circle of poets. The ambition of these writers and Mary Sidney was to banish the *"barbarism of English"* by propagating Italian culture and literature. This aim was greatly assisted by John Florio, linguist, translator and lexicographer: a protégée of the Countess. John Florio was the son of Michelangelo Florio the Italian protestant émigré who earlier had exerted a notable influence upon English letters.

The leading writers of the time were engaged in creating an English literary renaissance; these included Henry Constable, Christopher Marlowe, Thomas Nashe, Edward Dyer, George Gascoigne, Arthur Brooke, George Whetstone, Thomas Lodge, Barnabe Riche, Thomas Watson, Michael Drayton, Barnabe Barnes, Thomas Heywood, Philip Massinger, Thomas Kyd, George Chapman, Nicholas Breton, William Browne Abraham Fraunce, John Lyly, John Davies of Hereford, Hugh Sanford and Samuel Daniel. Both Sanford and Daniel were poets and tutors to William and Philip Herbert.

Many of the works of writers associated with the Wilton circle provided the basis for the plays in the First Folio

George Whetstone's *Heptamerone of Civil Discourses,* published in 1582, includes *The Rare Historie of Promos and Cassandra,* a play in two parts. This was drawn from the novel of Giraldi Cinthio's *Hecatommithi.* From Cinthio's prose version, the plots of *Measure for Measure* and *Othello* are drawn. Another Whetstone book provided the plot for *Much Ado About Nothing.*

Barnabe Riche claims the story of *Apolonius and Silla* as his own invention, the second in the collection from which the plot of *Twelfth Night* is taken. A possible collaboration between Michelangelo Florio and George Gascoigne's *Taming of A Shrew* formed the basis of the play *Taming of the Shrew.* Thomas Lodge's *Rosalynde, Euphues Golden Legacie* furnished the story of *As You Like It.*

John Lyly should be remembered as a primary influence on the First Folio's romantic comedies, particularly *Love's Metamorphosis:* an influence on *Love's Labour's Lost.* Lyly's *Galathea* is one of the sources for *A Midsummer Night's Dream.* A claim has also been made for the influence of Lyly's writing upon *Twelfth Night* and *As You Like It.*

The play "As You Like It" and the Wilton group

As You Like It is a pastoral comedy believed to have been written in 1599 or early 1600 and not published until printed in the First Folio of 1623. The play's first performance is uncertain, although a staging at Wilton House in 1603 as entertainment for King James on his journey from Scotland survives as a legend. The court was wary of entering London because of an outbreak of plague and resided with the Herberts at their country seat for several weeks.

As You Like It was "staied" in 1599, which could indicate that the authorities considered that it may have been written by Thomas Nashe or Gabriel Harvey – both of whom had their work destroyed at this time. Both Thomas Nashe and Gabriel Harvey were engaged with the Wilton group and may have collaborated on the play. The survival of this work is accounted for by a copy of the original text having been retained at Wilton and then revived in the Jacobean era. Both Samuel Daniel, the poet, and John Florio, the lexicographer, were resident in Wilton and also may have had a hand in the composition of this witty and lighthearted work.

The play "Cymbeline" and Mary Herbert

It may be significant that *Cymbeline* includes descriptions of Milford Haven in Pembrokeshire. The town is mentioned by name while the cave described in the play may relate to the cave below Pembroke Castle. The hills outside the town are also described, along with references to the Roman encampment nearby.

Whilst this is clear evidence that the author knew this town, the cave and the castle, none of the authorial candidates proposed over the years are known to have visited that far corner of Wales, except the writers enjoying the Countess of Pembroke's patronage.

The play itself was based on legends concerning the early Celtic British King Cunobelinus. Although listed as a tragedy in the First Folio, modern critics often classify *Cymbeline* rather differently; there are those who regard it as a romance, whilst others believe it to be a problem play because its central character confronts a specific moral concern.

Like *Othello* and *The Winter's Tale*, the play deals with the themes of innocence and jealousy. While the precise date of composition remains unknown, the play was certainly produced as early as 1611 when a performance of a version of the play was noted by the alchemist Simon Forman.

Cymbeline was first published in the First Folio in 1623. Some scholars claim the play shares notable similarities in language, situation and plot with Beaumont and Fletcher's tragicomedy *Philaster, or Love Lies a-Bleeding*, which was performed at court twice in the winter of 1612–13.

Plays inspired by the patronage of the Countess of Pembroke

Measure for Measure is based on George Whetstone's *Promos and Cassandra*. The Countess of Pembroke was a patron of the writer.

As You Like It is based on Thomas Lodge's *Rosalynde*. The Countess of Pembroke was a patron of Lodge.

Twelfth Night is sourced from Barnabe Riche, *Riche his Farewell to Militarie Profession*. The Countess was a patron of Riche.

Although many sources inspired *King Lear*, the source of the subplot involving Gloucester, Edgar and Edmund is a tale in Philip Sidney's *Countess of Pembroke's Arcadia*, with a blind Paphlagonian king and his two sons, Leonatus and Plexitrus.

Since Edward Capell first made the suggestion in 1780, scholars have been confident that the writer was familiar with Montaigne's Essays. John Florio's translation of Montaigne's *Essais* was available in English in 1603. John Florio was closely associated with the Wilton Group and the Sidneys.

The primary source for *Henry V*, as for most of the Folio chronicle histories, was Raphael Holinshed's *Chronicles*; the publication of the second edition in 1587 provides a *terminus ad quem* for the play. Edward Hall's *The Union of the Two Illustrious Families of Lancaster and York* appears also to have been consulted, and scholars have supposed the writers were familiar with Samuel Daniel's poem on the civil wars. Samuel Daniel was a resident writer at Wilton

A play called *Hamlet,* perhaps an early version of the play which appears in the First Folio, appears to have been written by Thomas Kyd, a notable member of the Wilton literary group.

All's Well that Ends Well is is based on a tale from Boccaccio's *The Decameron* which may have been familiar to Michelangelo Florio a protégée and tutor to the Cecil, Herbert and Grey households. (see Chapter Ten).

The plot of *Romeo and Juliet* – this Italian play may derive from Mariotto and Gianozza by Salernitano and may have been initiated by Michelangelo Florio together with the original of *The Two Gentlemen of Verona* which also echoes Edmund Spenser. Equally, however, the writing has a similarity to Robert Greene, and yet another candidate as the writer is Thomas Sackville, Earl of Dorset, the author of the very popular play *Gorboduc*.

Parts of *Timon of Athens* are derived from William Painter's *The Palace of*

Pleasure although it has been suggested that an early version of the play, called *The Solitarie Knight,* was performed at the Blackfriars Theatre during the 1576/7 season.

The characters in the royal history plays whose fictional accounts re-enforce the legitimacy of the royal Lancastrian line are ancestors from the same patron families, namely: the Earls of Oxford, Pembroke, Warwick and Shrewsbury.

The patronage of William Herbert, 3rd Earl of Pembroke

1613 was the year that saw a court performance of *Henry V,* as well as the investiture of William Herbert, 3rd Earl of Pembroke, with the Order of the Garter. The presence of Dafydd Gam in the play would have given an appropriate and memorable reminder of the Herberts' long and constant loyalty towards the Lancastrian monarchs. William's brother Philip was similarly invested in 1605, 1st Earl of Montgomery, later 4th Earl of Pembroke.

It has been suggested that a playwright familiar with the regional Monmouthshire accent wrote some of the speeches in the First Folio version of this play. A possible collaborator (or sole playwright) was Edward Dyer, born at Glastonbury, Somerset. Dyer was part of the Herbert literary group and, after some time abroad, appeared at Elizabeth's court. Traces of Christopher Marlowe have also been identified in the text which may indicate an updated version of an earlier play.

Edward Dyer's first patron was Robert Dudley, Ist Earl of Leicester and he is mentioned by Gabriel Harvey, along with Sir Philip Sidney, as one of the 'ornaments' of the court. Sidney, in his will, bequeathed his books equally between Fulke Greville and Edward Dyer.

William Herbert married Mary Talbot, daughter of Gilbert Talbot, 7th Earl of Shrewsbury. It was on their wedding day, 4th November 1604, when the *Merry Wives of Windsor* was performed at the court celebrations by the King's Players.

This old play performed for the Order of the Garter celebrations of 1597, was doubtless revised for the Jacobean court.

Patronage of Philip Herbert, 1st Earl of Montgomerey

On 27th December 1604, at the enthusiastic urging of James I, Philip married Susan de Vere, daughter of Edward de Vere, 17th Earl of Oxford. At the ceremony the King played a prominent role and provided generous financial gifts for the bride. The previous evening, a celebration at court included a performance of *Measure for Measure* and another First Folio play, *Comedy of Errors,* was performed on the day following the wedding.

An early version of this play was performed before Queen Elizabeth in 1577 by the Paul's Boys at court, as previously stated, may originally have been a translation by Philip Herbert's great aunt, Frances Radclyffe (née Sidney), Countess of Sussex.

Measure for Measure. In this thoughtful drama, an aspiring nun, Isabella, is faced with an impossible choice after her brother is sentenced to death for the crime of "fornication." When a corrupt deputy propositions her and says she can trade her virginity for her brother's life, Isabella refuses and her brother faces execution. The play presents social and moral issues to the audience.

Famous for its dark tone and obsession with death and judgment, *Measure for Measure*, first performed at the court of the newly crowned King James I in 1604, marks a major shift in the writing of the First Folio plays. As one of the later plays, it seems to anticipate the tragedies that would follow – *Othello, King Lear,* and *Macbeth.*

This play was possibly recalled by Philip Herbert as suitable for the court entertainment celebrating his marriage to Susan de Vere.

The significance of the 'bed-trick' deception in *Measure for Measure* is that Susan de Vere's mother Anne Cecil was abandoned on the night of her wedding by an unwilling husband, Edward de Vere, although she subsequently bore his children. It may be assumed that a similar deception was practised by Anne Cecil in the reconciliation with her husband.

A further play with the same 'bed-trick' theme is *All's Well That Ends Well*, written between 1604 and 1605 and originally published in the First Folio in 1623. The play is based on a tale of Boccaccio's *The Decameron* which was included by William Painter in his *Palace of Pleasure.*

Further significance of the Sidney family in the Jacobean court

Sir Robert Sidney, Earl of Leicester, Lord Chamberlain to Queen Anne

Sir Robert Sidney, 1st Earl of Leicester, born in 1563, second son of Sir Henry Sidney, was a statesman of Elizabethan and Jacobean England, as well as a patron of the arts and an interesting poet. Robert's mother, Mary Sidney née Dudley, was a lady-in-waiting to Queen Elizabeth I and a sister of Robert Dudley, 1st Earl of Leicester, adviser and favourite of the Queen.

Educated at Christ Church, Oxford, Sir Robert Sidney afterwards travelled on the Continent for some years between 1578 and 1583. In 1585 Sir Robert was elected Member of Parliament for Glamorganshire and in the same year he went, with his elder brother, Sir Philip Sidney, to the Netherlands, where he served in the war against Spain under Leicester. Sir Robert Sidney was present at the Battle of Zutphen where Sir Philip Sidney was mortally wounded and he remained with his brother until his death.

After visiting Scotland on a diplomatic mission in 1588 and France on a similar errand in 1593, Sir Robert Sidney returned to the Netherlands in 1606, where he rendered distinguished service in the war for the next two years. Having been appointed governor of Flushing in 1588, the nobleman spent much time in the Netherlands. In 1595, moreover, he sent his business manager Rowland Whyte to court to lobby for resources for Flushing, and to send him information about events and political gossip at the English court.

In 1603, on the accession of James I, Sidney returned to England and James raised him at once to the peerage, as Baron Sidney of Penshurst, and he was appointed Lord Chamberlain to the Queen consort, Anne of Denmark.

In 1605 Sidney was created Viscount Lisle, and in 1618, Earl of Leicester. The latter title had become extinct in 1588 on the death of his uncle. Sir Robert Sidney married twice: firstly Barbara Gamage, by Barbara, Sidney had eleven children.

Robert Sidney's eldest son, Sir William Sidney, predeceased his father and died unmarried in 1613. The 2nd Earl of Leicester, Robert Sidney's second son of the same name, became his heir.

His daughter, Lady Mary, married Sir Robert Wroth of Loughton Hall, was a poet like her father. Ben Jonson dedicated *The Alchemist* to her in 1612.

Robert Sidney's second wife was Sarah Blount, daughter of William Blount and widow of Sir Thomas Smythe.

The first Earl of Leicester was a man of taste and a patron of literature and music, whose cultured mode of life at his country seat, Penshurst Place, was celebrated in verse by Ben Jonson. It was also at Penshurst where Robert Sidney died in 1626. The earl was a patron of musicians, and was the dedicatee of Robert Jones's *First Booke of Songes and Ayres,* 1600, and *A Musicall Banquet,* 1610, compiled by Robert Dowland. Sidney had agreed to be godfather to Robert, the son of composer John Dowland, and *A Musicall Banquet* opens with a galliard by the latter, entitled *Syr Robert Sidney his Galliard.*

Though he was the brother of one of the most famous poets in the English language, it was not suspected that Sir Robert Sidney had himself been a poet until the 1960s, when his working notebook emerged through the dispersal of the library of Warwick Castle. Subsequent research shows it had been acquired in 1848, after passing through a number of sales, beginning with the dispersal of the library at Penshurst in the early 19th century. Sold again at Sotheby's and acquired by the British Library in 1975, the autograph is, as its first editor P. J. Croft points out, *"the largest body of verse to have survived from the Elizabethan period in a text entirely set down by the poet himself."*

Apparently dating from the latter half of the 1590s, when Robert Sidney was governor of Flushing, the collection comprises 66 sonnets, songs, pastorals, elegies and slighter pieces, apparently structured as a kind of reply to Philip Sidney's *Astrophel and Stella*. They present Robert Sidney as an advocate of the Neo-platonic philosophy of love, and a poet adept at a great variety of verse forms. In a reflection of his interest in music, several of the poems are based on identifiable tunes.

Other poets of the extended Sidney family

As stated previously, the Countess of Sussex was the second wife of Thomas Radclyffe, Viscount Fitzwalter and the daughter of Sir William Sidney of Penshurst, a prominent courtier during the reign of Henry VIII. As such, the Countess was the sister of Sir Henry Sidney and an aunt of the poets Sir Philip Sidney, Mary Sidney, Countess of Pembroke, and Robert Sidney, Earl of Leicester, father of the poet Lady Mary Wroth.

It is also of interest that Sir Richard Ratcliffe, one of Thomas Radclyffe's ancestors, appears in the play *Richard III*.

Two other poets of the Jacobean period reflected the high literary ambitions of the extended Sidney and Herbert family: Edward and George Herbert.

Edward Herbert, 1st Baron Herbert, born in 1583, was a metaphysical poet and notable philosopher. Herbert was also a leading courtier and diplomat recognised by contemporary thinkers of his time as the principal progenitor of English Deism and called *"the father of English Deism."*

George Herbert, born in 1593, was also a poet of the Metaphysical school and wrote in English, Latin and Greek. Herbert spent much of his short life as a parish priest in a village near Salisbury and his literary work was published in 1633, the year of his death.

Edward and George were the sons of Richard Herbert of Montgomery Castle, a member of a collateral branch of the Earls of Pembroke family.

Another family linked to the Herberts' may also be connected to three of the plays in the First Folio: Christina North, the sister of the notable translator Sir Thomas North, married into a branch of the Herbert family through William Somerset, 3rd Earl of Worcester. The earl was a patron of the arts, and sponsored, among others, the eminent Elizabethan actor Edward Alleyn.

Three of the First Folio plays *Antony and Cleopatra, Coriolanus* and *Julius Caesar* were drawn from North's translation of Plutarch's *Lives* and some of the play texts are taken directly from this translation. There is a possibility that there was collaboration within the family of some or parts of these three plays, all set in ancient Rome.

Sir Fulke Greville, 1st Baron Brooke 1554-1628. Statesman,
poet, playwright, literary patron and close friend of Philip Sidney.

CHAPTER SIX

Fulke Greville, Baron Brooke: an involvement in some writing and editing of the First Folio plays

WILLIAM Herbert, Philip Herbert and Fulke Greville, Baron Brooke, shared common ancestry to a great extent, largely through the Neville line. On this basis, and in the light of his lifetime affection for Mary Sidney, Greville may have been a participant in the production of the First Folio. As discussed in an earlier chapter, it is recorded that Fulke Greville said that *"I am the Master of Shakespeare."*

Greville's alleged remark about Shakespeare first appeared in print in David Lloyd's biography of him in *The Statesmen and Favourites of England since the Reformation* of 1670. The most likely source for the remark is Fulke Greville's elderly page, William Davenant.

That the statesman, playwright and poet may have played a part in the preparation of the publication is supported by research from Claremont McKenna College, Los Angeles. Computer analysis of First Folio texts by the college led them to the conclusion that some of the plays may have been composed by Fulke Greville. Equally arguable is that the hand of Greville has been detected in the editing of the publication.

Fulke Greville, statesman, literary patron, playwright and poet was a descendant of the Earl of Warwick through his mother's Beauchamp ancestry. One of these early ancestors was Thomas Beauchamp, first Earl of Warwick, one of the founders of the Order of the Garter and an experienced soldier. Beauchamp fought at Calais, Crecy and Poitier in the wars with France in the mid-14th century.

An early family chronicle of the Beauchamp family was the *Warwick Roll,* which centred on the life of the chivalric Richard de Beauchamp, 13th Earl of Warwick, who was born in 1382 and who died in 1439. The Earl appears as a major figure in the plays *Richard II* and *Henry VI*. Collated by chronicler John Rous, the *Roll* includes historically important illustrations of subjects connected with the families.

The Lancastrian history plays, featuring many Neville and Herbert characters, may be seen as a continuation of the earlier chronicle. The

Warwick or Rous Roll, presented a pro-Yorkist version of recent English history while glorifying the Warwick family, notably the Nevilles.

John Rous was a medieval English historian, best known for his two books: *Rous Roll* and *Historia Regum Angliae* (History of the Kings of England), which describes British and English rulers from Brutus of Britain to Henry VII of England.

Born at Warwick, most likely in 1411, Rous died in 1491. Educated at Oxford before taking holy orders, he remained in the vicinity of Warwick for most of his clerical career, though he spent time travelling to study archives for his historical research.

John Rous spent the majority of his adult life in the service of the Yorkist dynasty as chaplain of the chapel of Guy's Cliffe in the reign of Richard III and canon of the collegiate church at Warwick. In his chronicle, Rous lauds the character of Richard III as being benevolent to his people. Nevertheless, in writing *Historia Regum Angliae*, following the accession of Henry VII, Rous then perhaps not surprisingly describes the deposed King as a freakish and unnatural figure.

The *Rous Roll* features Anne Neville, wife of Richard III – and thus an important historical figure of which the Neville family descendants were keenly aware. Not least of these was Sir Fulke Greville, who was all too conscious of his noble heritage.

Early sources on Richard Neville, Earl of Warwick, fall into two categories. The first are the sympathetic chronicles of the Yorkist years, as in the *Rous Roll*, or works based on these writings such as the *Mirror for Magistrates* of 1559.

These accounts contradict the chronicles commissioned by Edward IV after Warwick's fall, such as the *Historie of the arrivall of Edward IV*, which cast a more negative light on the earl. *The Mirror* portrayed Warwick as a great man who was beloved by the people but betrayed by the Prince he had helped to gain the throne. In the First Folio's *Henry VI* trilogy Warwick is a supremely powerful nobleman driven by pride and egotism who had the power to create and depose kings at will.

The Earl of Warwick's actions were not considered unjust by his contemporaries, as is suggested by the earl's popularity, exceeding that of the king. Warwick could not easily suffer his seemingly unfair treatment by the king, but it was equally impossible for Edward IV to accept the Earl's presence on the political scene. As long as Warwick remained as powerful and influential as he was Edward could not fully assert his royal authority and an eventual confrontation became inevitable.

Literary historian E. K. Chambers held that Shakspeare had first been employed by Greville's father, the old Stratford Recorder, who *maintained domestic players at Beauchamp Court.* Historian Katherine Duncan-Jones also believed that *"Shakspere's earliest patron"* was Fulke Greville senior. In a chapter entitled *Sir Fulke Greville's Man?* she conjectured that perhaps it was as a performer in a Christmas or Whitsuntide play that Shakspeare was first *'spotted'* by Greville. According to this theory, Shakspeare served Greville in some capacity *probably as a player and possibly also as a clerk or secretary.*

Fulke Greville's early education was at Shrewsbury where Philip Sidney was a fellow pupil and the two of them were to share great friendship and common literary ambitions until Sidney's early death. During his extensive travels on the continent as a young man, Fulke Greville acted as an 'intelligencer' for Sir Francis Walsingham. Later, he advanced to high administrative office in the service of Queen Elizabeth, King James and lastly King Charles, during a forty year career as a statesman. Clerk to the Council of Wales, Treasurer of the Navy, and Chancellor of the Exchequer were positions that attest to Greville's abilities and the favour in which he was held by successive English monarchs.

History remembers Fulke Greville mostly as a literary figure of some importance: the romantic poet penning verse of adoration to Mary, Countess of Pembroke, sister of Sir Philip Sidney; as the writer of several historical dramas and as the author of an admiring biography of his idol, Sidney. Greville's closet drama *Antony and Cleopatra,* apparently destroyed, might have survived or became a memorial version of the play in the First Folio with the same name. The maturity and intellectual breadth of Fulke Greville would make him a good candidate for the authorship of *Measure for Measure.* Equally, his intimate knowledge of politics could be reflected by *Coriolanus* and possibly revised versions of *King Lear, Hamlet* and *Julius Caesar.*

As stated earlier Fulke Greville shared the Protestant and literary ambitions of the 'Areopagus' coterie, centred upon Mary Herbert's Wilton country seat, which was later to become the famed Wilton Literary Circle.

In his role as a man of letters, Greville was a generous patron of a number of the major writers of his age, such as Christopher Marlowe, Thomas Nashe, Samuel Daniel, Edmund Spenser, William Davenant, and especially the Poet Laureate, Ben Jonson.

Fulke Greville was on the inquisition committee that quizzed Guy Fawkes after his attempt to blow up Parliament on 5th November 1605 and was subsequently appointed Under Treasurer of the committee that investigated the rebuilding of the Banqueting House in Whitehall after a destructive fire. Rebuilding took place in 1619-1622.

James I created Fulke Greville, Baron Brooke, and awarded him the dilapidated Warwick castle and its grounds, upon which Greville spent 20,000 pounds, an enormous sum at the time. Brooke was also given Knowle Park in 1604. After Ambrose Dudley's death Warwick Castle had reverted to the Crown.

The extravagant restoration of Warwick Castle may have been an attempt by Greville to emulate the grandeur of Henry de Beaumont, the 1st Earl of Warwick, who was reputed to be the richest man in England. It was a source of great frustration and continual disappointment to Fulke Greville that despite being awarded Warwick Castle he failed to obtain the Earldom of Warwick for which he craved.

Baron Brooke took enormous pride in his Neville ancestry. Greville's mother Anne Neville daughter of Ralph Neville, 4th Earl of Westmorland KG, was the grandson of Ralph Neville, 3rd Earl of Westmorland.

The Earldom of Warwick was awarded to John Dudley, 1st Viscount Lisle. He had already been created Viscount Lisle in right of his deceased mother, Elizabeth Grey, in 1543, and was made Earl of Warwick in the Peerage of England in 1547. In 1551 he was further honoured when he was created Duke of Northumberland. In January 1553 Parliament passed the earldom to his eldest son John, the second Earl. John died young in 1554, and since it was attainted along with his father in August 1553, the title became extinct until it was revived in 1561 for his younger brother Ambrose, the third Earl. On his death in 1590 the earldom became extinct.

The title was re-created when Robert Rich, 3rd Baron Rich, was made Earl of Warwick in 1618. The second son of Robert Rich the Honourable Henry Rich was created Baron Kensington in 1623 and Earl of Holland in 1624.

The Earldom became extinct in 1759, only to be revived that year in favour of Francis Greville, 1st Earl Brooke, which meant that the title and castle were joined after more than a century. This creation remains extant although Warwick Castle has been sold by the family.

Further significant ancestors of Fulke Greville mentioned or participants in the history plays include other Earls of Warwick, Salisbury, Westmorland, Northumberland, Abergavenny, Buckingham, Baron Willoughby de Eresby, Shrewsbury, Waterford, and the surnames Ratcliffe and Stanley.

The distinguished courtier, statesman, author and patron of the arts Fulke Greville may be viewed as the personification of the Renaissance man. Greville was a person who thought deeply about morality, philosophy and faith, all encompassed within his deep regard for the well-being of England and the cause of international Protestantism.

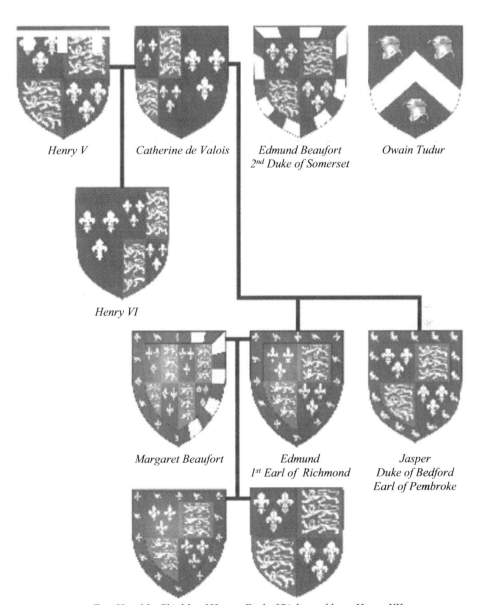

Henry V

Catherine de Valois

Edmund Beaufort
2ⁿᵈ Duke of Somerset

Owain Tudur

Henry VI

Margaret Beaufort

Edmund
1ˢᵗ Earl of Richmond

Jasper
Duke of Bedford
Earl of Pembroke

Two Heraldic Shields of Henry, Earl of Richmond later Henry VII

Beaufort and Tudur shields

Earlier there had been a proclamation from Richard III against "Henry Tydder," pretender to the throne, *whereunto he hath (in) no manner interest, right title or colour, as every man knoweth, for he is descended of bastard blood, both of father side and of mother side.*

In an apt description of Henry's position in 1485, it has been stated that *"For all his high words about his just title, it was in fact as shaky as could be without being non-existent."* Thereafter, most of the revolts he faced were similar pieces of manoeuvering over which family to put on the throne. As a consequence of these threats Henry VII's subsequent policy was to murder, or neutralise by threat, as many potential rivals as he could reach. Indeed, there were so many plots against the Tudor king that a court poet compared the first twelve years of his reign to the Labours of Hercules.

A number of the English history plays in the First Folio may be perceived as a public acknowledgement of the presence of certain noble families and military commanders who were involved in the Wars of the Roses: all supporters of a Lancastrian monarch. The loyalty they had to Henry, Earl of Richmond (later to become Henry VII), half-brother of Henry VI, underpins the legitimacy of the Beaufort-Tudor royal line, despite Henry's questionable claim and eventual seizure of the English crown. This period of England's royal history may be said to parallel that of the usurpation of the throne by John of Gaunt's son Henry IV in 1399.

Despite the endorsement of these leading noblemen the accession of Henry, Earl of Richmond, and his claim for the throne continued to be called into question during his reign – and the same doubts therefore applied to his royal successors. There was good reason for later generations of royalty to present the Lancastrians in a favourable light and thus reaffirm their heritage.

Several of the influential noble families of the Elizabethan age owed their high position to the support given by their ancestors for the Tudor royal line, and this loyalty is recorded in the history plays. The power and status of noblemen was derived from and dependent upon the acceptance of the 'Tudor' myth.

Henry, Earl of Richmond, the son of Lady Margaret Beaufort and grandson of Katherine de Valois, widow of Henry V, gained the support of many noblemen for his royal claim because of his true Beaufort-Lancastrian lineage. This was despite the earlier 'questionable marriage' claim of a union between the dowager Queen Catherine and her servant, Owain Tudur.

Richmond's mother Margaret, through her father John Beaufort, the son of John Beaufort, 1st Earl of Somerset, was a great-granddaughter of John of Gaunt, 1st Duke of Lancaster and his mistress (later his third wife), Catherine

Swynford. Thus he was descended from King Edward III. The Beaufort name relates to a French possession of John of Gaunt. This was the royal bloodline that motivated many of the noble houses to fight for the English Kings Henry IV, V, VI and VII.

Following Gaunt's marriage to Katherine Swynford, their children, the Beauforts, were legitimised, but the act approving their legitimacy carried a condition that their descendants were barred from inheriting the throne. Lady Margaret's own son, Henry VII (and all English, British, and UK sovereigns who followed), are descended from Gaunt and Swynford. Henry VII gained the English throne, therefore, not through a better claim than Richard III, but by force of arms. Richard, Duke of Gloucester, was a descendant of Lionel of Antwerp, third son of Edward III and consequently senior to John of Gaunt, the fourth son of Edward.

It was on behalf of the last surviving member of the House of Lancaster, Henry, Earl of Richmond, that leading English noblemen rallied at Bosworth Field in 1485 to defeat the rightful Yorkist king Richard III.

Nevertheless, there remains an additional question regarding Henry VII's royal claim in respect of his true parentage and the subsequent adoption of the Tudor name.

As Gerald Harriss writes in *Cardinal Beaufort* in *Medieval History*, *"it is not unlikely that the Beauforts finally succeeded to the English throne under cover of a Welsh name."* Harriss also explains the circumstances surrounding the birth of Edmund Beaufort, later known as Edmund Tudor.

In England in the mid-1420s, speculation was circulating in court circles of Edmund Beaufort's love affair with Henry V's widow Catherine de Valois. Significantly, Catherine gave birth to a son at Much Hadham, at the house of the Beaufort Bishop of London. Whilst the date remains uncertain the records show the dowager queen named him Edmund.

Possibly as an additional barrier to any unwise marriage with dynastic consequence, Parliament passed a statute in 1427/1428 stating that if a dowager Queen married without the king's consent (which could be given only when he reached his majority) the suitor would lose his lands and possessions. Any children resulting from the match would, however, still be members of the royal family.

> *... Item, it is ordered and established by the authority of this parliament for the preservation of the honour of the most noble estate of queens of England that no man of whatever estate or condition make contract of betrothal or matrimony to marry himself to the queen of England without the special*

licence and assent of the king, when the latter is of the age of discretion, and he who acts to the contrary and is duly convicted will forfeit for his whole life all his lands and tenements, even those which are or which will be in his own hands as well as those which are or which will be in the hands of others to his use, and also all his goods and chattels in whosoever's hands they are, considering that by the disparagement of the queen the estate and honour of the king will be most greatly damaged...

According to *Giles Chronicle,* moreover, it was rumoured that Catherine would marry Edmund Beaufort, grandson of Gaunt, who was born in 1406 and would have been sixteen when Henry V died. Catherine left court when her young son's regents, John, Duke of Bedford and Humphrey, Duke of Gloucester (brothers of Henry V), denied her permission to marry Edmund Beaufort, Count of Mortain, Duke of Somerset, and scion of a legitimised Plantagenet line.

No documentation survives whatsoever of Catherine's claimed marriage in 1429 to Owain Tudur, the presumed grandfather of Henry VII, which casts the union in doubt. This historical deception may be exposed by considering the known class structure that existed within the social and political context of the time. Upon analysis the Catherine de Valois-Owain Tudur marriage appears to be a fabrication, yet thereafter the deceit of the Tudor name has prevailed over the centuries.

The accepted history of Henry Tudur / Tudor records that several powerful English magnates fought on Henry's side at Bosworth. By allying themselves with the Earl of Richmond in preference to King Richard III these noblemen ensured victory for the Lancastrian cause. What is questionable is whether these landowners would have placed their great estates and high social rank in jeopardy in order to back Owain Tudur, the son of an obscure Welsh Squire, whose own lowly status meant he had to be granted the rights of an Englishman.

Owain Tudur was a household official, possibly Keeper of the Wardrobe, but clearly occupied the role of a servant. Although of low rank, Owain Tudur had supposedly married the high-rank dowager Queen Catherine, previously the Queen of France as well as of England, yet astonishingly there is no record of the ceremony. This is highly unlikely for such an important royal figure.

No witnesses of this marriage have ever been identified, nor was any contemporary written comment recorded about this unique situation: a royal marrying a commoner. Yet this secretive union was a matter of high political sensitivity. It was an act which contravened the wishes of England's protectors, Bedford and Gloucester, who opposed a remarriage of Catherine since it would have led to serious political complications in respect of the royal succession.

Within six months of Queen Catherine's death in January 1437, Owain Tudur was imprisoned at Newgate Prison. Presumably the cause of the imprisonment was his forbidden 'marriage', but he managed to escape. After recapture, he was sent to Windsor Castle where he remained until 1439, when he was pardoned by the king and released with a restoration of goods and lands. This freedom was possibly granted in the absence of any evidence of the marriage.

In December 1444, as Owain Tudur, Esquire, he was appointed Captain of Règnéville in Normandy, a post he held until Sept. 1449, when he surrendered it to Admiral de Coëtivy after six days of siege. In 1459 Tudur was granted an annuity of £100 for life by King Henry VI and in 1460 Tudur was granted the office of Parker of several parks in the lordship of Denbigh in Wales.

It is worth noting that in widowhood Catherine continued to style herself proudly, *"Catherine, Queen of England, daughter of King Charles of France, mother of the King of England and Lady of Ireland."* This tale of the low-born yeoman marrying the self-important ex-Queen of England is preposterous given the period's rigid class divisions and the tradition of arranged marriages organised in the interest of combining land, property, wealth and social aspiration. In this respect it may be noted that a century later Queen Elizabeth was horrified by an unauthorized court "love-match" to the extent that the partners were sent to prison for a time.

As stated previously, during the time of the challenge of Henry, Earl of Richmond, there had been a proclamation from Richard III against "Henry Tydder", pretender to the throne, *'whereunto he hath (in) no manner interest, right title or colour, as every man knoweth, for he is descended of bastard blood, both of father side and of mother side'*. This assertion can only be understood if it is assumed that Richard III knew the earl was a descendant of the illegitimate Beaufort line both through John Beaufort, Margaret Beaufort's father and the Catherine de Valois.

The deception that found its way into the history books is based upon the fiction of an Italian historian, Polydor Virgil (or Vergil). It was at the instigation of King Henry VII that Virgil commenced his *Historia Anglica* – a work which apparently began as early as 1505, but was not completed and published until, respectively, August 1533 (the date of its dedication to Henry VIII) and 1534.

Henry VIII, who wanted to distance himself from his father Henry VII, as much as possible, also hired Virgil to document both his and his father's lives. Naturally, the historical accuracy of Virgil's account has come into question especially concerning the heritage of Henry VII.

Catherine de Valois entered Bermondsey Abbey in 1436/7 and made her will just three days before her death on 3 January 1437. It was only after his mother's death that King Henry VI acknowledged Edmund and Jasper as half brothers.

Catherine de Valois was accustomed to a profligate style of court behaviour in France, and it is recorded that the French court she left was one of personal excess and loose sexual morals. There is no doubt that her first child was fathered by Henry V, but her other children, Edmund, Earl of Richmond, Jasper, Earl of Pembroke, Owain and her daughter Tacinda may have each had a different father: no evidence is recorded of their paternity.

Edmund and Jasper were sent to live for a time at Barking Abbey in Essex by the council of Henry VI, cared for by the Abbess of Barking, Katherine de la Pole, the Earl of Suffolk's sister. Around 1442 their half-brother Henry VI brought them to London and they were ennobled in 1542: Edmund, born in 1430, was created Earl of Richmond and Jasper, born 1431, was created Earl of Pembroke. The brothers then became the premier Earls of England and, excluding dukes, had precedence over all other laymen. As half-brothers to King Henry VI they received recognition of the highest order: the king gave the earls estates and other gifts. Thereafter, Henry VI continued to grant lands and annuities to Edmund and Jasper.

It is extraordinary that such honours should be awarded to the sons of Catherine's Keeper of the Wardrobe. Perhaps less extraordinary, however, than the fact that the brothers were honoured after the death of their mother and any royal knowledge of her marriage to Owen Tudur. It seems most likely that Edmund and Jasper were honoured because of their true lineage from John of Gaunt.

Furthermore, there is evidence that Edmund and Jasper appear to be recognised as the continuation of the Lancastrian house of Plantagenet. Both brothers carried the Beaufort arms on their shields, and neither of them carried the heraldic device held by Owain Tudur. It was customary for the son to continue with their father's heraldic device.

According to Boutell's *Heraldry* each brothers' shield carried a different bordure (border) Edmund's shield carried martlets and fleur-de-lys – suggesting his position as fourth son, and possibly one with French ancestry. However Jasper's shield also featured martlets in the bordure azure without the fleur de lys. Both shields publicly present their close relationship with their half-brother Henry VI.

The martlet symbol first featured in the arms of the Valence family Earls of Pembroke to difference them from their parent house of Lusignan. William de Valence, 1st Earl of Pembroke who died in 1296 displays the martlet in the shield on his effigy in Westminster Abbey. Martlets are also present in the arms of Pembroke College.

The independent historian John Ashley-Hill has provided further corroboration of the doubt concerning the 'Tudor' claim. A century after his father's accession Henry VIII retrieved only two bodies from Monasteries destroyed in his Dissolution of Church property: that of his sister Mary and his grandfather Edmund Tudor. The historian notes that Henry failed to retrieve his great-grandfather Owen Tudur's body, Ashdown-Hill asks, *"Could it have been that Henry VIII knew more about his true paternal ancestry than later historians?"*

In time, the brothers Edmund and Jasper took part in several of the battles of the Civil War and in 1453 the brothers received the joint wardship of Margaret, daughter of the legitimised John Beaufort, 1st Duke of Somerset, who was the heiress to the powerful Beaufort family. In 1455, Edmund, Earl of Richmond, married Lady Margaret Beaufort, who was then aged twelve

In 1461, Jasper was subject to attainder for supporting King Henry VI against the Yorkists, who eventually deposed the King, although later Jasper held Denbigh Castle for the House of Lancaster. Jasper had been the protector of his nephew Henry until the said time, when custody was taken over by William Herbert. Following the Yorkist King Edward IV's return from temporary isolation in 1471, Jasper took the teenage Henry with him into exile, this time to Brittany, where they were protected by Duke Francis. Edmund, 1st Earl of Richmond died in 1456.

On Henry's accession, in 1485, Jasper was restored to all his former titles forfeited by the House of York. These honours included becoming Knight of the Garter and Duke of Bedford. In 1488 Jasper took possession of Cardiff Castle, but on his death without heirs in 1495 the title became extinct.

The dubious parentage of King James I

The Earl of Richmond (Henry VII) was succeeded by his son, Henry VIII and though his father was a Lancastrian, Henry VIII could also claim a right to the throne through the Yorkist line, as his mother Elizabeth was the sister and heiress of Edward V.

The royal line continued through to Elizabeth I who was succeeded by King James VI of Scotland, her first cousin twice removed, even though this succession violated Henry VIII's will. This will stated that Lady Anne Stanley, heiress of Mary Tudor, Duchess of Suffolk, Henry VIII's sister, was intended to succeed. James V1 asserted that his hereditary right was superior to statutory

adviser, led to the Calvinist Protestant James acceding to the English throne. The accession had become a *fait accompli*, even though James was not born in England and thus was debarred by statute from the Crown.

The group of 'history' plays which historically legitimise the Beaufort line of Royal usurpers fulfil the role of an historical record that justifies the right of the Crown for King James

A description of James I by Sir Anthony Weldon

Sir Anthony Weldon, who died in 1648, was a courtier and politician in James' Court. Weldon is also the purported author of *The Court and Character of King James I*, although this attribution has been challenged. According to Weldon, James:

> *Was of middle stature, more corpulent through his cloathes then in his body, yet fat enough, his cloathes ever being made   large and easie, the doublets quilted for stiletto proofe, his breeches in great pleits and full stuffed; hee was naturally of a timorous disposition, which was the reason of his quilted doublets; his eyes large, ever roving after any stranger that came in his presence, inasmuch, as many for shame have left the roome, as being out of countenance; his beard was very thin his tongue too large for his mouth, which ever made him speak full in the mouth, and made him drink very uncomely, as if eating his drink, which came out nto the cup of each side of his mouth; his skin was as soft as taffeta sarsenet, which felt so, because hee never washt his hands, onely rubb'd his fingers ends slightly with the wet end of a napkin; his legs were very weake having had (as was thought) some foulplay in his youth, or rather before he was born, that he was not able to stand at seven years of age, that weaknesse made him ever leaning on other mens shoulders; his walke was ever circular, his fingers ever in that walke fiddling about his codpiece; he was very temperate in his exercises and in his dyet, and not intemperate in his drinking....he drank very often....rather out of a custom than any delight,...he was very constnt in all things, (his favourites excepted,) in which he loved change...in his apparel so constnt, as by good will he would never change his cloathes until worn out to very rages (11,1).*

James' oversize tongue and habit of speaking thickly, spraying spit and food and drink around him implies an inheritance from the dwarfish, misshapen, ugly David Riccio.

The King, whose weak legs caused him to be tied to his mount when hunting, was so passionate about staying in the field that he would urinate into his saddle rather than dismount. James also delighted in such practices as *"taking the assay of the stag,"* by thrusting his hands into the entrails of a newly killed beast. James also fondled young men in public and had a succession of male lovers.

The distinctive ornaments of the Order of the Garter

CHAPTER EIGHT

The Order of the Garter

The very special significance attached to the Order of the Garter was an Elizabethan tradition. There had been a great revival of the Order, its ceremonies, processions and ethos, during the reign of Elizabeth and James they both used the Order as a means of drawing their noblemen together in common service to the Crown.

IT was during the 11th and 12th centuries that the idea of the medieval notion of chivalry and knighthood first developed within the warrior-classes. The Crusades in the Middle East had released these men from the previous constraints of feudalism. They could now express their new-found identity by the creation of religious and military orders of chivalry. The earliest orders of knighthood were amongst groups of like-minded men who, being drawn from a particular social class, were therefore bound together in a common purpose.

First Folio Plays and the Order of the Garter

The genesis of the Order of the Garter has more than one explanation, although both of them draw upon the legends of Chivalric literature as the fundamental inspiration for the noble order.

The first account has its origin in the end of the reign of Edward I, who initiated the distinctive Order of the Feast of Swans, held at Westminster in 1306. Prior to the feast, the king invited knights from the English shires to London in order to receive their military accoutrements and ceremonial robes for the ceremony at Whitsuntide. After a Vigil and Mass, and prior to the ceremony, the Crown Prince was knighted by the King. The youngest knight then dubbed his fellow knights into the Order and the banquet followed.

The alternative version of the first beginnings of the Order of the Garter is that in 1344 King Edward III, inspired by the legend of King Arthur and the Knights of the Round Table, made a demonstration of his interest in Arthurian legend during a spectacular joust at Windsor Castle.

Edward promised to renew King Arthur's fraternity of knights with all the paragons of knightly virtues. Work even began on a gigantic circular building, two-hundred feet across, within the upper ward of the castle to house this so-called Order of the Round Table. The renewal of war with France interrupted this project, but in 1348 it was revived in a different guise.

The Order of the Garter was originally intended to consist of twenty-four knights; however, during 1349/50 it consisted of the Sovereign and twenty-five Knights Companion, one of whom was the Prince of Wales, the Black Prince.

These 'founder knights' were military men, skilled in battle and tournaments. Few of them were much over the age of 30, and there were even four under the age of 20. The other founder knights had all served in the French campaigns of the time, including the battle of Crécy, and three were foreigners who had previously sworn allegiance to the English king, making twenty-six knights in all. Edward III intended the Order to be reserved as the highest reward for loyalty and for military merit.

These knights included some who owed allegiance to King Edward – not as King of England but as Lord of Gascony. These Companions were known as Stranger Knights (a distinction from subjects of the English Crown). During the next hundred years, foreign monarchs were admitted to the Order as Stranger Knights in addition to the number allowed by statute.

The insignia of the Order has gradually developed over the centuries, starting with a garter and badge depicting St George and the Dragon. A collar was added in the 16th century, with the star and broad ribbon being added in the 17th century. Although the collar could not be decorated with precious stones (the statutes forbade it), the other insignia could be decorated according to taste and affordability.

As part of the original College of St George, Edward III established a community of twenty-six impoverished military veterans known as 'Poor Knights', who were required to pray daily for the Sovereign and the Knights of the Garter during their lifetime, and even for their souls after death. In return they received maintenance and lodgings in Windsor Castle. This number of twenty-six was reduced to thirteen by Elizabeth I at the request of her father Henry VIII.

The importance of the Order was recognised in the extant 15th century manuscript, *The Bruges Garter Book,* which contains portraits of the founder knights. The book was commissioned by William Bruges who died in 1450, Garter King of Arms.

The Most Noble Order of the Garter is one of the oldest and most important of all such Orders throughout the world, championing the concept of a like-minded brotherhood dedicated to service and chivalry. Almost a thousand appointments have been made since 1348, including royalty, soldiers, statesmen, court favourites, magnates and even a few traitors.

To this day, the Order requires all members to assemble at Windsor on the eve of the feast day. The Knights and Ladies put on the mantle of the Order and the Greater George, and go to St George's Chapel for a service of thanksgiving. The members then attend supper at the Dean's House. On St George's Day itself the members have lunch in the Waterloo Chamber.

At the installation ceremony all members process to the Chapel for a service, wearing the full robes of the Order, including black velvet hats with white plumes, and any new members are installed. On the day after this only the mantle is worn, but the Garter is worn throughout the occasion. The Greater George must be worn on all official holidays, on Ascension Day, at the funeral of a member of the Order and when a member of the Order is created a Peer. The British sovereign and Prince of Wales are always members of the Order.

The Order of the Garter in the Jacobean era

The Garter ceremony, St George's Feast, could be held at various times of the year and in various places, including the Palaces of Windsor, St James, Greenwich and Whitehall.

After James' accession, the King reinstated a part of the ancient ceremony of the Order of the Garter which had fallen into disuse, thus indicating his particular interest in the Order, and in the twenty-six nobles who comprised the group at that time.

James I sought a revival of the pageantry of the Order in the fourteenth year of his reign, when he held the feast on March 20th and he assembled a Chapter at Whitehall on March 2nd. A further five ceremonies were held within the next two years.

> *The ancient custom which for some years had been intermitted, wherein, the solemnity of this feast all the Knight's Companion were wont to go attended, each with a large Train was recalled and brought back into use...*

> *... September 13 the next following at Windsor, on 26 May at Greenwich which was changed to 22-24 April until 16-18 August, thence again until October 4, 5, and 6 and lastly to 23-25 November at Windsor.).*

> *Elias Ashmole, celebrated English antiquarian, 1617 – 1692.*

For almost two centuries thereafter, the Sovereign and Knights of the Garter met at Windsor Castle for a Festival which lasted for three days, usually at St

George's 'tide' in April. The participants gathered in Chapter, feasted in St George's Hall and occupied their stalls in St George's Chapel for Matins, the Eucharist, Evensong and Requiem for departed Knights.

Garter celebrations and some First Folio plays

"The Merry Wives of Windsor", the Duke of Württemberg and other noblemen

Some scholars have suggested that in Queen Elizabeth's reign the play *The Merry Wives of Windsor* was performed as part of the celebration for the investiture of several noblemen. These included Frederick, Duke of Wurttemberg, who was awarded the Order of the Garter in 1597.

Queen Elizabeth pointedly made the Garter ceremony at a time when the Duke was unable to attend, reportedly because of his impertinence in requesting the Order of the Garter honour. The Duke was eventually installed many years later, when his Order was delivered to him in Stuttgart in November 1603.

The date of composition of *The Merry Wives of Windsor* is unknown and the play was registered for publication in 1602. However, textual allusions to the Order of the Garter suggest that the comedy may have been intended for performance in April 1597, prior to the installation of the Knights-Elect of that order at Windsor in May.

If that was the case the work was probably performed when the Queen attended the Garter Feast on 23rd April 1597, as stated by Dr Leslie Hotson in his historical investigation *Justice and Shallow*.

The title page of Quarto 1 states that the play was acted by the Lord Chamberlain's Men, *"Both before Her Majesty, and elsewhere"*. The earliest confirmed performance, however, occurred on 4th November 1604 at White-hall Palace.

Other noblemen invested in 1597 may have also enjoyed the play as part of the Garter celebrations, possibly in the presence of an Ambassador from Württemberg.

Other recipients of the Order of the Garter in that year were George Carey, 2nd Lord Hunsdon, who died in 1603 and was cousin to Queen Elizabeth; Thomas, 1st Lord Howard de Walden, afterwards 1st Earl of Suffolk, who served in the Fleet against the Spanish Armada; Charles Blount, 8th Lord Mountjoy, afterwards Earl of Devonshire, who died in 1606; and Sir Henry Lee, who died in 1611, the "Personal Champion" to Queen Elizabeth.

The Carey family

Lord Chamberlain George Carey, 2nd Lord Hunsdon KG, was the eldest son of Henry Carey, 1st Baron Hunsdon, and Anne Morgan; Henry was first cousin or half brother to Elizabeth I of England.

In 1560, at the age of 13, George matriculated at Trinity College, Cambridge. In 1566 he accompanied the Earl of Bedford on an official mission to Scotland, to attend the baptism of the future King James VI. During the Northern Rebellion of 1569, George was knighted in the field by the Earl of Sussex for bravery. George had challenged Lord Fleming, the commander of Dunbar Castle, to single combat.

George served as a Member of Parliament in the Commons for several terms (for Hertfordshire in 1571, for Hampshire in 1584, 1586, 1588–1589, 1592). During the threat of the Spanish Armada invasion, George was sent to Carisbrooke Castle on the Isle of Wight and later assumed command of the Isle's defences.

In July 1596, following his father's death, George Carey became the second Baron Hunsdon, and the following year he was appointed Lord Chamberlain – a position which had also been held by his father.

Both Henry and George Carey were patrons of the professional theatre company in London known as The Lord Chamberlain's Men" (later The King's Men), which featured talents such as Richard Burbage, Augustine Phillips and William Kempe.

Significantly, George Carey was the major patron of Thomas Nashe for many years and was on unusually friendly terms with the poet. Sir George and Lady Carey helped the impetuous playwright on several occasions when Nashe's wit and anarchic behaviour brought him official disfavour and even imprisonment; most notably for his contribution to the supposedly seditious play, *The Isle of Dogs*.

As the favoured poet of George Carey, Lord Chamberlain, the skilled and witty poet Thomas Nashe may have had a hand in the comedic *Merry Wives of Windsor*. It is also possible that an earlier play, *The Two Angry Women of Abington* by Henry Porter, an English dramatist known only for this one surviving work, may be the original source for the farcical plot of *The Merry Wives of Windsor*. Both of these plays have been compared favourably in style, plot and dramatic humour.

Some elements of both plays may, in turn, have been adapted from *Il Pecorone*, a collection of stories by Ser Giovanni Fiorentino. One of these texts was included in William Painter's *The Palace of Pleasure*.

In 1597 George Carey was invested as a Knight of the Garter, and it is likely that the first performance of *Merry Wives of Windsor* was held to commemorate the occasion.

George Carey was married to Elizabeth Spenser, who was related to the poet Edmund Spenser. Like her husband, Elizabeth was a cultured patron of the arts. The Carey's had one daughter, named Elizabeth. George Carey died in 1603 and his brother John, the next eldest, became the third Lord Hunsdon.

A further recipient of the Order of the Garter in the same year was Charles Blount, born 1563, the 2nd son of James, 6th Lord Mountjoy, he was educated at Winchester, Oxford and Clifford's Inn; Middle Temple.

Historical accounts record the lengthy liaison of Charles Blount with Lady Penelope Devereux, wife of Robert Rich, 3rd Baron Rich, by whom she bore several children. After her divorce from Rich, Penelope married Blount in an unlicensed ceremony in December 1605, becoming Countess of Devonshire, but she died two years later. The daughter of Walter Devereux, 1st Earl of Essex, the noted beauty Penelope, was also a popular figure at court and she is claimed to be Sir Philip Sidney's idealised *'Stella'* in his *Astrophil and Stella* sonnet sequence.

Knighted in 1587 and awarded the Order of the Garter in 1597, Charles Blount succeeded his brother as 8th Lord Mountjoy in 1594 and was created the Earl of Devonshire in 1603. Charles Blount was a member of the extended Sidney family.

Camden described Blount *as "a person famous for conduct, and so eminent in courage and learning that in these respects he had no superior, and but few equals."* It was Blount's youthful ambition to *'rebuild the ancient house,"* and to retrieve the declining fortunes of his family. In this endeavour Charles Blount would have succeeded, but for the lack of legitimate heirs.

Besides studying law, Blount spent his leisure hours with scholars able to direct him, and he gradually established his own reputation as a scholar, learning to read French and Italian alongside history, cosmography, mathematics and natural philosophy. As a young man, Charles Blount was *"addicted to popery,"* but eventually conformed to the established religion.

Apart from the Blount ancestors of Mary, Countess of Pembroke, a further significant figure was the wife of Sir Robert Sidney, Sarah Blount.

"Love's Labour's Lost", the French King Henri IV and Anthony Bacon

Love's Labour's Lost is a play that may have been intended as a court performance to celebrate the award of the Order of the Garter to Henri IV of France

142

in 1590 by Queen Elizabeth. Appropriately, the work staged the behaviour of noblemen with great humour at Henri's earlier court of Navarre, which was then an independent country. Henri of Navarre succeeded to the crown of France as Henri IV.

It is credible that Anthony Bacon wrote the play while in France, under the auspices of Francis Walsingham, his patron or his uncle William Cecil, and that it was commissioned for a performance before the King of Navarre in London. However, the French King did not attend the Garter investiture ceremony in that year and the award was delivered to him later.

Love's Labour's Lost is set in the court of Navarre in the mid-to-late 1580s; the knowledge of the court and its courtiers could only have been obtained by someone very familiar with the Navarre setting and the aristocrats portrayed in the play. The most likely candidate for authorship of the work is thus Anthony Bacon who was resident at the court of Navarre for a lengthy period of time.

Major characters in *Love's Labour's Lost* echo the names of the members of the court of Navarre: Biron (Berowne), Mayenne (Dumain) and de Longueville (Longaville).

There is, however, another explanation of the authorship of the play as put forward by James Greenstreet in his *A hitherto unknown writer of Elizabethan comedies*. This view asserts that the writer of the play is the 6th Earl of Derby, William Stanley, who was at the court of Navarre between 1582 and 1587. Although William Stanley was known to have written comedies, no identifiable work of the earl has survived. However, in support of this opinion there are records indicating that the Stanleys were associated with the theatre and were patrons of the Earl of Derby's Men. The young Stanley had been accompanied on his Continental stay by his tutor Richard Lloyd, whose version of the town of Chester 'Pageant' in the *Nine Worthies* was cleverly parodied in *Love's Labour's Lost*.

The origin of the play is certainly obscure. As one of the First Folio's early comedies, it is believed to have been revised in the 1590s and first published in quarto in 1598 by the bookseller Cuthbert Burby. The title page states that the play was *"Newly corrected and augmented by W. Shakespere,"* which has suggested to some scholars that it is a revision of an earlier version. The play next appeared in print in the First Folio in 1623, with a later quarto in 1631. This is the first play that carries the name of William Shakespeare. Yet how the claimed author became so familiar with the Navarre court and its noblemen remains inexplicable. Again, the sophisticated use of language in the play would indicate a writer of higher education and literary skill than Shakespeare's background would suggest.

It can only be conjectured how this play became the property of William Shakespeare. One explanation is that the text may have been used as a pledge for a cash loan that was not redeemed, or possibly the text was simply purchased but authorship acquired by the new owner. Equally, the text was was an unpaid commission of a copy of the original at the scriptorium of Francis Bacon.

Similarly, George Peele's play *The Rape of Lucrece,* whose part authorship is affirmed conclusively by Professor Brian Vickers, may have been another example of a play acquired as a commercial transaction.

The title of this play is nowadays given as *Love's Labour's Lost.* In its first 1598 quarto publication, the title appears as *Loues Labors Lost.* In the 1623 First Folio it is *Loues Labour's Lost* and in the 1631 edition it is *Loues Labours Lost.* In the Third Folio it appears for the first time with the modern punctuation and spelling as *Love's Labour's Lost.*

It has been suggested that the title derived from a line in John Florio's *His Firste Fruites of* 1578 *"We neede not speak so much of loue, al books are ful of lou, with so many authours, that it were labour lost to speake of Loue;"* a source from which the author also took the untranslated Venetian proverb, *"Venetia, Venetia/Chi non ti vede non ti pretia".*

Love's Labour's Lost, along with *The Tempest,* is a play without any obvious sources. *Cymbeline* also falls into this category to some extent, although it does draw strands of its narrative from some texts agreed on by modern scholars. Some possible influences can be found in the early plays of John Lyly, Robert Wilson's *The Cobbler's Prophecy* (c.1590) and Pierre de la Primaudaye's *L'Academie française* (1577 [available in translation from 1584]). This volume summarised the philosophical and scientific knowledge of the era. Stuart Gillespie describes it as a *"prose compendium of scientific, moral and philosophical knowledge."*

The earliest recorded performance of *Love's Labour's Lost* occurred before Queen Elizabeth at Christmas time, 1597, at court. A second recorded performance occurred in the first half of January 1605, played either at the house of the Earl of Southampton or that of Robert Cecil, Lord Cranborne, a cousin of Anthony Bacon.

Love's Labour's Lost is often thought of as a most flamboyantly intellectual play. The comedy abounds in sophisticated wordplay, puns and literary allusions and it is filled with clever pastiches of contemporary poetic forms.

It is often assumed that the work was written for performance at the Inns of Court, whose students would have been most likely to appreciate its style. However, it is more probable that it had been written for the sophisticated and educated members of the English court. The style of the work is the principal reason why it has never been among one of the most popular First Folio plays. The pedantic humour and subtle dialogue makes it largely inaccessible to contemporary theatre goers.

Anthony Bacon, poet and authorial candidate

Anthony Bacon was a son of Sir Nicholas Bacon, a senior English administrator and his second wife, Anne (née Cooke), daughter of Sir Anthony Cooke the tutor of Edward VI. Through the marriage of his mother's sisters Anthony was nephew to Sir Henry Killigrew, Sir Thomas Hoby, and to Elizabeth I's Secretary of State, later Lord Treasurer, William Cecil, Lord Burleigh.

Mary Sidney's mother Mary Dudley was a close friend to the Cooke sisters, Sir Anthony's daughters received an exceptionally high level of education and of them perhaps Mildred was the most intellectually able: she was the mother of the statesman, Sir Robert Cecil.

Anthony grew up with his younger brother, Francis, at his parents' Hertfordshire estate of Gorhambury, where they were tutored. Anthony and Francis studied for three years at Trinity College, Cambridge from April 1573, under John Whitgift, but without graduating.

Anthony Bacon was admitted to Gray's Inn, and following his father's death in February 1579 – through which he inherited estates worth £360 per annum – Anthony decided at twenty-one to go abroad. It was in December 1579, with letters of recommendation from Burleigh and the French ambassador, Michel de Castelnau, Seigneur de Mauvissière, he set off to Paris, where he began to provide intelligence reports for Burleigh and Sir Francis Walsingham, principal secretary.

By October 1584, Anthony Bacon was established in the Huguenot stronghold of Montauban, embraced by Navarre's court – the poet Du Bartas included. However, his status deteriorated during 1585 and 1586, when Bacon and one of his pages were accused of the capital offence of sodomy. Details are scarce, but interrogations took place in August 1586 and November 1587. Bacon may have been formally tried, given that Navarre certainly intervened to commute a sentence against him. None of these problems were known in England where Bacon's failure to return home was regarded with increasing anger by Queen Elizabeth.

In 1590 Bacon returned to Bordeaux, where he engaged in a merchants' controversy, renewed his acquaintance with Montaigne (sending one of the last known letters to the writer) and befriended the imprisoned Catholic double agent, Anthony Standen. Hearing of this, Lady Bacon claimed that he was *illegitimate and not to be born of her body* and encouraged his brother Francis to shun him. But when Anthony Bacon finally returned home in February 1592 after a twelve-year absence, Francis welcomed him into his Gray's Inn lodgings. Anthony had hoped to profit from his long-standing intelligence service to his uncle Burleigh but soon found that path blocked.

Anthony Bacon's relations with Burleigh and his cousin Sir Robert Cecil remained strained, but this rejection paved the way for Bacon's better future. Francis Bacon introduced Cecil to his own patron, Elizabeth's controversial favourite, Robert Devereux, 2nd Earl of Essex. Anthony Bacon soon enhanced Essex's remarkable secretariat by co-ordinating (on an unpaid basis) a massive foreign intelligence operation with contacts across Europe. Bacon's associates included Thomas Bodley, Sir Thomas Chaloner, Dr Henry Hawkins, John Napier and Sir Anthony Sherley.

In May 1594 Anthony bought a London house in Bishopsgate Street, much to his mother's concern as the property adjoined the popular Red Bull theatre thus attracting London's 'riff-raff.' Bacon's activities between 1597 and 1601 are difficult to reconstruct. This was a turbulent period, during which the Earl of Essex fell from favour several times until controversially leading English forces in Ireland, which ended in his failure and disgrace.

Anthony Bacon remained in Essex House until Elizabeth ordered him and others to leave in March 1600. However, when the Earl of Essex attempted his rebellion in February 1601, Anthony was apparently not involved and he was not called to give evidence against the earl. By then, living in Crutched Friars in London, Bacon was terminally ill and whilst the date of his actual death is unknown he was buried in May 1601.

James I granted Francis Bacon the office of learned counsel, and a life pension of £60 per annum in August 1604. The patent was awarded *"on account of the good, faithful and commendable service, until recently, of our beloved servant Anthony Bacon."*

Anthony's younger brother, Francis the statesman, senior lawyer and pioneer of scientific reason, was also known as a 'hidden' poet. Francis Bacon the versifier has been put forward as the most convincing candidate for authorship of the plays in the First Folio.

Both Anthony and Francis could have sought patrons through the author-ship of a group of plays created between 1594 and 1596, which include *Richard 11, King John* and *A Midsummer Night's Dream,* like their father Sir Nicholas Bacon, they were noted sonneteers.

The Order of the Garter and "Henry VI Part I"

Three distinct connections to the plays *Henry VI, Part I* and *Part II* can be made between Mary Talbot, Countess of Pembroke, the wife of William Herbert, 3rd Earl of Pembroke; Fulke Greville, Baron Brooke; and William Stanley, Earl of Derby in that their common ancestor was John Talbot, 1st Earl of Shrewsbury and 1st Earl of Waterford. Talbot was better known as "Old Talbot" a famed military commander.

Gilbert Talbot, 7th Earl of Shrewsbury, who was awarded the Order of the Garter in 1592 was a descendant of John Talbot. There exists the possibility that *Henry VI, Part I*, in which the 1st Earl of Shrewsbury is highly praised, could have been performed during this Garter celebration. Perhaps the Garter play was later included in the First Folio at the request of Mary Herbert (Talbot), Countess of Pembroke and wife of the Lord Chamberlain, the senior patron of the volume and one of the *'Illustrious Pair'*.

Sir Fulke Greville, could well have used his influence to include the play in the First Folio. Greville would have been able to claim his family link with the legendary Talbot through his Beauchamp and Neville lineage.

The first Earl of Shrewsbury is praised highly in the two historical plays, *Henry VI, Part I* and *Part II*. In the second act of *Henry VI, Part I* the Countess of Auvergne refers to the fact that the Talbot name created such a terror in France *that mothers with his name still their babes.*

The valiant Lord Talbot, the famous General, is taken prisoner by the French at the retreat of Orleans, alluded to in Act I, Scene I, of *Henry VI Part 1*, wherein descriptions are made of his bravery in battle. The Duke of Bedford also mentions Talbot and St. George's Day in Act I:

> *His ransom there is none but I shall pay:*
> *I'll hale the Dauphin headlong from his throne:*
> *His crown shall be the ransom of my friend;*
> *Four of their lords I'll change for one of ours.*
> *Farewell, my masters; to my task will I;*
> *Bonfires in France forthwith I am to make,*
> *To keep our great Saint George's feast withal:*
> *Ten thousand soldiers with me I will take,*
> *Whose bloody deeds shall make all Europe quake.*

Talbot first appears in person in Act I, Scene IV of *Henry VI Part 1*, with other English noblemen having been exchanged for Lord Ponton de Santrailles.

Talbot's successes in Burgundy are enumerated in Act III, Scene IV of this play in a Palace room in Paris, wherein he is created Earl of Shrewsbury before King Henry and English noblemen.

Talbot, having been described by the French General, *Our nation's terror and their bloody scourge!* conducted the siege of Bordeaux and took the town. However, he was outnumbered, defeated and killed with his son John, who is also praised for his selfless bravery, in Act IV, Scenes V and VI of *Henry VI.* This event actually occurred in 1453, long after the execution of Joan of Arc, which is not the way it was represented in the play.

The Talbot family's presence, in a dramatic era of English history, when much of France was lost, is affirmed once again with Gilbert Talbot. This Talbot is mentioned in *Richard III*, Act IV, scene V as one of the adherents of the Earl of Richmond, later Henry VII, alongside Sir Walter Herbert, Sir William Stanley, the Earl of Oxford and the Earl of Pembroke.

John Talbot, 1st earl of Shrewsbury, commissioned the *Talbot Shrewsbury Book* in Rouen in 1444-5. This extant and richly-illustrated manuscript was presented to Margaret of Anjou by Talbot in honour of her marriage to King Henri VI.

Although William Herbert, Earl of Pembroke, was married to Margaret Talbot in the Jacobean era and the play's inclusion may be in remembrance of her ancestor the actual play has its origins in the Elizabethan period. The scholars Bakeless, Tucker Brooke, and Rosenblum, amongst others, assert that the play *Henry VI* Parts *1 and 2* are likely to have been written by many hands and revised several times over the years. Academic research has shown text attributable to Thomas Nashe, Christopher Marlowe, and Robert Greene, with subsequent revisions by other writers during a period when collaboration was commonplace.

The printed quarto of 1594 of *Henry VI* and the *"careless"* quarto reprint of 1600 did not carry William Shakespeare's name on the title page. It did appear, however, on the third edition in 1619, twenty-five years after the first printing, which contained a number of major and minor changes to the text; by this date Shakespeare had been dead for seven years.

One analyst of the two early plays mentioned in 1591 claims that the composition of *The First Part of the Contention* and *The True Tragedy of Richard Duke of York* were early, memorial reconstructions of a fuller original text of the second and third parts of *Henry VI,* possibly played at court.

It was soon after the first Henslowe record of these early plays in 1592 that the poet Robert Greene mounted a printed attack on Shakespeare and his fellow actors purporting to be writers in his *"Greene's Groatsworth of wit..."* He described Shakespeare's life and career as *"bought with a Million of Repentance. Describing the follie of Youth, the falsehood of makeshift flatterers, the miserie of the negligent, and mischiefes of deceiving Courtesans."*

Written shortly before his death, the poem was published at his dying request by another fellow writer, Henry Chettle. Greene's posthumous pamphlet complains that:

> those Puppits (I meane) that speake from our mouths, those Anticks garnish in our colours. Is it not strange that I, to whom they all haue beene beholding; shall (were ye in that case that I am now) be both at once of them forsaken? Yes trust them not: for there is an upstart Crow, beautified with our feathers, that with a tigers heart wrapt in a Players hide, supposes he is as well able to bombast out a blanke verse as the best of you; and being an absolute Iohannes factotum, is in his owne conceit the only Shake-scene in a countrie.
>
> O that I might intreate your rare wits to be imployed in more profitable courses; & let those Apes imitate your past excellence, and never more aquaint them with your admired inuentions. I know the best husband of you will never proue an Usurer, and the unkindest of them all will neuer prooue a kinde nurse; yet whilst you may, seek you better Maisters ; for it is pittie men of such rare wits, should be subject to the pleasures of such rude groomes.
>
> In this I might insert two more, that both have writ against these buckram Gentlemen but let their owne works serue to witnesse against their owne wickednesse, if they perseuer to maintaine any more such peasants. For other newcomers I leaue them to the mercie of these painted monsters, who (I doubt not) will driue the best minded to despise them: for the rest it skills not though they make a ieast at them.
>
> But now I return again to you three, knowing my miserie is to you no news: and let me heartily intreate you to bee warned by my harmes... Trust not then (I beseech yee) to such weak staies : for they are as changeable in minde, as in many attires.
>
> Well, my hand is tired and I am forst to leaue where I would begin; for a whole booke cannot containe these wrongs, which I am forst to knit vpin some few lines of words. Desirous that you should lieu, though himself be dying, Robert Greene.

There is little doubt that in this tirade against imposter writers Greene is complaining that actors are taking the work of the university-educated playwrights and presenting it as their own. The three playwrights he appears to mention are Marlowe, Nashe (or Lodge) and Peele. Marlowe is obvious, Nashe was called '*Juvenal*' by his contemporaries and Peele, '*Sweet St George*'.

An explanation for this pirating of existing work may well be that the original authors, Greene, Marlowe and Nashe, had written these plays for the noble families who were their patrons, to be performed at court or their noble houses. The players taking part had then 'cobbled together' simpler and crude versions of these plays, with lots of sword fighting, for the popular stage. Therefore, the actors concerned gained revenue from the later stage performance in addition to payment for the text by the printer. The income generated thus was not shared by the original writers. The Greene tirade parallels the *Poor Poet Ape* attack on literary pirating by Ben Jonson; these angry protestations confirm the problem of maintaining written ownership at the time.

These attacks by Robert Greene and Ben Jonson appear to identify William Shakespeare and his fellow actors as the culprits. Greene's resentment is seen by some scholars to be actuated by the success of *The Contention...*, *The True Tragedie of the Duke of Yorke...* and *Henry VI, Part I and II*. This bitter resentment could also refer to other plays attributed to Shakespeare: *The Taming of the Shrew*, *Titus Andronicus*, *A Midsummer Night's Dream* and the old *King John*.

The True Tragedie was published as having been "*sundrie times acted by the Right Honourable Earl of Pembroke his Servants.*" William Shakespeare is not known to have any connection with Pembroke's company in 1594. Adding to proof of Shakespeare's deception is the testimony of Nashe that, "*Greene was Chief Agent of the companie* [Pembroke's company] *for he wrote more than four other.*" In this paragraph, Nashe concludes with the words "*he would show himself either incompetent or foolhardy, I think, who denied that Greene's title to the older version of two plays for one is but the continuation of the other.*"

There is another clear contemporary reference to plagiarism in the same vein, in a poem included within a pamphlet composed by the writer R.B. Gent:

> *Greene is the pleasing on an eie;*
> *Greene pleased the eies of all that lookt upon him;*
> *Greene is the ground of eurie Painters die*
> *Greene gaue the ground of all that wrote vpon him,*
> *Nay more, the men that so eclipst his fame*
> *Purloyned his plumes, can they deny the same.*

Henry VI Parts II and III and *Richard III* form a distinct and separate group in the opinion of historian Miss Lee in a postscript to her main paper *On the order of Shakespeare's historical plays.* Lee finds in them a singular resemblance to Christopher Marlowe (as do other scholars), and believes that *Part II* and *III* were written as early as 1590–1, and *Richard III* no later than 1592–3. As stated, other scholars have seen the hands of Greene and Peele in these early works that have later additions and rewriting of the original text.

The academic consensus as to the authorship of the two old plays and the three final parts is that the works contain a good deal of the language and style of Marlowe, Greene and Peele, with the latter two predominating. It may also be noted that in some instances of Peele's writing he made free use of Kyd, either directly copying the dramatist or working with him; Marlowe and Kyd shared a room for a time until Marlowe was murdered in 1593. The use of Kyd's writing is particularly marked in *Henry VI, Parts II* and *III*.

The authorship of the English history plays: contemporary collaborators

Five contemporary writers have been identified as contributors to the early history plays: Robert Greene, Christopher Marlowe, George Peele, Thomas Lodge and Thomas Kyd.

Robert Greene was best known for the posthumous pamphlet attributed to him: Greene's *Groats-Worth of Wit*. Born in Norwich in 1558, Greene attended Cambridge University, receiving a B.A. in 1580, and an M.A. in 1583 before moving to London, where Greene became one of the first authors in England to support himself with his pen.

Greene published in many genres, such as autobiographies, plays and romances, including *Mamillia, Pandosto* and *Menaphon*. Short poems and songs incorporated in some of the romances also gave him a reputation for and high rank as a lyrical poet.

In his notorious *Coney-Catching* pamphlets, Greene fashioned himself into a well-known public figure by telling colourful, inside stories of rakes and rascals duping solid citizens out of their hard-earned money.

Greene's plays include *The Scottish History of James IV, Alphonsus* (his greatest popular success), *Friar Bacon and Friar Bungay* (c. 1589), as well as *Orlando Furioso*, based on Ludovico Ariosto's epic poem. Robert Greene may also have had a hand in numerous other plays, and may have written a second part to *Friar Bacon,* which may survive as *John of Bordeaux.*

In addition to his acknowledged plays, Greene has been proposed as the author of a range of other dramas, including *The Troublesome Reign of King John, George-a-Greene, Fair Em, A Knack to Know a Knave, Locrine, Selimus,* and *Edward III,* among others – *Titus Andronicus* is another candidate.

Though some writers argue that the early date of Greene's remark precludes a reference to Shakespeare (who in 1592 had no published works to his name), some scholars think that Greene's comment refers to Shakespeare, who would in this period have been an 'upstart' actor, writing and contributing to plays such as *Henry VI, Parts I–III* and *King John*. These were most likely written and produced – though not published before Greene's death. Other scholars argue that the remarks refer to another actor, Edward Alleyn, whom Greene had attacked in an earlier pamphlet using much the same language.

Some academics think that all or part of *The Groats-Worth* may have been written shortly after Greene's death by one of his fellow writers (the pamphlet's printer, Henry Chettle, being the favoured candidate) hoping to capitalize on a lurid tale of deathbed repentance. Hanspeter Born argues that Greene wrote the whole of *Groats-Worth* and that his deathbed attack on the *"upstart Crow"* was provoked by William Shakespeare's interference with Greene's play *A Knack to Know a Knave*.

Christopher Marlowe, baptised in 1564, was an English dramatist, poet and translator of the Elizabethan era. Marlowe was the foremost Elizabethan tragedian of his day and his plays are known for their use of dramatic blank verse and their overreaching and vividly presented protagonists. Marlowe's colourful use of language has been identified by various scholars in the early Lancastrian history plays.

Marlowe attended The King's School in Canterbury and Corpus Christi College, Cambridge, where he studied on a scholarship and received his Bachelor of Arts degree in 1584. The Privy Council intervened on his behalf when his M.A. was withheld because of his alleged Roman Catholic sympathies, and commended him for his *"faithful dealing"* and *"good service"* to the Queen. The nature of Marlowe's service was not specified by the Council, but its letter to the Cambridge authorities has provoked much speculation, notably the theory that Marlowe was operating as a secret agent working for Sir Francis Walsingham's intelligence service.

Of the dramas attributed to Marlowe, *Dido, Queen of Carthage* is believed to have been his first, and performed by the Children of the Chapel acting company between 1587 and 1593. The play was first published in 1594 and the title page attributes the play to Christopher Marlowe and Thomas Nashe: yet another example of collaboration by writers.

Marlowe's first play was *Tamburlaine the Great*, about the conqueror Timur, who rises from shepherd to warrior. It is among the first English plays to be written in blank verse, and, with Thomas Kyd's *The Spanish Tragedy*, is generally considered the beginning of the mature phase of the Elizabethan theatre. *Tamburlaine* was a success, and was followed with *Tamburlaine the Great, Part II.*

The two parts of *Tamburlaine* were published in 1590, but all of Marlowe's other works were published posthumously. The sequence of the writing of his other four plays is unknown and, in character with their author, they all deal with controversial themes.

Alongside *Tamburlaine,* the quartet of plays for which Marlowe is acclaimed are: *The Jew of Malta,* about a Maltese Jew's barbarous revenge against the city authorities printed in 1633.

Edward II is a history play about the deposition of King Edward II by his barons and the Queen, who resent the undue influence that the King's favourites have in court and state affairs. The play was entered into the Stationers' Register on 6 July 1593, five weeks after Marlowe's death.

The Massacre at Paris is a short and luridly written work. The quarto is the only surviving text of *The Massacre,* a likely reconstruction from memory of the original performance text. The play portrays the events of the Saint Bartholomew's Day Massacre in 1572, which English Protestants frequently invoked as the blackest example of Catholic treachery.

The Tragicall History of the Life and Death of Doctor Faustus, based on the German *Faustbuch,* was the first dramatised version of the Faust legend of a scholar's ill-fated dealings with the devil. *Dr Faustus* is a textual problem for scholars as it was highly edited, possibly censored and rewritten after Marlowe's death.

Shortened versions suited to a small stage were enormously successful – thanks in part, no doubt, to the imposing stage presence of Edward Alleyne. unusually tall for the time, well suited to the haughty roles of Tamburlaine, Faustus and Barabas. These simplified plays were the foundation of the repertoire of Alleyn's company, the Admiral's Men, throughout the 1590s.

In May 1593 the Privy Council ordered the arrest of those responsible for the libels posted about London threatening Protestant refugees – one of which was signed *Tamburlaine*. Marlowe's colleague Thomas Kyd was arrested and his lodgings were searched before a fragment of an heretical tract was found. Kyd asserted that it had belonged to Marlowe, with whom he had been writing *in one chamber* some two years earlier. At that time they had both been working for an aristocratic patron, probably Ferdinando Stanley, Lord Strange.

Various accounts of Marlowe's death were current over the next few years. In his *Palladis Tamia*, published in 1598, Francis Meres says Marlowe was *"stabbed to death by a bawdy serving-man, a rival of his in his lewd love"* as punishment for his *"epicurism and atheism."*

The official account only came to light in 1925 when the scholar Leslie Hotson discovered the coroner's report of the inquest on Marlowe's death, held two days later on Friday 1st June 1593, by the Coroner of the Queen's Household, William Danby. Marlowe had spent all day in a house in Deptford, owned by the widow Eleanor Bull, and together with three men: Ingram Frizer, Nicholas Skeres and Robert Poley. All three men had been employed by Walsingham, the spymaster.

Marlowe's death is alleged by some to be an authorised assassination; the three men who were in the room with him when he died were all connected both to the state secret service and to the London underworld. Frizer and Skeres also had a long record as loan sharks and conmen, as shown by court accounts. Bull's house also had *"links to the government's spy network."*

Marlovian themes were re-used in *Antony and Cleopatra*, *The Merchant of Venice*, *Richard II*, *Macbeth*, *Dido, Queen of Carthage*, *The Jew of Malta*, *Edward II* and *Dr Faustus* respectively.

In *Hamlet*, after meeting with the travelling actors, Hamlet requests the Player perform a speech about the Trojan War, which at 2.2.429–32 has an echo of Marlowe's *Dido, Queen of Carthage*. In *Love's Labour's Lost*, the poet brings on a character "Marcade" (three syllables) in conscious acknowledgement of Marlowe's character "Mercury," also in attendance on the King of Navarre, in *Massacre at Paris*. The significance to the audience, who had read *Hero and Leander*, was Marlowe's identification of himself with the god Mercury.

Thomas Lodge was a dramatist and writer of the Elizabethan and Jacobean periods, and traces of his work have been detected in the early English history plays.

Lodge was born about 1558 at West Ham, the second son of Sir Thomas Lodge, who was Lord Mayor of the City of London in 1562–3. Thomas' brother, William, married Mary, the daughter of the Master of the Revels, Thomas Blagrave. Thomas Lodge was educated at Merchant Taylors' School and Trinity College, Oxford where he took his BA in 1577 and MA in 1581.

In 1578 Thomas Lodge entered Lincoln's Inn, where, as in the other Inns of Court, a love of letters and drama were common. The budding writer, disregarding the wishes of his family, took up literature. When Stephen Gosson in 1579 published his *Schoole of Abuse*, a critical attack of the stage and players, Lodge responded with *Defence of Poetry, Music and Stage Plays* in 1579 or 1580.

From 1587 onwards the author seems to have made a series of attempts at playwriting, though most of those attributed to him are mainly conjectural. Having been to sea with Captain Clarke in his expedition to Terceira and the Canaries, in 1591 Lodge made a voyage with Thomas Cavendish to Brazil and the Straits of Magellan, returning home by 1593. During the Canaries expedition, to beguile the tedium of his voyage, he composed his prose tale of *Rosalynde, Euphues Golden Legacie*, which, printed in 1590, afterwards furnished the story of *As You Like It*.

Before starting on his second expedition, Thomas Lodge had published an historical romance, *The History of Robert, Second Duke of Normandy, surnamed Robert the Devil*. Lodge also left behind him for publication *Catharos Diogenes in his Singularity, a discourse on the immorality of Athens signifying London*, both of which appeared in 1591. Another romance in the manner of Lyly, *Euphues Shadow, the Battaile of the Sences* of 1592, appeared while Lodge was on his travels.

The quantity of Thomas Lodge's confirmed dramatic work is small in comparison, such as the odd – but far from feeble – play, *A Looking Glass for London and England*. The author had already written *The Wounds of Civil War*, produced perhaps as early as 1587 and published in 1594, and put on as a 'play reading' at the Globe Theatre on 7th February 1606.

However, the 19th century scholar Frederick saw grounds for assigning *Mucedorus and Amadine* to Lodge, played by the Queen's Men about 1588, along with a share with Robert Greene in *George a Greene, the Pinner of Wakefield*, and collaboration in *Henry VI, Part II*. Fleay also regards Lodge as at least part-author of *The True Chronicle of King Leir and his three Daughters* of 1594 and *The Troublesome Raigne of John, King of England* (c. 1588).

In the latter part of Lodge's life – possibly about 1596, when he published his *Wits Miserie and the World's Madnesse* and the religious tract *Prosopopeia*, he became a Catholic and engaged in the practice of medicine, for which Wood says he qualified himself by a degree at Avignon in 1600. Two years afterwards the author received the degree of M.D. from Oxford University.

Lodge's second historical romance, the *Life and Death of William Longbeard* of 1593, was more successful than the first. Lodge also brought back with him from the new world *A Margarite of America*, published 1596, a romance of the same description interspersed with many lyrics. Already in 1580 Lodge had given to the world a volume of poems bearing the title of the chief among them, *Scillaes Metamorphosis, Enterlaced with the Unfortunate Love of Glaucus* (more briefly known as *Glaucus and Scilla*): to this tale the poet of *Venus and Adonis* was indebted.

If Thomas Lodge, as has been supposed, was the Alcon in *Colin Clout's Come Home Again*, it may have been the influence of Edmund Spenser which led to the composition of *Phillis*, a volume of sonnets. This sonnet sequence was published with the narrative poem, *The Complaynte of Elsired*, in 1593. *A Fig for*

Momus, on the strength of which he has been called the earliest English satirist, contains eclogues addressed to Samuel Daniel and others. An epistle addressed to Michael Drayton and other pieces appeared in 1595.

Henry, Prince of Wales and "Macbeth"

There is a possibility that the play *Macbeth* was written for Crown Prince Henry Stuart and perhaps performed during the celebration of the Order of the Garter in 1603 when he was awarded the honour.

Macbeth has a particular significance for Prince Henry inasmuch as the narrative of the play legitimises a fictional Scottish history and infers his descent (and that of James I) from Banquo: an ancient Scottish King. This flattering fiction of Scottish royal legitimacy is not, however, borne out by the facts of the king's lineage.

Others receiving the Order of the Garter in that year were: John Erskine, 2nd Earl of Mar, companion from boyhood of James I, High Treasurer of England; Ludovick Stuart, 2nd Duke of Lennox, afterwards also 1st Duke of Richmond; Henry Wriothesley, 3rd Earl of Southampton and William Herbert, 3rd Earl of Pembroke.

The tragedy of *Macbeth* is believed to have been written between 1603 and 1607 and is most commonly dated to 1606. The earliest account of a probable performance of the play is April 1611, when Simon Forman recorded seeing such a performance at the Globe theatre. It was first published in the First Folio of 1623, possibly from a prompt book. The source for the tragedy is the account of King Macbeth of Scotland, Macduff, and Duncan in *Holinshed's Chronicles* of 1587, a history of England, Scotland and Ireland. However, some scholars think that George Buchanan's *Rerum Scoticarum Historia* is a more notable match for the First Folio version. Buchanan's work was available only in Latin.

Banquo was thought to be a direct ancestor of the Stuart King James I, but this association was disproved in the 19th century, hence the Banquo portrayed in historical sources is significantly different from the Banquo created for the First Folio play. As a primary example it would have been dangerous to portray the king's ancestor as a murderer as in the chronicle. Instead, the later Banquo was portrayed more acceptably in the play as a nobleman.

The play appears to celebrate King James' ancestors and adds credibility to the Stuart accession to the throne in 1603. Scholars suggest that the vision of the witches, in Act IV, which reveals a number of earlier Scottish kings, is a compliment to King James' 'wisdom' on the subject of witchcraft.

Macbeth was first printed in the First Folio of 1623 and this publication is the only source for the text, which has been plainly altered by later hands. Most notable is the inclusion of two songs from Thomas Middleton's play *The Witch*. Middleton is conjectured to have inserted an extra scene involving the witches and Hecate and these scenes have proved highly popular with audiences.

Macbeth is an anomaly among the First Folio tragedies in certain critical ways. It is short: more than a thousand lines shorter than *Othello* and *King Lear*, and only slightly more than half as long as *Hamlet*. This brevity has suggested to many critics that the received version is based on a heavily-cut source, later corrected. Other unusual features pointed out are the rapid pace of the first act, which contains much action, the comparative flatness of the characters other than Macbeth and the uniqueness of Macbeth himself compared with other First Folio tragic heroes.

One convincing candidate for the original authorship is Sir Robert Aytoun (also spelt Ayton or Aiton), who was a Scottish poet and the son of Ayton of Kinaldie House in Fife. Aytoun and his elder brother entered St Leonard's College in St Andrews in 1584.

It is noteworthy that Robert Aytoun appears to have been well-known to his literary contemporaries in Scotland and England and became court poet to Queen Anne. A favourite of King James too, Aytoun's major work was *Diophantus and Charidora*. The courtier poet composed poetry in Latin, Greek and English and was one of the first Scotsman to write his poetry in the English language.

After graduating MA from St. Andrews in 1588, he studied civil law at Paris, became Ambassador to the Emperor, and held other court offices. Sir Robert Aytoun is buried in Poet's Corner in Westminster Abbey, which has a particular significance in regard to the other putative authors of the First Folio canon.

Thomas Middleton, born in 1580, has also been connected to the authorship of the play *Macbeth* and stands with John Fletcher and Ben Jonson as among the most successful and prolific of Jacobean playwrights, composing both comedies and tragedies. Middleton was also a prolific writer of masques and pageants.

Middleton attended Queen's College, Oxford, matriculating in 1598, where he wrote and published three long poems in popular Elizabethan styles although one, his book of satires, ran afoul of the Anglican Church's ban on satire and was burned.

In the early 17th century, Middleton wrote topical pamphlets, including one – *Penniless Parliament of Threadbare Poets* – that became the subject of a Parliamentary inquiry. At this time, Philip Henslowe's Diary records that Thomas Middleton was writing for the Admiral's Men. However, Middleton's early dramatic career was marked by controversy when the writer's friendship with Thomas Dekker brought him into conflict with Ben Jonson and George Chapman in the so called 'War of the Theatres'. The grudge with Jonson continued as late as 1626, when Jonson's play *The Staple of News* contains a slur on Middleton's great success with the political satire *A Game at Chess*.

Plague closed the London theatres in 1603, during which time Middleton composed prose pamphlets before returning to drama with great energy and producing close to a score of plays, for several companies and in several genres. These works were most notably city comedies and revenge tragedies. A continuing collaboration of Middleton and Dekker produced *The Roaring Girl*, another stage success.

In the 1610s, Middleton began his fruitful collaboration with the actor William Rowley, producing *Wit at Several Weapons* and *A Fair Quarrel*. Working alone as a playwright he also produced his comic masterpiece, *A Chaste Maid in Cheapside*, in 1613. Some scholars believe Middleton was earlier called upon to revise *Macbeth* and *Measure for Measure*, and at the same time as playwriting he was involved in composing civic pageants.

The 1620s saw the production of Middleton and Rowley's tragedy *The Changeling*, and several tragicomedies. It was in 1624 when Middleton reached a pinnacle of notoriety, after his dramatic allegory *A Game at Chess* was staged by the King's Men. The play used the concept of a chess game to present and satirise the recent intrigues surrounding the Spanish Match, the diplomatic marriage. The Privy Council shut down the play after nine performances following the complaints of the Spanish Ambassador. Middleton faced an unknown, but probably frightening, degree of punishment. Since no play later than *A Game at Chess* is recorded, it has been hypothesized that his punishment included a ban on writing for the stage.

There is extensive evidence not only for Middleton's authorship of *The Revenger's Tragedy*, but also for his collaboration on *Timon of Athens* with an unidentified writer.

A Chaste Maid in Cheapside, produced by the Lady Elizabeth's Men, skillfully combines London life with an expansive view of the power of love to effect reconciliation. *The Changeling*, a late tragedy, returns Middleton to an Italianate setting, like that of *The Revenger's Tragedy*.

"Hamlet"

The investiture of Christian IV, King of Denmark and Norway, brother of Queen Anne, to the Order of the Garter in 1603 may have been the occasion of celebration with a performance of *Hamlet, Prince of Denmark* – evidently a revised play dating from two decades earlier. Christian IV was unable to attend the ceremony and on 28th June 1603 Francis Manners travelled with his brother to Denmark to present the Order to Christian IV.

At a later investiture in 1605, the Order of the Garter was awarded to Ulric, Duke of Schleswig-Holstein, son of the King of Denmark and Norway, and Henry Howard, Earl of Northampton, Lord Privy Seal. Otherwise, *Hamlet* may have been played during the second visit of Christian IV in 1614.

Hamlet is the longest play in the First Folio with complex, philosophical, yet dramatic content. The plot dramatises the revenge Prince Hamlet exacts on his uncle Claudius for murdering the Danish king, Hamlet's father, before succeeding to the throne and taking the widow Gertrude, Hamlet's mother, as his wife. The play explores themes of treachery, revenge, incest and moral corruption, dramatised within the individual consciousness of the introspective Hamlet.

Three early but different versions of the play are extant, the first Quarto (Q1, 1603), the second Quarto (Q2, 1604), and the First Folio (F1, 1623). Each of the versions includes lines, and even entire scenes, missing from the others.

According to a popular theory, the main source of *Hamlet Prince of Denmark* is believed to be an earlier play – now lost – known today as the *Ur-Hamlet*, written by Thomas Kyd. The *Ur-Hamlet* would have been in performance by 1589 and the first version of the story is known to incorporate a ghost. The Chamberlain's Men may have purchased and performed this early play.

Clearly scholars cannot assert with any confidence how much material was taken from the *Ur-Hamlet*, or derived from legends written in Latin. Or even how much was developed from de Belleforest's version of 1570, a translation and adaptation of the *histoires tragiques* by the Italian Matteo Bandello, based upon Pierre Boaistuau. Interestingly, original elements of Belleforest's work are not in the traditional story but do appear in the 1623 play.

Scholars have often speculated that Hamlet's character Polonius might have been inspired by William Cecil, Lord Burleigh, Lord High Treasurer and chief counsellor to Queen Elizabeth. Literary historian E. K. Chambers has suggested that Polonius's advice to Laertes may have echoed Burleigh's counselling of his son Robert Cecil. The historian John Dover Wilson thought it almost certain that the figure of Polonius caricatured Burleigh, while in recent times the critic and historian A. L. Rowse also speculated that Polonius's tedious verbosity might have resembled that of the Elizabethan statesman.

In Francis Mere's *Palladis Tamia Wits Treasury*, twelve of the First Folio plays are named but *Hamlet* is not among them, suggesting that it had not yet been written. As *Hamlet* was very popular, Bernard Lott, the series editor of *New Swan*, believes it unlikely that Meres would have overlooked *so significant a piece.*

The phrase *little eyases* in the First Folio (F1) may allude to the Children of the Chapel, whose popularity in London forced the Globe Company into provincial touring. This became known as the *'War of the Theatres'*, and supports a 1601 dating. Historian Katherine Duncan-Jones accepts a 1600–1 attribution for the date *Hamlet* was written.

Comparison of the *To be, or not to be* soliloquy in the first three editions of *Hamlet,* exemplify the varying quality of the text in the *Bad Quarto,* the *Good Quarto* and the *First Folio.* The discovery in 1823 of Hamlet Q1, whose existence had been unsuspected, caused considerable interest and raised many questions of editorial practice and interpretation.

Scholars immediately identified apparent deficiencies in Q1 which was instrumental in the development of the concept of a 'bad quarto'. Yet Q1 still has value since it contains stage directions that reveal actual stage practices in a way that Q2 and F1 do not. The new text contains an entire scene (usually labelled 4.6) that does not appear in either Hamlet Q2 or F1 and it is useful for comparison with the later editions.

The Q1 scene order is more coherent, without the problems of Q2 and F1 of *Hamlet* seeming to resolve something in one scene and enter the next drowning in indecision. The major deficiency of Q1 is in the language, particularly in the opening lines of the famous *To be, or not to be* soliloquy, which are markedly different: *"To be, or not to be, aye there's the point. / To die, to sleep, is that all? Aye all: / No, to sleep, to dream, aye marry there it goes."*

Q1 is considerably shorter than Q2 or F1 and may be a memorial reconstruction of the play by an actor who played a minor role, possibly *Marcellus*. Scholars disagree whether the reconstruction was pirated or authorised. Yet another theory, considered by New Cambridge editor Kathleen Irace, holds that Q1 is an abridged version intended especially for travelling productions.

A view held by some analysts of the First Folio works is that the final revision of *Hamlet* for publication shows the hand of Sir Fulke Greville, Lord Brooke. The play's superior intellectual content indicates one of the more scholarly poets of the Jacobean era and Fulke Greville, an intelligent, gifted writer with a philosophical turn of mind, could well be considered as the writer or principal editor of the version of *Hamlet* in the First Folio.

Thomas Kyd, born in 1558, the author of *The Spanish Tragedy* and one of the most important figures in the development of Elizabethan drama. Although well known in his own time, Kyd fell into obscurity until 1773 when Thomas

Hawkins, an early editor of *The Spanish Tragedy*, discovered that Kyd was named as its author by Thomas Heywood in his *Apologie for Actors* in 1612.

A century later, scholars in Germany and England began to shed light on Kyd's life and work, including the controversial discovery that he was probably the author of a *Hamlet* play pre-dating that in the First Folio.

Thomas Kyd was the son of Francis Kydd, described as *Citizen and Writer of the Courte Letter of London;* a scrivener and in 1580, also recorded as a warden of the Scriveners' Company. In October 1565 the young Kyd was enrolled in the newly founded Merchant Taylors' School, whose headmaster was Richard Mulcaster – an early lexicographer of English who later became High Master of St Paul's School. Fellow students of Kyd included Edmund Spenser and Thomas Lodge.

At Merchant Taylors' Thomas Kyd received a well-rounded education thanks to the humanist Mulcaster's progressive ideas. Apart from Latin and Greek, the rigorous curriculum included music, drama, physical education, and *good manners*. There is no evidence that Kyd progressed to either of the English universities, but he may have followed his father's profession for a time: two letters written by him are extant and his handwriting suggests the training of a scrivener.

Evidence suggests that in the 1580s Kyd became an important playwright, but little is known about his early activity. Francis Meres in his *Palladis Tamia: Wit's Treasury* placed him among *"our best for tragedy"* and Heywood elsewhere called him *"Famous Kyd."* Ben Jonson places him in the First Folio encomium alongside Christopher Marlowe and John Lyly.

Kyd's famous work, *The Spanish Tragedie* was usually known simply as *Hieronimo,* after the protagonist, and was probably written in the mid to late 1580s. The earliest surviving edition of *The Spanish Tragedy* was printed in 1592. The play set new standards in plot construction and character development and in 1602 another version of the play was published with *"additions"*.

Other works by Kyd are his translations of Torquato Tasso's *Padre di Famiglia* (published as *The Householder's Philosophy* in 1588) and Robert Garnier's *Cornelia* (1594). Plays attributed in whole or in part to Kyd include *Soliman and Perseda, King Leir, Arden of Feversham* and *Edward III*.

Some poems by Kyd also exist, but it seems that the majority of his work is lost or unidentified. The success of Kyd's plays extended to Europe. Various versions of *The Spanish Tragedy* and his *Hamlet* were popular in Germany and the Netherlands for generations after their appearance in England.

From 1587 to 1593 Kyd was in the service of an unidentified nobleman, perhaps in a secretarial role, since, after his imprisonment in 1593 (see below), he wrote of having lost *"the favours of my Lord, whom I haue servd almost theis vi yeres nowe."* The various noblemen who have been proposed as Kyd's patron include the Earl of Sussex, the Earl of Pembroke, Lord Strange and Edward de Vere, Earl of Oxford. Around 1591 Christopher Marlowe also joined the service of Kyd's patron. Both poets were imprisoned for *"divers lewd and mutinous libels"*. Kyd was eventually released, but was not accepted back into his lord's service. Believing he was under suspicion of atheism himself, he wrote to the Lord Keeper, Sir John Puckering, protesting his innocence, but his efforts to clear his name were apparently fruitless. The last one may hear from the playwright on this ordeal accompanies the publication of *Cornelia* in 1594, where he alludes in the dedication to the Countess of Sussex to the *bitter times and privy broken passions* he had endured. Thomas Kyd died later that year and was buried on 15 August in London at only 35 years of age.

"King John"

The play *King John* found a welcome reception within the strongly Protestant political climate of Queen Elizabeth's reign. The anti-papists saw John as the one British King before Henry VIII who defied the Pope and the Protestant Chronicles had made a reformation hero of this independent monarch.

Later, however, Roman Catholic writers stressed John's subsequent surrender of his crown authority to the Pope, which effectively meant that Henry VIII was subordinate to him. The king's subsequent Church Reformation thus became a civil and ecclesiastical rebellion against Christendom the higher power in Europe.

A forerunner of the First Folio historical drama may be found firstly in John Bale's 'Kynge Johan' of 1536, written some two years after Henry's Act of Supremacy. It is arguably the first time the history play begins to emerge from the Morality play.

Half a century after Bale's play another drama on the subject was published anonymously in 1591, although it was probably written several years earlier. The work was entitled *The Troublesome Reigne of King John of England*. The later work supports Bale's picture of the English King as a victim of Papal and French plots, eventually emerging as a Protestant martyr. Most scholars have regarded this version as the source play from which the First Folio's *King John* draws both historical events and its political slant.

There were perceived similarities between the reigns of King John and Elizabeth I, too giving the play a topical relevance when it was written in the 1590s. Queen Elizabeth also defied the Pope, who not only had her excommunicated, but promised to canonize the assassin who could kill her. Like King John, Queen Elizabeth was attacked by a Catholic monarch, Philip II of Spain, who attempted to invade England in 1588 until the Spanish Armada was blown off course and destroyed.

In addition to these historical parallels, neither King John nor Queen Elizabeth was entirely secure in their own claim to the throne and both had credible rivals who enjoyed powerful support. John's rival claimant was Arthur, son of his elder brother Geoffrey, who enjoyed the backing of both King Philip of France and the Papacy.

Elizabeth's rival was Mary Stuart, Queen of Scots, supported by both the Spanish King and the Papacy, as well as many English Catholics. John's desire for Arthur's death, and subsequent remorse for it, could be seen as comparable to Elizabeth's handling of the problem of Mary Stuart's execution and her own subsequent troubled feelings. It is significant that of the total cast in King John, some two thirds are past and distant relations of Mary Sidney.

Recipients of the Garter in 1593 were: Henry Percy, 9th Earl of Northumberland, a relation of the Sidney family, to whom George Peele wrote the introductory poem *The honour of the Garter: displaied in a Poeme gratulatorie,* Edward Somerset, 4th Earl of Worcester; Edmund, 3rd Lord Sheffield and afterwards 1st Earl of Mulgrave; Sir Francis Knollys, a first cousin of Queen Elizabeth, who was prominent in her reign as a consistent champion of the Puritan cause and Thomas, 5th Lord Borough (or Burgh) of Gainsborough, Lord Deputy of Ireland.

Knollys daughter, Lettice, Countess of Essex and of Leicester, who died in 1634, married firstly Walter Devereux, 1st Earl of Essex, secondly Robert Dudley, 1st Earl of Leicester, and thirdly Sir Christopher Blount.

Engraving of the balcony scene from Romeo and Juliet

Love looks not with the eyes, but with the mind
All thoughts, all passions, all delights
Whatever starts this mortal frame
All are but ministers of Love,
And feed his sacred flame

Love by Samuel Coleridge Taylor

CHAPTER NINE

Love and courtly entertainment

THE plays in the First Folio, excluding the English royal chronicles, are concerned with aspects of love: a subject well suited for court entertainment.

Unlike the plays concerned with Lancastrian history, which were included for their own separate purpose, aspects of love pertained to the overarching theme that encompassed the bulk of the works in the First Folio.

England's educated society and the poets of the early Elizabethan age had inherited their social mores from the much earlier tradition of Courtly Love. This is expressed in Chaucer's early poem *Court of Love*, which depicted the concept as a regal court – the central sovereign of Love's authority. Here statutes are discussed and decrees issued, upon which tribunals frame their proceedings, all centred upon a concept of love that finds its echo in the Christian faith: "Love One Another."

Courtly Love was a concept of love that became a central theme of lyric and epic poetry in both France and England. The philosophy of courtly love is made manifest in works such as the 12th century Chrétien de Troyes' *Lancelot*, Guillaume de Lorris's *Roman de la Rose* in the 13th century and notably Chaucer's *Troilus and Criseyde* in the late 14th century.

A fourteenth century near-contemporary of Chaucer, the poet John Gower also followed the medieval mindset of Courtly Love in his long poem *Confessio Amantis*. However, here love allowed for the moral challenges of the seven deadly sins, which impinge upon and taint pure love.

The advent of humanism brought the new perception of self-determinism to England around the 1570s, influencing its intellectuals and poets such as Philip Sidney and also served to widen the interpretation of the word 'love'.

Different forms of love were recognised, drawn from classical descriptions:

Agape, unconditional or pure love; *Philia,* familial love and *Eros,* romantic love. The definition of Courtly Love – noble and chivalrous love – had grown to measure many more manifestations of love from the base and unpleasant to the admirable and selfless. These forms of love were thought to govern the character of individuals and indeed mankind generally.

The idealised virtues of love: romantic, filial, patriotic, brotherly and compassionate, by their very existence cause the unacceptable distortions of human behaviour: greed, avarice, excessive ambition, hatred, cowardice and deceit.

By the end of the 16th century the concept of a utopian Courtly Love had been superseded by a concept of love that more truly accorded with the reality of human behaviour. Here was the broadest possible subject for dramatic presentation, providing virtually unlimited characters and plots for plays that raised moral issues and personal decisions, of virtue or vice, that could be personified on stage.

In court circles this multifaceted question of *"What is Love?"* provided both intellectual and emotional entertainment, from the witty and light-hearted comedy to the sombre and judgmental tragedy.

The new perspectives of humanity, viewed so differently from earlier theological and ethical positions, were well-suited to the vibrant and questioning minds that were so apparent in the Elizabethan age and the early Stuart period. It was a pre-requisite of a play at the Elizabethan court that it was concerned with an aspect of love.

Romeo and Juliet

The story of Romeo and Juliet remains a classical ideal of romantic love that often ends in tragedy, in the tradition of *Troilus and Cressida* or *Hero and Leander.* The drama derives from an old Italian tale by da Porto published between 1530 and 1535 and the *Decameron.* A later version of 1561 is listed in the *Annals of English Drama* which may be linked with the Italian migrant, tutor and author Michelangelo Florio resident in England 1550-1554.

Based upon an earlier cautionary tale of unacceptable social behaviour, the play dramatises the intensity of the young lovers' passion, which is thwarted and finally destroyed by family rivalry.

Twelfth Night

Unrequited love provides the continuing theme throughout the complex plot of *Twelfth Night.* The insanity of romantic desire is represented by the behaviour of Duke Orsino, Countess Olivia and Lady Viola. The farcical events are offset by the unhappy experience of Olivia's steward Malvolio, who is tricked into believing his love for his mistress is reciprocated. Further comic complications arise as a result of cross-dressing and confusion over identical twins of different sexes.

All's Well that Ends Well

The play applauds the triumph of a woman's love for a man, who is indifferent to her. As a result of her devotion and determination to win him, the heroine Helen eventually succeeds in her quest for Bertram by means of a witty sexual deceit. The play is drawn from a tale by Boccaccio that appeared in *The Decameron*, a story known to Michelangelo Florio and included in William Painter's *Palace of Pleasure*.

Antony and Cleopatra

The grand passion of the two lovers presents at one level an extraordinary, almost transcendental intensity, yet their great love is humanised by their own frailties and their roles in a drama of the political conflict of opposing states.

As You Like It

Sourced but refashioned from the popular *Rosalind*, written by Thomas Lodge in 1590, a far more sombre play. *As You Like It* provides witty observations on the universality of love. The principal character is the forceful and independent Rosalind, who challenges the stereotypes of male and female behaviour in her roles, particularly by playing the part of each sex in disguise.

The Comedy of Errors

Brotherly love, expressed by the reuniting of long-lost identical twins, is the essential plot of *The Comedy of Errors*. The play is based upon the *Menaechmi* written by the Roman dramatist Plautus and also draws from Gower's *Confessio Amantis* of 1390 and George Gascoigne's *Supposes* of 1566. A short comedy that verges on farce, the plot also illuminates serious aspects of the emotional relationship between women and men.

Coriolanus

The valiant, martial Coriolanus prizes honour and plain-speaking and, above all, suffers from overwhelming pride but demonstrates great contempt for the Roman plebeians and their noblemen. Banished from the city, Coriolanus plans its destruction with the help of the tribal enemy of Rome, but is persuaded to desist by his mother, Volumnia, for whose approval he has strived to achieve fame.

It is the love of Coriolanus for Volumnia and his inability to resist her power over him that resolves the impending sack of Rome. This familial love however, ultimately invites his own death.

Cymbeline

The intricate plot of this tragicomedy bears a resemblance to the fairytale genre with its crude characterisations and mystical happenings. The subject of a mistaken infidelity by the heroine Innogen notably dramatises the misogyny and heartlessness of the male characters – much contrasted with Innogen's faithfulness and the sincerity of her love for her husband Posthumous.

Hamlet

Essentially a revenge play centring on the troubled mind of the philosophic and brooding Prince, the work dramatises the frustration of Hamlet's disturbed love for his widowed mother, Gertrude, and his deceitful love for Ophelia. Hamlet's urge of normal love has been poisoned by the suspicious death of his father and the Queen's subsequent errant behaviour in, to his mind, remarrying too soon. A tragic sub-plot is the unrequited love of a cruel Hamlet by Ophelia, resulting in her madness and suicide.

Julius Caesar

A play of political intrigue, assassinations and other deaths triggered by the pride and ambition of Caesar who, with popular support, is seen to be within reach of the Roman crown before he is killed.

Julius Caesar's self-love is thwarted by the conspirators, who are motivated by their love for republicanism and the preservation of Rome as the home of liberty and democratic ideals. Yet this idealism leads to treachery and assassination.

King Lear

The foolish English king's casual resignation from power in return for a public display of love from his three daughters sets the scene for a tale of personal tragedy, disappointment and near-insanity.

Misled by the spurious claims of love by his two eldest daughters, Goneril and Regen, King Lear's faith and sanity is redeemed finally by the true love of his youngest daughter, Cordelia. With the State imperilled by Lear's actions, the play warns against mixing 'love' with politics and the danger of dividing the nation.

Love's Labour's Lost

A game of love set in the Court of Navarre with a farcical plot and a host of comic characters. The actions of the male courtiers, who are impossibly romantic, are well counterbalanced by the astringent responses of their adored aristocratic females. The text delights in complex wordplay including literary allusions, sustained alliterations and double meanings; the writing altogether indicates an author of considerable education and literary skill.

The writer also demonstrates a great familiarity with the real court of Navarre, as fitting for a member of the English court.

Macbeth

The love of glory and power, fueled by the ambitious Lady Macbeth, is the motivation that leads Macbeth to savagely murder the Scottish king Duncan, fellow general Banquo and the monarch's two guards.

Measure for Measure

The characters of the play reflect a love of justice, morality, political power and the blessing of mercy, as well as romantic love. These many aspects of love both pose concurrent questions and form dimensions that deal essentially with ethical issues – notably the question of ends and means. How love can be measured is at the heart of this convoluted plot.

Merchant of Venice

Whilst the overriding subject of the play is a love of money, as exemplified by Shylock, the spendthrift Venetian merchants and the Casket challenge, other aspects of love are also portrayed. Significant sub-plots are the romance between Portia and Bassanio, and the love of justice and mercy expounded by Portia.

The Merry Wives of Windsor

This social comedy concerns itself with cuckoldry and its consequent distortions of love. The contortions of behaviour are contrasted with the harmony of the united married partners. Romantic love is displayed by the elopers Anne Paige and Master Fenton.

The Merry Wives is the only play in the First Folio to deal exclusively with contemporary English middle class life.

A Midsummer Night's Dream

This romantic comedy dramatises, through its various manifestations of love, the emotions of fairies and the complications encountered in the romantic life of four Athenian lovers. The Dream deals especially, although in comic vain, with impossible illusions of love that might verge on insanity for those smitten.

Much Ado About Nothing

A witty yet thought-provoking story that dramatises the uncertainties and deceptions of two pairs of lovers, who endure trials and tribulations before their mutual happiness is resolved.

Othello

A classic tragedy in which the confused Othello is wrongfully convinced by the persuasive and manipulative Iago of his wife's infidelity and juxtaposes his deep love of her with uncontrollable jealousy.

The Taming of the Shrew

One interpretation of this farce is that of an unruly wife tamed by her new husband, yet the play concludes with a new relationship between Kate and her husband that may blossom into genuine love.

The Tempest

Set on a magical island, and possibly an allegory of love conquering evil, the play embraces revenge at the hands of the island's wizard and ruler Prospero, having been banished there after he was usurped from the throne by his brother Antonio. A subplot portrays the great love of Prospero for his daughter by his blessing of her marriage with Ferdinand, the son of Alonso, King of Naples – an ally of Antonio.

Timon of Athens

This morality-style tale is centred on the hedonistic lifestyle of Timon and the loss of his fortune that exposes the avarice of Athenian society. Forced into poverty and rejected by his materialistic followers, Timon becomes a misanthrope due to his disillusionment. Having fallen victim to the false love of his subjects he descends into madness and is led to an untimely death.

Titus Andronicus

A sensational and bloodthirsty drama Titus has many classical parallels, including *Ovid*. Its theme of revenge for senseless rape, mutilation, murder and cannibalism reverses the natural familial love and loyalty of Titus. The hatred and violence expressed by the play's characters demonstrate the opposite of human love.

Troilus and Cressida

Set within a period during the lengthy Trojan War, the play, nihilistic in character, highlights the impermanence and misguided nature of the futile love affair of Troilus and Cressida that ends with Cressida's ultimate betrayal. All of the characters in the drama are portrayed as cynical and self-serving.

Two Gentlemen of Verona

A comedy of two friends falling in love with the same woman and the difficulties this situation presents for their deep friendship. The male protagonists, Valentine and Proteus, are characterised as shallow and greedy, much in contrast to the two female characters in love with them: Julia and Sylvia, who both exemplify the ideals of romantic love.

The Winter's Tale

A whimsical story about a king, Leontes, whose unreasonable jealousy of his Queen, Hermione, loses him his wife, young son and baby daughter.

After many improbable events the play concludes with the miraculous resurrection of the dead Hermione and the return of the play's heroine, their daughter Perdita, now an adult. This provides a literal portrayal of the overarching theme: death is banished by love.

En virtute suâ contentus, nobilis arte,
Italus ore, Anglus pectore, uterq; opere.
Floret adhuc, et adhuc florebit: floreat vltra
FLORIVS, hâc specie floridus, optat amans.

John (Giovanni) Florio 1553-1625

Leading linguist, lexicographer, a tutor to Queen Anne and noble English families,
translator of Montaigne's Essays. Son of Michelangelo Florio Crollalanza a
Protestant exile in London 1550-1553, also a linguist, tutor and translator.

CHAPTER TEN

The early Italian plays

"...knowledge of all things Italian..."
John Paul Roe, researcher and writer

T HERE is a surprising emphasis upon Italian settings and characters in the early plays of the First Folio, bearing in mind that the works were supposedly written by a provincial Englishman of humble stock: the Stratford Bard. The plays themselves display an attention to detail that suggests the first-hand knowledge of the author. Yet there is no record of William Shakespeare visiting Italy in his lifetime or indeed travelling abroad on any occasion.

Equally, one of the principal alternative authors of the First Folio, Edward de Vere, while having travelled extensively in Italy was unlikely to have become sufficiently familiar with the minute details of the places, terrain and ancient history of the cities in which the First Folio plays are set. This is not the knowledge obtained by a visitor.

There is a strong likelihood that the reason for the appearance of many Italian plays in England is due to their whole or part authorship by a native Italian and this explanation is detailed later.

There are a number of First Folio plays set in Italy and nine are early plays: *Romeo and Juliet, The Two Gentlemen of Verona, The Taming of the Shrew, The Merchant of Venice, Othello: Act 1 only, A Midsummer Night's Dream, All's Well That Ends Well, Much Ado About Nothing* and *The Winter's Tale*. Three other plays are set in ancient Rome: *Coriolanus, Titus Andronicus* and *Julius Caesar*.

In comparison, there are ten English history plays, another ten plays set in different foreign countries and a single English domestic comedy. Virtually a third of all the First Folio plays are intimately linked to Italy and feature aspects of life in Florence, Venice, Padua and Verona. Again not subjects familiar to the untravelled son of a tradesman in rural England.

Richard Paul Roe and *"The Shakespeare Guide to Italy"*

This deeply researched study of the Italian plays in the First Folio sets out the case that references in the texts do indeed reflect reality. The author of the plays was in possession of first-hand knowledge of the local scenes in which parts of the plays were dramatised, obscure place names and detailed knowledge of Italian history. Roe states that the First Folio author's *"knowledge of all things Italian is astonishing."*

It must be added that some of the books to which the Italian plays were indebted had not been translated into English at the dates they were purportedly written, while some lines in play texts were translated literally from the Italian, indicating recourse to the original manuscript in that language. A major source, the tales by Giovanni Battista Giraldi, entitled *Gli Hecatommithi* and published in Venice in 1565 had no English translation before 1753.

A significant aspect concerning the authorship of the First Folio is that the works of Plato were used for some of the plays in the First Folio, yet all of Plato's works were untranslated when the plays were written. This is likewise the case with the works of Herodotus and the plays of Seneca.

Poems written by French and Italian authors – Ronsard, Jodell, du Bellay, Desportes, Aretino and Petrarch especially – were echoed in the plays. A few of these poems were available, having been paraphrased into English, but there are insufficient indications that the playwrights of the First Folio read them in their original forms. The ability to read all these untranslated works could only have resulted from private tuition, or having the facility of a native speaker. French, Italian and Spanish were not taught in the grammar schools, or at an English university.

In *The Shakespeare Guide to Italy* by Richard Paul Roe, an American lawyer sets out the research which demonstrates the knowledge of Italy possessed by the author of these plays in meticulous detail.

Roe gives *The Taming of the Shrew* as a prime example of the detailed knowledge exhibited in the Italian plays. In that work the obvious familiarity with Italian customs and the small details of domestic life could hardly be gained from books, or by means of conversation with travellers from Italy.

The Taming of the Shrew

This comedy exploring love's submission and dominance begins with a framing device, often referred to as the Induction, in which a mischievous nobleman tricks a drunken tinker named Christopher Sly into believing he is actually a nobleman himself.

The main plot depicts the courtship of Petruchio, a gentleman of Verona, and Katherina, the headstrong, obdurate shrew. Initially, Katherina is an unwilling participant in the relationship, but Petruchio tempers her with various psychological torments – the 'taming' – until she becomes a compliant and obedient bride. The sub-plot features a competition between the suitors of Katherina's more desirable sister, Bianca.

Set in Padua, a University City, the character Lucentio demonstrates a great knowledge of Italy, including Lombardy and Venetian Veneto, as well as the land and water routes to Padua. There was a canal system within Padua by the 16th century, of which the author is clearly well aware.

Roe emphasises the likelihood that the action occurring when Lucentio first arrives, involving a wharf or quay and a hostelry or house on a street or plaza, on which the characters interact is portrayed realistically for the period in question. Roe also proposes the modern location in which the play's original writer may well have set the scene.

The play shows specific knowledge of Italy's banking practices, including financial instruments such as *"bills for money by exchange."* The business of issuing, discounting and then redeeming bills of exchange was carried out in many Italian cities, including Mantua, Padua, Venice, Florence and Rome. The author also knew there were receiving banks in Tripoli, North Africa, a fact only likely to have been known by a native of Italy; the author also uses the Italian term "Mercantant" [without the e ending] instead of the English "Merchant" for the bearer of such bills of exchange.

The supposedly false declaration by Tranio in *The Taming of the Shrew* regarding the Duke of Mantua's 'seagoing' ships was proved correct by Roe's analysis, since Governolo, adjacent to the River Po in Mantua, enjoyed access to the rivers Po, Adige and thence the Adriatic sea.

In the same way, a reference in the play to a 'saile-maker' in Bergamo, far inland, has been derided as ignorance. In fact, a writer acquainted with Italy would be aware that Bergamo, where canvas was produced, was the principal source of sails for the ships of the Mediterranean world in that era.

The author of *The Taming of the Shrew* provides a detailed description of a contemporary, richly-furnished interior of a wealthy Italian home, verified by a villa preserved in modern-day Venice: it is a description clearly unlike that of a 16th century home of an Englishman. In the same exploration of the play, Richard Paul Roe locates the Church of St Luke in a modern landscape; this is the parish in which the characters Baptista Minola and his daughters lived and worshipped.

The volume and variety of alterations and additions to the original text of

16th century plays is well illustrated by *The Taming of the Shrew*. Modern scholars accept that the play has undergone no less than three hundred and fifty insertions, substitutions or amendments by the end of the twentieth century. No doubt some of these emendations were because of the assumption of ignorance on the part of an English writer and a lack of awareness of the local knowledge of a native Italian author.

John Paul Roe continues his thesis with an analysis of the other 'Italian' plays:

Romeo and Juliet

This early tragedy from the First Folio, regarding two young star-crossed lovers whose deaths ultimately reconcile their feuding families, is set in Verona.

In his investigative journey in Verona, John Paul Roe was able to locate the surviving remains of the grove of Sycamore trees described in the first scene of the play, just outside the western wall. The accepted source of *Romeo and Juliet* is namely an old Italian tale by Luigi da Porto, who adapted the story as *Giulietta e Romeo* and included it in his *Historia novellamente ritrovata di due Nobili Amanti*, published between 1530 and 1535.

Da Porto drew on Pyramus and Thisbe and Boccaccio's Decameron, giving the story much of its modern form, including the names of the lovers, the rival families of Montecchi and Capuleti and its location in Verona. The ultimately tragic romantic tale was then later embellished by the Italian Matteo Bandello.

Another *Romeo and Juliet* of 1561 may be the work of Michelangelo Florio mentioned earlier who was in England between 1550 and 1554. In later versions of the Romeo and Juliet story the Sycamore grove does not appear, but it was clearly known to the author of the play in the First Folio.

Similarly, Roe was able to locate the medieval Franciscan Church of St Peter, the parish Church of Juliet Capulet, as well as the 'Villafranca' stronghold, a court of princely judgements named in the play. Roe also established the precise area in which the first confrontations of the warring Veronese families took place. Such close knowledge of the topography points to an author with first-hand observation of Verona.

The Two Gentlemen of Verona

This play, which deals with the themes of friendship and infidelity, the conflict between friendship and love, and the foolish behaviour of people in love is full of descriptions of and allusions to all things Italian. This familiarity was long thought to stem from artistic invention, or assumed to be a result of ignorance on the part of the playwright. A major doubt in the authority of the text has been the journey undertaken by the play's characters: first Valentine and then Proteus sailed by boat from Verona to Milan when both cities are inland.

John Paul Roe points out the word 'roads' used in the play has a nautical meaning and there are references to 'tide' and 'flood' in the play's sense of time; these were apposite given that Milan boasted a vast quay in the past, catering for international shipping. Thus this centre of trade and commerce was navigable on the River Po from the Tyrrhenian Sea. With its city-wide canal system, Milan was classified as one of Italy's major maritime ports until the middle of the twentieth century.

Furthermore, the Adige River, flowing through Verona, was an important commercial waterway for a city that was a centre for shipping, and from which the Adriatic Sea could be reached via the mouth of the river. Verona also enjoyed internal boat travel on its network of city canals.

By means of extensive and extremely diligent research, Roe has uncovered the water-borne route that enabled boats to make the journey from the centre of Verona to the gates of Milan. The remarkable evidence put forward by the author clearly indicates that there was indeed a route between these two cities; it is not an absurd description demonstrating the ignorance of the writer.

From Verona, the journey was made possible by means of canals dug in and before 1269 at the river points of Legnago, Ostiglia and Martesana on the Rivers Adige, Tartaro, and the major river Po. This was then joined with the La Fossa canal as the final connection to Milan.

This water route, accessed by a system incorporating rivers and canals, was practicable and the references in the play are accurate despite the derision of many academics and critics over the years. It is quite clear that the detailed knowledge of this shipping thoroughfare between these two great cities could have only been known by a native of Italy.

Another criticism levelled at the writer of the play is the supposed ignorance surrounding the Veronese Valentine and Proteus' ambition to present themselves at the 'Emperor's Court' in Milan, which was a Duchy and therefore ruled by the Duke and his court.

The references in *Two Gentleman of Verona* to the Emperor and his Court are not, however, inconsistent with the historical facts. There was an invasion in 1494 by Charles VIII of France at the invitation of the Duke of Milan and much of Italy was overrun; this was followed by further intrusions by the French over the next thirty years.

Then the Holy Roman Emperor and Charles V, King of Spain, defeated the

French king Francis I and his ally the de Medici Pope Clement VII at Pavia in 1525. The brutal 'Sack of Rome' followed the Spanish invasion, but two years later the Emperor restored the rule of the de Medici Pope, and by 1529 Milan had become a Spanish dependency by the Treaty of Cambrai.

The Dukedom of Milan owed an oath of fealty to the Emperor and submission to the Imperial power. In 1533 great preparations were made in the city for a visit of the Emperor, including an *"Imperial Arch of Triumph,"* and grand entertainments, although in the event, Charles V stayed in the embellished Milan for only four days after his arrival on May 10th, quickly continuing on his way to Spain.

Valentine and Proteus expected *"To salute the Emperor, and commend their service to his will,"* travelling to Milan for his visit by rivers and canals. In the play their ambition was not achieved, but the presence of the Emperor in Milan is recorded and would be a matter of great significance to an author closely aware of recent Italian history.

In his verification of references in *The Two Gentleman of Verona*, Roe also uncovers the fact that *St Gregory's Well* was not a source of water, but a name given to the vast plague pit, or graveyard, of St Gregory's Church, close by the Lazaretto enclosure for the confinement of lepers. This discovery adds extra colour to Proteus directing his bitter rival to meet at a place of horror and danger at night.

Another of Roe's revelations is the awareness of the play's author of the terrain on the overland route from Verona to Milan. This area is correctly described in the text as a "wilderness" and not a "forest" as incorrectly inserted by later editors of the play; the forest is actually three leagues (nine miles) further on.

Interestingly, Roe conjectures that the Irish Franciscan Friar Patrick O'Hely, who was involved in the attempted overthrow of English rule in Ireland, was probably the real world origin of Friar Patrick in *The Two Gentleman of Verona*.

A date could be suggested for this play by the appearance of the clown and his dog, both of whom echo Richard Tarlton and his dog Crab, favourites of Queen Elizabeth. Tarlton, who died in September 1588, was the most famous clown of his era, known for his extempore comic doggerel verses, which came to be known as 'Tarltons'. After the actor' death many witticisms and pranks were attributed to him and were published as *Tarlton's Jests*. Tarlton was also an accomplished dancer, musician, fencer and writer, authoring a number of jigs, pamphlets and at least one full length play. There is a strong possibility that the comic and his dog were cast as part of the 'Rude Mechanicals' in *A Midsummer Night's Dream*.

The Merchant of Venice

This play could be described as a play about the love of money, or it may be viewed in another way: as anti-Semitic propaganda. Here, a Christian merchant becomes indebted to a Jewish moneylender who demands repayment of his loan as a pound of the debtor's flesh. Another possibly anti-Semitic reading of the play is the downfall of Shylock. Shylock the Jew is abused by the Christians of Venice and robbed and deserted by his own daughter, being finally humiliated and forced to abandon his religion and convert to Christianity. The complex play is capable of various interpretations; this is typical of many of the First Folio plays.

The Shakespeare Guide to Italy notes that the author displays an intimate understanding of the laws, traditions, culture, banking, commerce and structure of Venetian society. The central financial district of the Rialto, too, is given its proper importance.

A familiarity with its topography is exhibited when there is a reference to a boat going aground in the lagoon. The writer is well aware, too, of the laws forbidding Venetian merchants hiring foreign vessels, the 'Argosies' and 'Andrews or Andreas,' for their trading in food and fabric merchandise.

There are two source tales claimed for *The Merchant of Venice*; one was Giovanni Fiorentino's *Il Pecorone* written in 1378, not printed until 1596, and the other was *The Casket Story*, from a collection of stories in Latin *Gesta Romanorum* of 1472, printed in English in 1595.

There are no foreign ships in *The Casket Story* or in *Il Pecorone* so Antonio's hired foreign merchant vessels are an invention of a writer precise in relevant detail: that the destination ports of those ships were forbidden to Venetian vessels.

Another astute observation of Richard Paul Roe is that the writer of *The Merchant of Venice* was conscious of the different origins of the Jews of Venice, which included Ashkenazi from Germany, the Levantines from Turkey, Syria and other parts of the eastern Mediterranean, as well as the Sephardic from Spain. The play also notes the distinctive 'gabbano' worn by Jewish men in . Venice and refers correctly to working horses that critics have wrongly denied existed in the 16th century city. The play's author mentions several synagogues in the Ghetto area.

In exploring the 'penthouse' in Shylock's house, Roe identified the house in present day Venice, supported on columns as defined in this historical period; this is the only structure of its kind in the Ghetto.

In the Belmont country villa part of *The Merchant of Venice* there is an allusion to "The Tranect" where Portia and Nerissa are to meet Balthazar. Richard Paul

Roe reveals that this is most likely to be the meeting place of 'Fusina', where travellers would leave their coach and go across the water to Venice: a practice well documented in both books and travel journals. Through analysis of the mileage estimated by Portia in the play, Roe has identified Belmont as the Villa Foscari near Malcontenta village on the Brenta canal. The author also explains that Portia wears a dagger rather than a sword on her journey was because carrying a sword was forbidden in Venice.

As in other Italian plays the ease with which the author writes of locations, behaviour and custom in *The Merchant of Venice* must infer that its writer was a native of the country.

Othello

This play of love and jealousy revolves around four central characters: Othello, a Moorish general in the Venetian army; his new wife, Desdemona; his lieutenant, Cassio; and his trusted ensign, Iago. It explores themes of racism, love, jealousy and betrayal.

In his book, Roe identifies the place named *"Sagittary,"* where Othello is sought, as the Venetian street Frezzaria, from the Italian *frecciaria*, [a place for arrows and arrow smiths], and the Latin equivalent *Sagittarius* or Sagittary, the street of arrow makers: the author's street knowledge is accurate.

A remarkable acquaintance with Venetian custom is also displayed, notes John Paul Roe. The author knew that Venetian young men of the time had their hair curled, with a lock falling onto their foreheads, while noble women dyed their hair blonde and wore elevated clogs or 'Zoccoli'. The clogs were often so high the ladies had to lean on the shoulder of a servant when they walked, as is indicated in the text.

Roe comments that the author was fully aware of recent history and current events with regard to the colony of Cyprus and the military garrison that Venice maintained on the island.

A Midsummer Night's Dream

This comedy about love portrays the events surrounding the marriage of the Duke of Athens, Theseus, and Hippolyta, and include the adventures of four young Athenian lovers and a group of six amateur actors, all of whom are controlled and manipulated by the fairies who inhabit the forest in which most of the play is set.

The play set in *"Athens"* and refers to *"Athenians"*, yet strangely does not mention Greece, Greeks, Grecians or the region of Attica. In *The Shakespeare Guide to Italy* however, John Paul Roe explains that on his travels in Italy he chanced upon the small walled city of Sabbionetta, near Mantua, built in the mid-16th century by Duke Vespasiano Gonzaga Colonna.

Here Roe visited the ducal palace and adjoining buildings, as well as the impressive, idealistic architecture of Sabbionetta, which, as a result of its cultural life and scholarly interest in art, history and literature, became known as '*Little Athens*'.

It was at the Porta della Vittoria, the architectural main gate of the city, that Roe heard from the guide that the passageway was also known as '*Quercia dei Duca*' or the '*Duke's Oak*'. From this clue of the "*Duke's Oak*", where the "*Rude Mechanicals*" meet to rehearse their own play, and the thirty references to Athens in the text, Roe concludes that *A Midsummer Night's Dream* was set in Little Athens, Sabbionetta. Additional support is given to Roe's conclusion in that the play refers to a temple, more accurately capitalised, and in Sabbionetta there is a little Church referred to as '*The Temple*.'

All's Well That Ends Well

The central love story appears to be more socially optimistic than other plays in the First Folio. The uncomfortable truth exposed by the play is that fairy-tale endings rarely meet human aspirations; the poor heroine needs to convince her aristocratic idol that she is worth marrying, but she eventually blackmails him into submission.

The tale is drawn from Boccaccio's *The Decameron* and is predominately set in France with nearly half of the scenes set in or near an Italian city, supposedly Florence. John Paul Roe suggests the writer had a personal knowledge of this city and its environs, hence his inclusion of the play in his Italian collection of works within the First Folio canon.

From England, Helen, the play's heroine, follows her husband Bertram, who has rejected her after their unconsummated marriage, to Italy where he has volunteered to fight in the Tuscan war between Florence and Siena. There were many skirmishes and battles between Florence and Siena over the centuries, involving a number of alliances with nearby states. The play no doubt refers to the final Tuscan war of 1555.

In *The Shakespeare Guide to Italy* the author suggests that *the many subtleties, circuitous descriptions and allusions about Florence found in scene 5, Act III* persuaded him that the playwright displays a most precise knowledge of that city and Roe comments:

His descriptions are a first-person testament to his having walked its streets, visited its sites and learned of its colloquialisms – and also of having acquainted himself with a most ordinary building located near a most ordinary square, which once had a particularly local name.

In analysing the standard but corrupted text, Roe proposes that Bertram and his troops are heard *within*, not *outside*, the city walls when returning from Siena, as in the traditional reading. This mistake has occurred because the word *city* should be capitalised, thus indicating a specific district. This 'City' within the city was probably the area containing a central Plaza and the citadel of Fortezza da Brasso. It would seem sensible for the battle-weary, muddy and tired soldiers to refresh themselves at this vast military complex before the official march and welcoming ceremony.

The victory route uncovered by Roe accords precisely with the narrative of the play and, equally significantly, places the lodgings of St Jacques Le Grand as adjoining the Port area – indeed an ancient port.

Once again John Paul Roe has demonstrated that without question the writer enjoyed a truly learned knowledge of this great Italian city.

Much Ado About Nothing

Much Ado About Nothing is generally considered one the best comedies concerning love in the First Folio, because it combines elements of robust hilarity with more serious meditations on honour, shame, and court politics. Similar to *As You Like It* and *Twelfth Night*, the play *Much Ado About Nothing* is a comedy that ends with multiple marriages and no deaths.

The play chronicles two pairs of lovers: Benedick and Beatrice (the main couple), and Claudio and Hero (the secondary couple). Although the young lovers Hero and Claudio provide much of the impetus for the plot, the courtship between the wittier, wiser lovers Benedick and Beatrice is what makes *Much Ado About Nothing* so memorable. Benedick and Beatrice argue with delightful wit and their journey is developed from antagonism to sincere love and affection with a rich sense of humour and compassion.

Set almost entirely in the city of Messina, north eastern Sicily, the play is sourced from a collection of stories by Matteo Bandello, published in 1554, although *Much Ado About Nothing* has a more complex plot, namely in unravelling the troubles of the young lovers: Claudio and Hero.

In analysing the text John Paul Roe states that *...the author has woven elements in his story which demonstrate first-hand knowledge of places, things and comportment unique to Italy.*

Roe puts forward a prime example of this Italian awareness in the wording *pleached alley or arbour,* used five times by the characters throughout the play. In Messina, climbing vines were 'pleached,' that is to say, densely woven to cut out the strong sunlight. Sometimes the arbour was made of trees planted in two rows and their branches were bent and intertwined to make a cool tunnel: such alleys are to be found in Messina today.

Commenting upon the natural conversation between mistress and servant in *Much Ado About Nothing* Roe also opines that such a degree of class informality would not have been tolerated in Elizabethan England, but was perfectly acceptable in southern Italy.

Roe uncovers three other points of Italian interest: the first of which identifies that the disbanded wedding of Hero and Claudius, a Florentine Count, takes place in The Temple Church of St John the Baptist, long associated with its local community of Florentine settlers. Again, Roe notes that the printed text does not capitalise the 't' of *The Temple,* which is the familiar local identification of this ancient Church.

Secondly, John Paul Roe reveals that the line of Beatrice in the play *I would eat his heart in the market place!* is a direct echo of a Massinian threat *I will eat your heart* and is a dire warning only familiar to one from the region.

Thirdly, the Friar's words after the failed wedding *And on your family's old monument Hang mournful epitaphs* refers to the burying of Hero in the family monument present in the immense walled Cimiterio Monumentale, the Great Cemetery, set on a hillside outside the city's walls.

Finally Roe suggests that the play's spiteful portrayal of Don John the Bastard is because he is a personification of Don John of Austria who has been deeply frustrated in his international political ambition. Don John of Austria's intention of marrying Mary, Queen of Scots, invading and subduing England was known and the script aims to play on or arouse hostility against him in England. This explanation accords with *Much Ado About Nothing* having been written in 1576, rather than at the accepted date of 1598.

The Winter's Tale

A further play concerning love and jealousy; the first three acts of the play are filled with intense psychological drama, while the last two acts are comedic and supply a happy ending. The play relates the story of a King whose jealousy is so strong that, although unfounded, it loses him not only his wife but his young son and baby daughter.

This play has the most widely diverse geographies of any of the Italian plays:

set in medieval Sicily and Bohemia in central Europe. It is a mix of events, historical periods, places and people.

The main seeming error in this play, long debated by scholars, is the play's reference to the coastline of land-locked Bohemia, now within the Czech Republic. It appears however that this description is not incorrect as critics claim.

Roe explains that the author of the work was aware that Bohemia had acquired territory in the thirteenth century, adjoining Trieste, on the Adriatic Sea's Gulf of Ponanzo, for a short time. This stretch of coast which Bohemia held for nine years provided the base for the King of Bohemia's fleet.

The Shakespeare Guide to Italy analyses the return journey time taken by the two courtiers from the Sicilian court to the Oracle at Delphi of twenty three days. John Paul Roe concludes after mapping the most likely sea and land route from Palermo to Delphi that the journey duration matches the time claimed in the play.

Roe adds that the writer was well aware of the topography of Sicily and features such as the ancient Temple of Segesta which by the sixteenth century was an object of great pride by the Sicilians.

The Tempest

The play is set on a remote island, where Prospero, the deposed Duke of Milan, plots to restore his daughter Miranda to her rightful place using illusion and skilful manipulation. Prospero conjures up a storm, to lure his usurping brother Antonio and the complicit King Alonso of Naples to the island. There, his machinations bring about the revelation of Antonio's lowly nature, the redemption of the King, and the marriage of Miranda to Alonso's son, Ferdinand.

The island upon which the action of *The Tempest* takes place is identified by John Paul Roe as Vulcano, situated in the Tyrrenian Sea off the northern shore of Sicily. The volcanic nature of the island and its unusual geology, topography, flora and fauna is accurately described by the author who, by virtue of this intimate knowledge, must have had first-hand knowledge of the play's physical background.

In his book, Roe also explains that the lengthy, most impractical journey of Prospero and Miranda from the city of Milan, via the Adriatic Sea, to the mystical island was a falsification of the original composition. The only logical route from northern Italy, Roe claims, was from the city of Florence and travelling via the Arno River and by canal to the port of Livorno, which had access to the Tyrrenian Sea, and then south to Vulcano Island. Vulcano is the sister island of Stromboli and lies twelve miles from the Sicilian mainland.

Roe explains this alteration from Florence to Milan in the play was a response to the fear of giving offence to the Tuscan, ruler Grand Duke Francesco de Medici 1541-1587. The Duke's character, particularly his lifelong absorption with alchemy and magical powers, mirrored the paranormal skills of Prospero. Since Francesco died in 1587 it is likely that the alteration to the manuscript was made prior to this date and, although not published until 1623, the play may have been performed earlier, though there is no record of this.

In *The Shakespeare Guide to Italy* the author also studies the sea journey from Tunis to the Kingdom of Naples during which the royal fleet of King Alonso was blown off course by the stormy seas around the Sicilian Island. Roe observes that Alonso's journey is a parallel of Virgil's epic poem *The Aeneid,* where Aeneas leaves Dido of Carthage, or Tunis, for Rome. Aeneas of Troy met Dido, founder of Carthage, after having been shipwrecked in North Africa. The sea journey of Aeneas also begins with violent storms

The precise detail of Vulcano portrayed in *The Tempest,* combined with the knowledge of Italy and Roman history and legend once again points to a native Italian writer for at least part of the play or an earlier version.

A possible author of the original Italian plays

During his four years in England from 1550, while enjoying the patronage of the Herberts, it is feasible that Michelangelo Florio wrote, translated or adapted traditional Italian tales and plays for the noble family, to be presented at court or in their residences. There is a strong argument that some of these works were later edited by his son John Florio, among others, and included in the First Folio. These works were thus preserved as part of the Herbert-Sidney remembrance of family history. Both Mary, Countess of Pembroke, and her brother Sir Philip, the famed poet, were intent upon developing a graceful, poetic English language: an ambition they shared with the Florio's - father and son.

Following the accession of Mary I in 1553 and the accompanying severe anti-Protestant repression instituted by the new monarch, Michelangelo Florio fled the country, settling with his wife and son John in Soglio, Switzerland. Two decades later upon his return to London in the 1570s, the well-educated John Florio was to follow in his father's footsteps in becoming the outstanding lexicographer and grammarian of his age.

John Florio was to have significant influence upon the literary output of late Elizabethan and Jacobean England as a result of his origination of Italian-English dictionaries and phrase books. This Italian tutor to Queen Anne was devoted to the improvement of the English language, both in terms of a more graceful style and a wider vocabulary. John Florio introduced over 1,200 new words into the English language as well as many idiomatic expressions drawn from the Italian language. Textual evidence demonstrates that many of these Italian words and colloquial phrases are used in the First Folio indicating that John Florio was likely to have been the principal editor. John Florio was well acquainted with the volume's co-publisher Edward Blount, who had published John Florio's translation of Montaigne's *Essaies*, as well as his Italian-English dictionaries. William Jaggard, the main printer of the First Folio had been responsible for publishing Florio's translation of Boccaccio's *The Decameron*.

The remarkable intimacy with Italian topography and Italian history exhibited in the 'Italian' plays in the First Folio provide further substantiation of the major participation of John Florio in the editing and some re-writing of the First Folio publication.

A further book in support of an Italian influence on the First Folio is *Shakespeare era italiano* (2002) in which retired Sicilian professor Martino Juvara draws on research carried out by two professors at Palermo University focusing on Michelangelo Florio Crollalanza, born in Messina, Sicily to Giovanni Florio, a doctor and Guglielma Crollalanza a Sicilian noblewoman.

A play *"Tanto traffico per niente,"* written by Crollalanza in the Sicilian dialect translated as *"Much Ado About Nothing,"* is set entirely in Crollalanza's birthplace of Messina. Michelangelo escaping the Spanish Inquisition fled to England. Inquisition officers killed Giovanni Florio in Treviso near Venice.

A painstaking tally taken by *"Shakespeare and Italy"* author Ernesto Grillo found that Italy is mentioned an astounding 800 times in the plays. Grillo maintains that the author had a "profound knowledge of Milan, Bergamo, Verona, Mantua, Padua, and Venice," that could only have been derived "from an actual journey through Italy."

Italian is spoken in some of the Italian plays. "Alla nostra casa ben venuto," says Petruchio in the *"Taming of the Shrew."* "Molto honorato signor mio Petruchio," Hortensio replies. *"Love's Labour's Lost,"* which is rooted in the Italian theatre tradition of Commedia dell'Arte, and features accurate descriptions of Italian customs and laws, espouses a popular Venetian proverb: "Chi non ti vede, non ti pretia" ("He who does not see you, cannot appreciate you.")

It is suggested that Michelangelo was educated by Franciscan monks in Latin, Greek and history. Crollalanza is reputed to have fallen in love with a 16 year old Milanese countess called Giulietta. Because her aristocratic family was opposed to their relationship, they sent her off to Verona, when Crollalanza failed to rescue her, Giulietta committed suicide in despair.

*Executions of Protestant believers during the reign of
Mary 1st reinforced anti-Catholic fear in England
and thereafter for many generations*

CHAPTER ELEVEN

Spain: the Roman Catholic threat to England

The inquisitorial body of the Papacy was later to create a catalogue of forbidden books known as the Index Librorum Prohibitorum, or List of Forbidden Books, in 1559. The Index existed for many succeeding centuries as a powerful censoring mechanism throughout the Roman Catholic world.

As soon as there were books or writings of any kind generally available the English and European authorities, of either the Church or state, were obliged to take measures to control the written word. When the number of books was small because of the limitation of hand written copies the problem was manageable. However, following the introduction of the printing press, the multiplication and dissemination of all kinds of printed material began and, in tandem, the expansion of censorship grew to try to control the flood. There is a modern equivalent: governments today experience a comparable problem in controlling communication on the internet through Facebook, Twitter, texting and secret sites.

More than five centuries ago, in 1479, the Pope granted the fullest powers of censorship to the Bishop of Würzburg and the Archbishop of Mainz. In Venice the decree of 1491 ordered the censorship of theological and religious books only, but by 1515 the first papal censorial decrees were given for the whole Church which was universally accepted: all writings without exception were thus subjected to censorship.

Similar catalogues of unacceptable writings had been published since the 1520s by political and ecclesiastical authorities, particularly in England, France, Germany, and Venice, Milan and Lucca in Italy. The Protestant Reformation had weakened the powers of the Roman Catholic Church and every effort was being made in these countries to limit or stop the spread of heretical thought and practice.

Examples may be found of official licensors in the mid-part of 15th century England, authorised by the Church, who controlled the written word before its circulation: here, the censorship principally employed as an anti-Lollardy measure.

In England, more formal censorship, with the control of publications by the state, was inaugurated primarily under Henry VIII in the early 1520s as a reaction to the controversy caused by the Reformation. This was well illustrated by the burning of the works of the reformists Tyndale and Luther. In 1526 a citizen T. Berthelet was summoned for questioning for not having his book examined before its circulation.

The King's policy of separation from Rome a decade later, after his divorce from Katherine, led to him turning to the religious reformers and the printing press for new evangelical publishers. Two English biblical versions, partly based upon Tyndale's work, were now welcomed: Matthew's Bible of 1537 and the Great Bible of 1539.

Three proclamations of Henry VIII against heretical or seditious books in 1529, 1530 and 1536, all asserting the censoring power of the monarch, were followed in 1538 by a fourth. This edict forbade the printing of any English book except one with a license issued by the Privy Council, carrying the words 'seen and allowed'. The succeeding Act of 1543 for "the advancement of true religion" was aimed at suppressing drama, books, sermons or any other expression of contrary views likely to stir up sedition or heresy.

In matters of religious dissent occurring in England, the Crown and Church showed little mercy. In 1543, as an example, eight stationers were imprisoned by the Privy Council for printing unlawful evangelical books.

In Europe, following a Papal Bull of 1542, the Catholic General Inquisition took charge of the supervision of books, chiefly within Rome and Italy, with emphasis on suppression of writings that were deemed heretical.

The inquisitorial body of the Papacy was later to create a catalogue of forbidden books known as the *Index Librorum Prohibitorum* or List of Forbidden Books in 1559. The *Index* existed for many succeeding centuries as a powerful censoring mechanism throughout the Roman Catholic world.

The *Index*, as it is normally called, was an official list of writers and books which Roman Catholics were forbidden to own or read. Some notable examples were *The Praise of Folly* by Erasmus 1509, *On the Revolution of Heavenly Bodies* by the astronomer Copernicus1543 and Galileo's *Dialogues on the Two Chief World Systems 1632*.

The Index also listed the names of Roman Catholic writers dissenting from orthodoxy. These individuals included religious reformers such as Martin Luther and English philosophical writers such as Francis Bacon and Thomas Hobbes.

At the Council of Trent, 1546, in response to the growth of Protestantism the assembled Fathers insisted on the censorship and prohibition of any books containing heresies. The outcome of these deliberations was the so-called *Index Tridentinus* of 1564, which extended the existing powers of control.

Adding to a revised catalogue of forbidden books, this Index also contained ten general rules, since known as the *Tridentine Rules,* dealing with the order and content of the Mass.

In England during the last years of Henry VIII's reign the monarch ordered a sixth proclamation which laid down that every book, 'ballet' or play must bear the names of the printer and author, as well as the date of printing – and that an advance copy must be placed in the hands of the local mayor two days before publication.

Henry's proclamations lost their validity upon his death in 1547, but the policy of licensing was continued by his royal successors. Under Edward VI, a Privy Council order of 1549 directed that all English books printed or sold should be examined. This order was followed by a Proclamation of 1551, which required approval by the King or six of his Privy Councilors for any books produced. A year later a special license of the Privy Council was declared necessary for any dramatic performance. In the same year, after the Duke of Somerset, Lord Protector during Edward VI's early reign, was overthrown by Northumberland, plays and interludes (short pieces played between the acts of a longer play or at Court supper) were prohibited throughout the realm for three months as they could contain seditious matter.

England's six decades of religious hostility and censorship

The contentious beginning of Queen Mary's rule was a portent of the discord which was to be ever-present in her reign, caused by her intention of returning England to the Catholic faith and obedience to Rome. During her short reign Mary issued three proclamations against heretical books and these appeared in the years 1553, 1555 and finally in 1558, the year of her death.

The 1553 proclamation ordered her subjects to *"neither... print any books, matter, ballad, rhyme, interlude, process, or treatise, nor to play any interlude except they have her grace's special licence in writing for the same."*

In 1557 Mary granted a charter of incorporation to the London Company of Stationers, an organisation traceable as far back as 1404. During the 16th century it had come to include printers as well as booksellers. By this action the government was likely to have been seeking the aid of the Stationers' Company in establishing a more effective control over the printed promulgation of 'inconvenient' doctrines, i.e. seditious and heretical opinions.

England's official change of religion resulted in extreme hostility to Protestants by the Crown and the Ecclesiastical authorities. This enmity led to two hundred and eighty 'martyrs' tortured and eventually burned at the stake for heresy within five years. Consequently, an exodus of around eight hundred Protestants from England also took place during Mary's reign, with religious refugees fleeing to Strasbourg, Frankfurt, Basle, Zurich and Geneva.

The foreign Protestant church reformers were ordered to leave the country with their followers. They were accompanied by many of the English clergy and laity who feared that the part they took in Church reform would put them in danger of imprisonment or worse.

When Mary's first Parliament met in 1533 it declined to repeal 'en bloc' the religious statutes of Henry VIII and Edward VI and Henry's divorce, but it did agree to repeal the ecclesiastical laws of Edward's reign and legitimise Queen Mary by annulling Queen Katherine's divorce.

Mary did not at that time, however, restore Papal supremacy and for two years the Royal writs ran *"Mary by the Grace of God, Supreme head on earth of the Church of England."*

A repeal of the Edwardian statutes abolishing the English service books followed in favour of the old Latin Missals and Breviaries. The Six Articles Act, which enforced clerical celibacy, was also restored, leading to the deprivation of office for many of the married clergy.

The 'first fruits and tenths', a tax on the clergy which Henry had appropriated for the Crown, were ordered to be repaid to Rome. Mary also restored the greater part of Church lands and revenues that had remained in the hands of the Crown.

The Catholic Mass was restored, Holy Communion was banned and all priests had to be Catholic. The plain furniture in the Protestant churches was replaced with the colourful furniture and paintings of the old faith. Catholic Church services were held in Latin and Cranmer's English prayer book was banned.

Imprisoned Bishops who had challenged Edward's reforming policies were released to the palaces and diocese' of which they had been deprived. The Anglican Bishops in occupation were in turn deprived and similar action was taken with all other dissenting clergy. Steps were taken to obtain legal sanction for extreme measures against the imprisoned Bishops and clergy by reviving the Statutes that were enacted early in the reign of Henry IV to counter the Lollards.

The Statutes against Lollards were revised, soon enforced, and Bishops were appointed Commissioners in order to try all persons suspected of heresy. The trials took place in St Saviour's Church Southwark.

In effect, the Crown also controlled Convocation becoming a body subservient to royal views in as much as Bishops, Deans, and other senior church clergy were crown appointments. Additionally, the power given to the monarch by the Act of Supremacy allowed for the imprisonment and punishment of all who resisted royal decree. Early in Mary's reign it was decided that those who favoured the ecclesiastical views of Edward VI ought to be prevented from attending Convocation.

Further expressions of Mary's attitude followed. A Proclamation was issued which forbade all unlicensed preaching; those leading preachers among the reformers who disobeyed were arrested and confined. The Anglican bishops Hugh Latimer, Nicholas Ridley and Thomas Cranmer Archbishop of Canterbury, supporters of Lady Jane Grey, were sent to the Tower as traitors and later burned at the stake: the 'Oxford Martyrs' featured in *Foxe's Book of Martyrs*.

An even more significant reversal was made by Mary I. The Pope was eventually recognised as the head of the Church once again and thus the English Queen was to give homage and ultimate political authority to the Pontiff in Rome.

Achieving the Queen's objective was not straightforward. The Pope was only prepared to accept reunion with England when church property disputes had been settled. For English landowners, this meant allowing those who had acquired former church property at low cost, or been awarded it by Henry VIII, to retain ownership.

Only when English landowners had secured their claims did Pope Julius III's representative arrive in November 1554 to reconcile the realm. Cardinal Pole arrived, as a Plenipotentiary, to become Archbishop of Canterbury in the place of Archbishop Cranmer, who had refused to recant his Protestant beliefs.

The new Parliament (and consequently a new Convocation) were required by the Queen to desire reconciliation and pardon from the Legate; the members humbly knelt to receive absolution. Parliament then repealed all the Acts of Henry VIII's latter reign directed against the Papal supremacy. The legislature was shrewd enough to insert in the Statute of Repeal the provisions of a legatine dispensation, which confirmed the titles to ecclesiastical property –despite the resistance of Cardinal Pole.

English people at this time greatly feared the power of Spain. In an attempt to find reconciliation between the two nations, as well as to counter concerns about her marital status, Mary accepted a marriage proposal from the king of Spain, Philip II. It was anticipated by those in favour of the betrothal that children of the union would facilitate an unarguable royal succession, and thus avoid further disputation over the English crown.

The situation provoked a rebellion led by Sir Thomas Wyatt and a number of noblemen who raised a force of some four thousand, mostly from Kent, who failed to overcome London's defences. The uprising was defeated. Wyatt and ninety rebels were hanged, drawn and quartered. Sir Thomas Wyatt was the son of the notable English poet Thomas Wyatt. Although accused of complicity in the failed rebellion, Princess Elizabeth was able to refute the charge and survived to succeed Queen Mary following the monarch's death four years later.

Queen Mary's marriage with Philip of Spain took place in 1554, to the consternation of many Englishmen; her husband was a committed upholder of his faith and supporter of the feared Spanish Inquisition. Philip brought with him to England a number of 'Romish' clergy whose mission was to reduce England to papal obedience and promote the extirpation of so called 'heretics'. One of them became the Queen's confessor and others succeeded the foreign Protestant reformers as professors in the Universities.

Writings of traditional theologians such as St Thomas Aquinas were made subjects of study in place of the Classics and the works of early Christian fathers that Bishop Colet and Erasmus, the Dutch reforming theologian, had introduced during the previous reign.

The marriage proved to be a complete disaster. Philip disliked England, spent much of his time in Spain and the two rarely saw one another. The marriage did not produce the children that were anticipated. This was an outcome welcomed by many of the people of England, at all levels of society, who feared that the King Consort would be able to dominate Mary and so control England politically and commercially in the interests of Catholic Spain.

Mary died in 1558, her marriage, on which she had placed so much hope, had failed and the people were now fearful of the prospect of yet further changes of religion with the accession of a new monarch.

Censorship in the reign of Elizabeth I

The new Queen, Elizabeth, set the same authoritarian tone as her predecessor. At the commencement of her reign Elizabeth issued proclamations asserting the control of plays. In 1559 Mayors and Justices of the peace were commanded to ensure that no plays with a religious or political theme be performed. This was later amended to allow for such plays, providing there was no critical content of public policy or state religion.

In 1599 Queen Elizabeth I confirmed the Stationers' grant, but had already taken steps to provide for the continuance of the old system as part of the ecclesiastical settlement.

Queen Elizabeth's Act of Uniformity of 1559 made it an offence *"in any interludes, plays, songs, rhymes, or by any other open words to declare or speak anything in the derogation, depriving or despising"* the Book of Common Prayer.

In the same year a body of *Injunctions,* a code of ecclesiastical discipline, was created and promulgated by a series of diocesan visits, one of the *Injunctions* is directly concerned with the abuses of the printers of books.

This injunction begins with the forbidding of any book or paper to be printed without an express written license from the Queen herself or six of her Privy Councillors. Alternatively, printing may instead be authorised by the perusal of two senior figures of the Church, those being either the Archbishop of Canterbury or York; the Bishop of London; the Chancellor of Oxford or Cambridge; or the Bishop or Archdeacon from the place of printing. The injunction also declares that the names of the Licensors are to be shown at the end of every book.

Commissioners were appointed in the City of London, the home of printing, to implement the requirements of the *Injunctions.* The High Commission was constituted under a royal patent in 1559 and renewed from time to time throughout Elizabeth's reign. The Privy Councillors or other bodies appointed by the Queen to advise on policy also participated in its enforcement. In investigating public disorder, sedition and treason they sometimes fabricated evidence and extracted false confessions by torture. Suspects were *'racked'* thus leading to two inevitable outcomes: death or an extracted confession that itself resulted in an execution.

The Stationers' Company was given the status of a Livery title by the Lord Mayor of London in 1560. The new monopoly of the company meant that no person who was not a member of the Stationers' Company was allowed to print a book. This situation simplified the task of heresy seekers by enlisting the help of the Company in restricting the setting-up of printing presses by license of any but the well-known, responsible craftsmen.

The earlier interest of printers in joining together for commercial benefit had been incorporated into an efficient means of administering state control and literary censorship. Because the implementation of approval procedures was impractical, some scholars believe that, in practice, the Stationers' Company itself acted as a licensing authority in ordinary cases.

The Privy Council Ordinance of 1566 imposed special duties upon the Stationers' Company which gave them special powers to search for and seize unlawful books, while also imposing greater penalties. The main features of the legislation included the following restrictions:

I.   *That no person should print ...or bring ...into the realm printed any book against the force and meaning of any ordinance ...contained in any statutes or laws of this realm or in any injunctions, letters patent or ordinances set forth by the Queen's authority.*

II. *That whosoever should offend against the said ordinances should forfeit all such books and from thenceforth should   never exercise ...the feat of printing; and to sustain three months imprisonment.*

III. *That no person should sell, bind or sew and such books, upon pain of forfeit all such books and for every book 20s.*

In tandem, the work of the supervision of drama and the licensing of players was entrusted to the Master of the Revels office in the King's household, operating directly under the Lord Chamberlain. First appointed under Henry VII, the Master's original function was to devise and control all court entertainments so as to ensure that they performed in an orderly manner and gave no offence to the King.

The function was then gradually extended to the licensing of drama, players and companies throughout the country. Both the Crown and the Lord Chamberlain could act independently in the granting of patents which exempted the holders from the necessity of obtaining licenses for the plays presented.

In 1564 a Star Chamber decree confined the printing presses to London, with the exception of one in Oxford and another in Cambridge.

An Order in Council of 1566 that dealt with control of print was followed in 1570 by a new proclamation which encouraged people to inform on authors of *seditious* books, with the inducement that they:

> *shall be so largely rewarded as during his or their lives they shall have just cause to think themselves well used.*

This action by the authorities was executed under the Treasons Act of 1571, which was drawn up to deal with opponents of Queen Elizabeth. The Act provided that any person who *shall in writing, printing, preaching, speech ...affirm that Queen Elizabeth is an heretic, schismatic, tyrant, infidel ...then such said offences shall be high treason.*

Another area of control were the rules enforced in 1574, when the London authorities drafted objections to acting in the existing great Inns. This prompted the building of The Theatre in 1576 by a carpenter James Burbage and a grocer John Brayne.

The fierceness of the Elizabethan State's response to any contrary opinion of Royal behaviour is well illustrated by the persecution of John Stubbs – an example that has been recorded in detail.

John Stubbs was a pamphleteer or political commentator, educated at Trinity College, Cambridge. After studying law at Lincoln's Inn, he lived at Thelveton, Norfolk. Stubbs was a committed Puritan and he opposed the negotiations for a marriage between Queen Elizabeth and the French Roman Catholic, Francois, Duke of Anjou, the brother of the French king.

In 1579 he put his opinions into a pamphlet entitled *The Discoverie of a Gaping Gulf whereinto England is like to be Swallowed by another French Marriage*. Copies of the text were later publicly burned in the kitchen stove of Stationers' Hall.

The Stubbs pamphlet argued that, at forty-six years old, Elizabeth was too old to have children and therefore had no need for marriage. The writer argued also that English values, customs, language and morality would be undermined by so close a relationship with the French monarchy.

Stubbs claimed that his objective was to protect the freedom of thought and free speech that he said was associated with Protestantism. The proposed marriage too, would lead to a restoration of Catholic orthodoxy with an accompanying diminution of liberty.

Stubbs undiplomatically described the proposed wedding as a *contrary coupling* and *an immoral union, an uneven yoking of the clean ox to the unclean ass, a thing forbidden in the law* as laid down by St. Paul,... and leave the English *pressed down with the heavy loins of a worse people and beaten as with scorpions by a more vile nation.*

Elizabeth and the court were greatly displeased by the publication. Circulation of the pamphlet was prohibited and Stubbs, his printer, and the publisher were tried at Westminster, found guilty of *"seditious writing"* and sentenced to have their right hands cut off by means of a cleaver driven through the wrist by a croquet mallet. Initially, Queen Elizabeth had favoured the death penalty but was persuaded by her adviser John Jovey to opt for the lesser sentence.

The printer was subsequently pardoned by Elizabeth, but in the case of Stubbs and his publisher the sentence was carried out. Stubbs always protested his loyalty to the Crown. Immediately before the public dismemberment, Stubbs delivered a pun: *"Pray for me now my calamity is at hand."* The author's right hand having been cut off he removed his hat with his left and cried *"God Save the Queen!"* before fainting.

Stubbs was subsequently imprisoned for eighteen months. On being released, the political commentator continued to write and he published, among other pamphlets, a reply to Cardinal Allen's *Defence of the English*

Catholics. Despite Stubbs punishment, he remained a loyal subject of Queen Elizabeth and later in life served in the House of Commons.

The 1581 Act *against seditious words and rumours uttered against the Queen's most excellent Majesty* designates the retribution given to offenders. The punishment for the first offence was the pillory and the cutting off of ears, a payment of £220, as well as three months imprisonment. For the second offence the punishment was death and forfeiture of goods. This punitive Act also covered any prophesying regarding the Queen's life and any comment or conjecture concerning the next in line to the throne.

In 1581 Elizabeth I authorized Edmund Tilney, the holder of the post of Master of the Revels to be responsible, not only for court productions, but also of the supervision of the performance of plays throughout the realm. The purpose of this extension of powers was to protect the crown from any critical or subversive writings that affected Royal interests.

In respect of the relationship between the Crown, Government and the Stage, extracts from *Documents of Control* have been collected in E. K. Chambers *The Elizabethan Stage Volume IV*.

These documents show there were over 150 instances of control of players or playhouses during Elizabethan times. Such actions were taken either because of London plagues or, frequently, due to concerns relating to the content of the plays, the accompanying disorderly behaviour of the playhouse audience, or general disorder nearby. E. K. Chambers has also collected over sixty documents of criticism regarding the plays and players from 1489 to 1616.

If stationers themselves were suspected, or found guilty, of distributing Roman Catholic propaganda, they were severely punished. In 1581, Robert Parsons, a printer, managed to escape to France when Walsingham's agents visited his printing premises in Henley but, ultimately, his five assistants were arrested and imprisoned in the Tower of London.

Similarly the printer known as 'Vestige' in Smithfield also surreptitiously disappeared after printing two subversive titles. Another printer, William Carter, succeeded in producing eleven illicit publications before a charge of treason resulted in his execution.

Meanwhile, the Earl of Leicester, himself a Privy Councillor, was infuriated to find himself in the satirical pamphlet *Leicester's Commonwealth* (1584) and encouraged the Privy Council to take action. Anyone discovered hoarding a copy faced imprisonment, while many individuals were interrogated in an attempt to identify the authors.

The government's paranoia intensified as Walsingham's network of informants moved among the general population, and on 6th September 1586, Hugh

Davies gave evidence of a conversation with a Robert Atkins who had praised the virtues of *Leicester's Commonwealth* *"at offensive length."* Moreover, Robert Poley was interrogated merely for possessing a copy. In the end, Walsingham's methods succeeded in that the authors were revealed: they turned out to be Catholic ex-courtiers then in exile.

The examining powers of the Stationers' were eventually limited by virtue of a decree from the Star Chamber Court in 1586, composed of members of the Privy Council, which demanded that all published works must secure approval from agents working for the Bishop of London or the Archbishop of Canterbury. As the 1590s approached, England, and particularly London, was a dangerous place to be publishing work of a controversial nature.

The early Tudor era had experienced the beginnings of a new expression of controversial political and religious opinion seen as harmful to the interest of the State. In later Tudor times, as interludes and pamphlets became instruments of political and ecclesiastical controversy, the State became still more committed to literary censorship and the creation of the machinery of state control.

Despite the difficulties occasioned by censorship of the stage, Queen Elizabeth enjoyed watching plays and used the opportunity to entertain ambassadors and foreign dignitaries. The Privy Council was content to keep the popular theatres open within limits. This ensured that the Queen had access to *entertainers* – tumblers, clowns, fencers and dancers. Some of these performers took minor roles in the plays prepared under the patronage of her leading nobles such as the Earl of Leicester. The major acting roles in court plays that needed an appreciation of verse, and a verbal felicity, were performed by the gentlemen of the household or the boy court players, such as the Children of the Chapel.

The sensitivity of the court to slander, whether real or imagined, was displayed in the well-recorded instance of unacceptable satire, namely the *Isle of Dogs* play, written by Thomas Nashe and Ben Jonson and performed at a late period of the Queen's reign.

The play was acted, probably by Pembroke's Men, at the Swan Theatre in Bankside in either July or August of 1597. It was reported to the authorities as a *lewd plaie* full of seditious and *slanderous matter*. While existing records do not indicate what gave offence a reference in *The Returne from Parnassus* suggests that the Queen herself was satirised. Other evidence indicates that Henry Brooke, 8th Lord Cobham, may have been the target.

The Isle of Dogs is a location in London on the opposite bank of the Thames to Greenwich, home of a royal palace, Placentia, built by Humphrey, Duke of

Gloucester, where the Privy Council met. However, the title alone does not indicate the play's content since this area was also known as an unhealthy swamp where river sewage would accumulate. The Isle of Dogs is also mentioned in *Eastward Hoe* (1605), another play for which Jonson was arrested. Thomas Nashe also referred to the location in *Summers Last Will*:

> *Here's a coyle about dogges without wit. If I had thought the ship of fooles would have stayed to take in fresh water at the Ile of dogges I would have furnished it with a whole kennel of collections to the purpose.*

Whatever gave offence, Richard Topcliffe, state investigator, informed Sir Robert Cecil, Secretary of State, who raised the issue with the Privy Council. Three of the players, Gabriel Spencer, Robert Shaa, and co-author Ben Jonson, were arrested and sent to Marshalsea Prison. The home of writer Thomas Nashe was raided and his papers seized, but he had fled to Yarmouth and so he escaped imprisonment but lived on in penury.

Nashe later wrote that he had given birth to a monster: *It was no sooner borne but I was glad to runne from it.* Nashe was afterwards to call it *an imperfit Embrion of my idle houres* and claimed to have written only the introduction and first act of the *Isle of Dogs*. For his part, Jonson recalled that he said nothing but *Aye and No.*

In 1599, regarding the licensing of the plays, the wardens of the Stationers' Company were instructed by the prelates that a number of satirical books were condemned by name to be burnt, and direction given to the masters and wardens:

> *That no Satyres or Epigrams to be printed except they be allowed by some of her maiesties privie Counsell; That noe playes be printed excepte they bee allowed by suche as have aucthoritie; That all Nasshes books and Doctor Harvyes bookes be taken wheresoever they may be found and that none of theire bookes be euer printed hereafter; That thoughe any booke of the nature of theise heretofore expressed shalbe brought vnto yow vnder the hands of the lord Archebisshop of Canterburye or the lord Bishop of London yet the said booke shall not be printed vntill the master or wardens haue acquainted the said Lord Archbishop or the lord Bishop with the same to knowe whether it be their hand or no.*

The list of burned works included Joseph Hall's *Biting Satires and Virgidemiarum*, John Marston's *The Metamorphosis of Pygmalion's Image* and *The scourge of*

Villainy, Everard Gilpin's *Skialetheia*; Thomas Middleton's *Microcynicon: Six Snarling Satires*, Thomas Cutwode's *Caltha Poetarium*, and John Davies' *Epigrams*, which was bound with the *Elegies* of Christopher Marlowe.

The play *As You Like it* was '*staied*' on August 4 1600, together with *Henry V*, *Every Man In his Humour* and *Much Ado About Nothing*. Apart from *Every Man in his Humour* by Jonson, the other plays may have been connected to the disgraced writers Nashe or Harvey.

Even two anti-feminist works that could be read as critical of the unmarried Elizabeth were burned: *The Book Against Women* and *The Fifteen Joys of Marriage*.

The Bishop's ban made clear that the vogue for topical satire was officially over: *No satires or epigrams were to be printed herafter* and *No English histories are to be printed except they be allowed by some of her Majesty's Privy Council*.

Another example of literary control in the reign of Elizabeth is that of the punishment of Sir John Hayward for a seditious account of recent history. In February 1599 the knight published a small book called *The first part of the life and raigne of King Henrie IIII*, a work which despite its title, deals with the last years of the reign of King Richard II.

The treatise appeared at a time when Robert Devereaux, Earl of Essex, was in personal difficulties with the Queen, and the history contained a Latin dedication to Essex which Elizabeth found objectionable. Furthermore, there are passages in the book where parallels had been drawn between Elizabeth and Richard II. Queen Elizabeth concluded that the hapless Hayward was purposefully evoking the story of a long-dead, deposed monarch in order to foment disorder. After some copies had been issued the dedicatory leaf was removed and the work was allowed to circulate.

However, a revised second edition was suppressed, and Essex himself seems to have been one of the first persons to object to the book. Hayward's *Henrie IIII* was later brought into evidence against Essex, probably the first at the private trial of 5th June 1600, when Essex was charged with mishandling affairs in Ireland.

Around mid-May 1599 some 1,500 copies of the new edition of Hayward's history were printed. This angered the Bishop of London, Richard Bancroft, who was responsible along with the Archbishop of Canterbury, for censoring printed works. After Whit Sunday on 27th May, Bancroft ordered the second print run to be seized by the wardens of the Stationers' and delivered to his house in Fulham, where he burned them.

Hayward himself was committed to the Tower following an interrogation by Sir Francis Bacon before the Star Chamber. Elizabeth's view was that Hayward should be racked so *that he might disclose the truth.* Sir John Hayward was subjected to two trials: the first in July 1600 and the second in January 1601. The author remained in prison until after the death of Queen Elizabeth, despite Bacon's opinion that Hayward was only guilty of *stealing sentences from Tacitus.*

Censorship in the Jacobean age

The fierce punishments inflicted upon wrongdoers who defied the rules of censorship, promulgated in the time of Elizabeth, were by no means relaxed upon the accession of James I: a believer in royal absolutism. The crown, government and Church regulated the principal avenues of communication by perpetuating the repressive measures of control instituted by Elizabeth I.

Parliament enacted statutes that defined illegal writing and specified penalties, while royal proclamations identified unacceptable books and called for the punishment of authors and publishers. The Church also dictated what could be printed through pre-print authorisation and used the High Commission to enforce its will.

The punishment for unlawful printing was three to six months imprisonment, while the penalty imposed for the publishing of unlawful books was increased from a fine of twenty shillings a book ,to three months imprisonment. Faced with such repression it would not be surprising to find printers, publishers and writers practising deceit to evade dire punishments for their transgressions.

In 1603, Ben Jonson was questioned by the Privy Council about *Sejanus*, a politically-themed play about corruption in the Roman Empire, and he was again in trouble for the topical allusions of a play (now lost) in which he took part. Ben Jonson was censured again in 1605, two years after Elizabeth's death, when his play *Eastward Ho*, with its derogatory reference to the Scots, offended King James and lead to his return to jail.

Eastward Hoe or *Eastward Ho*, a satire and city comedy written by George Chapman, Ben Jonson, and John Marston, was printed in 1605. The play was written in response to *Westward Ho,* an earlier satire by Thomas Dekker and John Webster.

Eastward Ho offended King James with its anti-Scottish satirical reference in Act III. The play resulted in Jonson, Marston and Chapman being thrown in jail for a time and which made their play one of the famous dramatic scandals of its era. As a result of its notoriety, a significant body of documentation exists regarding the play, including personal letters written by both Chapman and Jonson while they were in prison. Oddly, the play was never entirely banned or suppressed and *Eastward Hoe* was revived by the Lady Elizabeth's Men in 1613, the same company who performed the play again at court on January 25, 1614.

Another stage scandal was caused by John Day's *The Isle of Gulls* which had its premiere in 1606. The play was most likely written in 1605, it was acted by the Children of the Revels at the Blackfriars theatre in February the following year and published later in a quarto in 1606.

This edition was unusual in several respects. Firstly, it was not licensed by the Stationers' Company as it should have been. Then changes were made after the press run had begun – the publisher's name was removed from the title page and the characters of the *King* and *Queen* were altered to *Duke* and *Duchess*.

The play, written in prose rather than verse, draws upon the *Arcadia* of Sir Philip Sidney for its plot. The offensive content appears to have arisen from the play's satire on the political conditions and personalities of its day. The play's *Arcadians* and *Lacedemonians* were understood to be the English and the Scots: the boy actors used Scottish accents for the *Lacedemonians*. The title gives an unmistakably English frame of reference: referencing the real Isle of Gulls in the Thames. The character *Damoetas* in Day's play represented royal favourite Robert Carr, 1st Earl of Somerset. The King or Duke wastes public funds on himself and his Queen or Duchess. The courtier appoints corrupt counsellors and rewards unworthy men with knighthood through his influence while generally leaving the state in chaos.

The play was offensive to the Stuart monarchy, even more so than *Eastward Ho* had been a year earlier, when Jonson and Chapman went to jail for their involvement. In the case of *The Isle of Gulls,* John Day was questioned by the Privy Council and may also have been imprisoned for a time. Moreover, some of the juvenile cast members of the Blackfriars production were incarcerated in Bridewell prison for a brief interval. These child actors who seemed to shoulder the blame then ended up under new management.

The court play *The Tragedy of Philotas* staged in 1605 placed its writer Samuel Daniel in danger of imprisonment. The play describes the dilemma of *Philotas*, a military commander, who became unwillingly embroiled in a plot to unseat Alexander the Great. Daniel was summoned before the Privy Council and accused of using *Philotas* to dramatise, sympathetically, the failed insurrection against Queen Elizabeth by Robert Devereux, second Earl of Essex. A fulsome apology to both the authorities and Daniel's patron, Lord Mountjoy, prevented any further action against the poet. Daniel also claimed in his defence that the work had been passed by the Lord Chamberlain before its performance at court.

George Chapman was yet another playwright who incurred the wrath of King James. In this case his anger was inflamed by Chapman's two part play *The Conspiracy and Tragedy of Charles, Duke of Byron*. The play's central character Charles Duke of Byron, Marshall of France, was a genuine historical figure who was executed for treason in 1602.

In all likelihood, Chapman composed both parts of *Byron* in 1607–8 using Edward Grimeston's *A General Inventory of the History of France*, first published in 1607, as his primary source on the political events portrayed in the plays. The title page of the quarto states that the play was acted by the Children of the Chapel, and then known as the Children of the Whitefriars; the sequel is thought to have been performed in conjunction with Chapman's original *Bussy D'Ambois* play. In the quarto the play is prefaced by an Epistle by George Chapman addressed to Sir Thomas Howard, second son of the first Earl of Suffolk, later Earl of Berkshire.

The original production offended the French Ambassador to the court of King James I, Antoine Lefèvre de la Boderie, who complained to the King. The Ambassador was particularly irritated by a scene in which the French Queen slapped the face of her husband's mistress.

Later scenes in *The Tragedy* twice compare Byron's plotting with the rebellion of the Earl of Essex against Elizabeth in 1601. It has been suggested that the face-slapping scene that caused so much trouble was inspired not by anything in French monarchical history but by a rumoured incident in which Elizabeth struck Essex.

The plays were duly suppressed but when the court left London in the summer, the boys performed the plays again in their original versions, with the offending material included. James was incensed when he learned of this, and swore that he would punish the players severely. Subsequently, the monarch stopped all dramatic performances in London for a time; three of the Children of the Blackfriars were sent to prison and the troupe was ejected from the Blackfriars theatre. James' passion for drama ultimately got the better of his anger, however: the boy actors were eventually forgiven and even performed at court in the ensuing Christmas season.

The two parts of *The Conspiracy and Tragedy of Charles, Duke of Byron* were entered into the Stationers' Register on June 5th, 1608, and were published together, later that year, in a quarto printed by George Eld for the bookseller Thorpe.

The printed text was *ruthlessly censor*, particularly in Part I, Act IV (Byron's visit to England), and Part II, Act II (the mistress-slapping scene). The masque in act II of *The Tragedy* is thought to have been inserted to fill the void left by censorship.

Two major cases between 1608 and 1617 concerning the dissemination of contentious ideas and consequent state retribution were those of Edmund Peacham and John Cowell.

One outstanding example of state coercion in 1614/5 was the arrest, imprisonment and torture of the Reverend Edmund Peacham, a Puritan preacher from Somerset, following criticism of his Church superiors found in notes for a sermon. These were found after a search in his study that followed rumours of his subversive opinions. The sermon in question's content was also critical of James I and his counsellors. Peacham had previously been charged and examined by the authorities in 1603 when he was accused of *"uttering in a sermon seditious and railing words against the king, and more especially against his counsellors, the bishops and judges."*

In December 1614 Peacham was arrested on Bishop Montagu's complaint by order of the Court of High Commission and transferred to the Tower. Ten days later he was brought to trial before the Court of High Commission at Lambeth on a charge of libelling Bishop Montagu, he was found guilty and deprived of his orders but more serious accusations were soon brought against him.

While his house was being searched for his writings against Bishop Montagu, the officers discovered the prepared notes of a sermon in which the King and the government were denounced with reckless vehemence. Not only were James' ministers charged with misconduct, the king with extravagance, and the ecclesiastical courts with a tyrannical exercise of their powers, but the King's sudden death and a rebellion of the people were declared to be the probable outcome of the government's alleged misdeeds.

The council treated Peacham's words as evidence of treasonable intent and he was at once examined, but offered no defence, and declined all explanation. Although the common law did not recognise the legality of torturing a prisoner to extort a confession, it was generally admitted that torture might be lawfully applied by the Privy Council to a prisoner who deliberately refused to surrender information respecting a plot against the life of the sovereign or the security of the government. On these grounds Edmund Peacham was interrogated before, during and after torture, but he refused to admit any wrongdoing and was then sent for trial, found guilty and executed.

A secular publication which caused considerable controversy in the period from 1608–1617 was *The Interpreter* by John Cowell. Originally allowed and printed at Cambridge in 1607, this law dictionary contained definitions of royal power and the role of parliament which were perceived as absolutist by some in parliament.

including Lionel Cranfield, 1st Earl of Middlesex, Baron Cranfield and Lord Treasurer, who was impeached before the House of Lords in April 1624 for corruption having earned the enmity of Prince Charles and Buckingham because of his opposition to a war with Spain. Cranfield was imprisoned for a few days only and was pardoned in the following year.

The former Spanish ambassador to London, Diego Sarmiento de Acuña, Conde de Gondomar, was blatantly satirised and caricatured in the play as the Machiavellian Black Knight. The King's Men went so far as to buy discarded items of Gondomar's wardrobe for the role. Gondomar's ambassadorial successor recognised the satire and complained to King James of the insulting portrayal.

The description of the rowdy reaction of the audience to the play yields a vivid picture of the character of the popular theatre.

> *There was such merriment, hubbub and applause that even if I had been many leagues away it would not have been possible for me not to have taken notice of it*

The play was stopped after nine performances (August 6–16, Sundays omitted), but not before it had become the greatest box-office hit of early modern London. The Privy Council opened a prosecution against the actors and the author of the play on August 18, as it was then illegal to portray any modern Christian king on the stage. The Globe theatre was shut down by the prosecutors, although Thomas Middleton was able to acquit himself by showing that the play had been passed by the Master of the Revels, Sir Henry Herbert. Nevertheless, further performance of the play was forbidden and Middleton and the actors were reprimanded and fined: Middleton never officially wrote another play.

If Gondomar failed to secure the liberty of all the Jesuits and priests confined within the Clink and Bridewell prisons, he surely rejoiced at the improved conditions in the English jails, where *new altars were permitted to be erected at which in one morning thirty and more masses were celebrated with special prayers to God for the success of the Emperor and Spinola's army* and *for the defeat of James' son-in-law, Frederick Prince Palatine and his followers.*

The House of Commons apparently regarded the more relaxed policy of the King toward his Catholic subjects with little favour.

The Commons deplored the increase of popery, which was to be attributed to the vigilance of the Pope and his adherents. It referred to the distress of Protestantism abroad, the increase of recusants and *the printing of popish books and swarming Jesuits.* When Coke formed a sub-committee to establish freedom of speech and discuss the rights of the Commons, James announced that *you usurp upon our prerogative royal and meddle with things far above your reach.* The king first adjourned Parliament and then forbade the Commons from discussing *matters of state at home or abroad.*

Ignoring this ban, Parliament issued a *Remonstrance to the King* on 11th December 1621, authored by Sir Edward Coke, jurist, in which they restated their liberties and right to discuss matters of state, claiming that such rights were the *ancient and undoubted birthright and inheritance of the subjects of England.*

After a debate, the document was sent to James, who rejected it; the Commons instead resolved to enter it into the Journal of the Commons, which required no royal authorisation. In the presence of Parliament, the King reacted by tearing the offending page from the Journal, declaring that it should be *razed out of all memories and utterly annihilated,* then dissolved Parliament again. Sir Edward Coke was then imprisoned in the Tower of London on 27th December, but released nine months later.

Nonetheless, by August 1622, *all priests and Papists imprisoned were set at liberty and were no longer to be troubled for saying Mass or refusing the oath of allegiance or supremacy and the like.* A few months later Chamberlain reported that *our papists begin to hold up their heads again for whereas writs were gone out to inquire o'er their lands and charges for not paying according to their stature, letters are gone downe to suppress that course.*

A deeply disturbed country where emotions ran high over religious and political differences, England also faced serious economic problems by the early 1620s. A mistake by the Treasury in setting the ratio of gold to silver led to silver leaving the country entirely forcing the English to barter.

In 1622 cloth exports were forty per cent lower than four years earlier and a disastrous harvest that year worsened the outlook for England. During this decade the Catholic Imperial forces were triumphant. It seemed Catholic power in Europe was in the ascendancy while the English Parliaments reaction to this threat was financially inadequate and far too late.

Divisive opinions on Church doctrine also became apparent during the 1620s. The Bishops George Abbot, John Williams and Thomas Morton, all saw Catholics as the main threat, possibly influenced by the 'gun-powder' plot and Jesuit activities in England. These senior clerics agreed with the Puritans on all principal aspects of theology: most notably the doctrine of predestination.

Some Churchmen, however, were becoming suspicious of Calvinism. Led by Bishops Lancelot Andrewes, Richard Neile and William Laud and prelate Richard Montagu, they opposed Calvinist doctrines and minimised the points on which the Church of England differed from Roman Catholicism. In addition, there were intermittent disputes between secular and Ecclesiastical Courts, such as the *Book of Sports*. It would be fair to say in economic, political and religious controversies in England during the 1620s meant that English society was disturbed and fearful of what the future would hold.

James I, Spain and the Catholic threat

The trials of Protestant groups in Spain, often Lutheran, in the mid-16th century virtually ended Spanish Protestantism. It was the policy of Spain similarly to eradicate the national faith of England should the Armada invasion of 1588 or another later large-scale attack be successful.

The *Auto-da-Fé* or 'show trial' was anticipated should the Spanish occupy England. The Catholic Inquisition had lately gained the power to repress heretical ideas and prohibit books listed on the Index, including vernacular versions of the Bible. Certainly the persecution of Spanish Protestants and the anti-clerical remained active during the latter decades of the 16th century. Such actions confirmed the English view of Spain and the Papacy as inherently dangerous to England's established religion and the harmony of the State, even perhaps the nation's very existence. That deep-seated dread continued for many decades.

Internal subversion by Catholic malcontents lent additional weight to the nation's foreboding. Towards the end of the reign of Elizabeth I, it became known that the head of the Jesuits in England, Henry Garnet, showed a group of soldiers the secret Papal briefing that ordered all Catholics to oppose the crowning of James VI of Scotland, that Monarch having been deemed a heretic. The military group included the Essex rebel and future Gunpowder Plot conspirator Robert Catesby.

It was also known by the Elizabethan authorities that the Jesuit faction was desperate for the Spanish to fulfill their earlier promise to carry out an invasion of England. To this end a son of Lord Bathurst, the Catholic Thomas Sackville, was sent to Rome to expedite preparations.

The English Government was also well-informed of the plotting by various English noblemen, in league with foreign powers, to place the Catholic Arbella Stuart on the English throne instead of the Protestant Scottish King James VI.

Some Protestants at this time feared that James I, upon his accession, secretly intended to offer religious toleration for Catholics, while others also thought that, following the Scottish King's coronation, he was too pro-Catholic. As one gentleman commented:

It is hardly credible in what jollity the Papists now live. They are already labouring tooth and nail for places in Parliament and do so mightily prevail... as I cannot see how their dangerous course can be stopped unless some higher authority speedily interpose itself.

Another indication of the strength of the Anti-Papist feeling of these times, straddling the late Elizabethan and early Stuart reigns, is well illustrated by the *Bond of Association* of 1584. By this 'Bond' many Protestants, including Privy Councillors and senior Clergy, undertook to kill anyone harming the Queen's presence. Their belief was that the Queen's death would lead to the destruction of Protestantism. As it was assumed that Mary, Queen of Scots, would be implicated in any design against Elizabeth I, the signatories committed to kill Mary in response, or at least prevent her accession to the throne.

The accession of James to the Protestant English throne created more discord on matters of religion than anticipated, despite the king's Calvinistic upbringing and his own, publicly demonstrated, desire for harmony between the various faiths. The *Millenary Petition* of 1603/4 for example, overseen by James, suggested an invitation to men of faith to hear all sides of the contemporary religious disputes.

James also wrote to the Pope suggesting some form of Christian unification, or at least an understanding between the faiths, but apparently he did not receive a response. The hostility between the major religions was to be a feature of English society throughout the King's reign and continued the fierce struggle for power so marked during the age of Queen Elizabeth.

Nevertheless, in defiance of public disquiet, James did not oppose negotiations for the proposed marriage of his elder son, Prince Henry, to a Spanish Infanta, initiated by the Queen. Anne's Catholicism was a major force in the Queen's preference for the dynastic matches proposed for her children with European Catholic ducal and royal families, particularly with Spain. It was as early as 1604, during the signing of the Anglo-Spanish peace treaty, when Anne put forward the scheme for the marriage of her son, Prince Henry, with the Spanish Infanta, Anna Maria.

The King's own financial extravagance, coupled with his inability to negotiate funds from Parliament, had persuaded James to agree to this match of dynastic importance.

James VI's consort had actually adopted the Catholic faith ten years earlier in Scotland, which at the time had caused alarm among the Scottish Kirk and raised deep suspicions in England. The Calvinist James was seemingly tolerant of his wife's choice of religion in those years and accepted the presence of senior ladies of the Catholic persuasion in the Queen's household, who assisted her in Catholic practice.

Jane Drummond, later Countess of Roxburghe, was a major influence and some of her supposed servants were in fact disguised priests and thus able to access court. When Dunfermline castle became Anne's preferred residence she surrounded herself with Catholic friends.

Despite her Catholic inclinations the Queen was nevertheless willing to side with the Protestant Court faction in their plan to replace Robert Carr, the favourite of the Howard Catholic supporters with George Villiers, the Protestant candidate, in 1616.

Queen Anne's hopes for the intended royal marriage alliance with Spain foundered in 1610 upon the untimely death of the Crown Prince, who succumbed to typhoid fever. It was, however, alleged by some that Henry been poisoned: possibly a Protestant plot.

King James had prevented the proposed and unpopular union of Princess Elizabeth with a French Catholic husband, earlier arranged by Queen Anne. Instead, James married Elizabeth to the Protestant Frederick V of the Bohemian Palatinate in 1612. This was intended to create a diplomatic balance in Europe, but was to prove disastrous for the couple and cause major political problems for James abroad. Moreover, it created great unrest in England when Frederick was unseated by the Catholic Hapsburg powers and the royal couple fled their country.

This became an international problem for James that was to prove insurmountable in the face of Parliament's refusal to fund a military expedition to recover the Palatinate without concessions from the king that he found unacceptable. The Commons on the one hand, granted subsidies inadequate to finance serious military operations in aid of Frederick, and on the other, called for a war directly against Spain.

The unhappy Palatinate situation remained unresolved and by the 1620s events on the continent had stirred up anti-Catholic feeling in England to a new pitch with the Commons calling for Charles to marry a Protestant bride.

In November 1621 political antagonisms came to head. Led by Sir Edward Coke, the Commons framed a petition asking not only for a war with Spain but for Prince Charles to marry a Protestant and for enforcement of the anti-Catholic laws. James flatly told them not to interfere in matters of royal prerogative or they would risk punishment. To this provocation the Commons reacted by issuing a statement protesting their rights, including freedom of speech. Urged on by Buckingham and the Spanish ambassador Gondomar, James ripped the protest out of the record book and dissolved Parliament.

Thwarted by the death of Prince Henry earlier in the reign, steps had then been initiated in 1614 by the newly arrived Spanish Ambassador, Count Gondamar, for the marriage of Prince Charles and his prospective bride, Maria Anna, daughter of the Spanish king Philip III. The succeeding negotiation for the marriage of Prince Charles to the Spanish Infanta then gained the strong approval of the king for several reasons.

James' long-held desire was to end persistent European conflict and he hoped to gain Spanish support in solving the Palatinate question. James also stood to receive a most handsome dowry – a welcome replenishment for his greatly depleted treasury, which had declined dramatically following his coronation, and which Parliament refused to alleviate with financial subsidies. Gondomar offered a dowry of £500,000 (later increased to £600,000), joined with the additional offer that Spain would not interfere with James' troubled rule in Ireland if the king would restrain the English 'Privateers' operating in Spanish-American waters.

The policy and diplomacy surrounding the proposed negotiations for the marriage of Charles and Anna Maria was described as The Spanish Match. The proposed union was met with the hostility of a Protestant House of Commons, still mindful of the comparatively recent Anglo-Spanish War and the ever-present threat of Spanish Catholic domination. The negotiation, commencing in 1617, was in the hands of the Privy Council albeit some senior members were firm Protestants. The initiative and events on the Continent stirred anti-Catholic feelings to a new high.

The climax of the ensuing near decade of high-level negotiation to secure a marriage between the leading Protestant and Catholic royal families of Europe occurred in 1623 in Madrid, after the impulsive journey to Spain, initially clandestine, of Prince Charles and James' favourite, George Villiers, 1st Duke of Buckingham. In the event the wedding did not take place following lengthy delays by the Spanish court while criticism of the terms laid down by Spain mounted by the Commons led to another dissolution of Parliament. A resentful, angry Prince Charles and Buckingham returned to England without the Infanta much to the relief of the population.

It became clear, as the negotiations progressed, that the Spanish, supported by the Pope, would never agree to the marriage unless Prince Charles converted to Roman Catholicism. The other conditions of the agreement were entirely in favour of England's Catholic community. These terms included repeal of the recusancy and anti-Catholic laws, freedom of Catholic worship in perpetuity, as well as the exercise of her religion by the Infanta and thus the royal household in England including Catholic priests.

One especially worrying article was an insistence that any children of the union should be educated by the Infanta until the age of ten. This condition appeared to pre-suppose that thereafter the royal children would continue in the Catholic faith, with every likelihood of a future Catholic monarch in England.

There was nothing in the whole treaty concerning the Palatinate, the dowry or even the date of the wedding. Furthermore, it was insisted that a twelve-month period was required to ensure the treaty was observed before the Infanta could leave Spain. The alternative put forward by Spain was that Charles could marry the Infanta immediately, subject to Papal approval, but would have to live in Spain for twelve months: this was unacceptable to the English party.

In England, any such unity of State and the Church of Rome was perceived to threaten the freedom and independence of England. Deeply disturbing to Protestant Englishmen was that within the marriage terms laid down, and accepted by James I, an agreement would be in place for the conversion of the royal suitor to Catholicism.

Such a step would create a Catholic royal family with the right of a Catholic succession – a fundamental shift of regal power. For the Anglican Church, the independence of the Catholic Church hierarchy would mean that their bishops would then owe their ultimate allegiance to the Pope, and not the ruling English monarch.

The marriage treaty also incorporated several private Articles, namely,

- *The repeal of the penal laws against Catholics within three years*
- *'A perpetual toleration' of Catholics in England*
- *Free religious discussion between the Prince and his wife*

A new domination of the country by the Catholic Church could well be envisaged by its opponents if this arrangement were to pass into English law. This scenario involved a Church leadership in alliance with the leading Catholic states, hostile to England, and subject to the strong influence of the Pope.

Many in society thought this situation might well lead to England becoming subsumed by Catholic Spain in the foreseeable future. This feared outcome was present in Protestant English minds throughout every generation from the latter part of Henry VIII's reign to those living during the reign of King James I.

The fears of the English nobility were echoed by a population that was apprehensive of another change of religion. It was anticipated by most in the country that a reversal of this magnitude could well bring about the bloody conflict, repression and social upheavals experienced in earlier reigns and, in particular, the executions ordered when Mary I came to the throne. The repression of Mary's reign was marked by severe censorship, well illustrated by the burning of *"heretical and seditious"* writings and the punishment of authors.

The savagery inflicted upon Protestant believers during Mary's reign were well publicised throughout England; *Foxe's Book of Martyrs* was read throughout the country. The country had not forgotten that in those years hundreds of Protestants were put to death and a number more co-religionists fled abroad, including noble families, statesmen, churchmen and other leaders of society.

Embittered by their treatment in Spain, Charles and Buckingham now turned James' Spanish policy upon its head and called for a French match and a war against the Habsburg Empire. To raise the necessary finance, they prevailed upon James to call another Parliament, which met in February 1624.

For once, the outpouring of anti-Catholic sentiment in the Commons was echoed in court. Here control of policy had shifted from King James to Charles and Buckingham, who pressed the king to declare war. They engineered the impeachment and imprisonment of the Lord Treasurer, Lionel Cranfield, Earl of Middlesex, when he opposed the idea on grounds of cost.

The outcome of the Parliament of 1624 was ambiguous: James still refused to declare war, but Charles believed the Commons had committed themselves to financing a war against Spain, a stance which was to contribute to his problems with Parliament during his own reign. Charles eventually married Henrietta of France in 1625, who became the mother of Charles II and James II.

During these decades of religious turmoil King James, Calvinist by upbringing, had remained remarkably lenient in his attitude towards Roman Catholics in general. This tolerance continued despite the actions of Catholic assassins in several subversive incidents, such as the 'Bye', 'Main' and 'Gunpowder' plots, all of which failed. James also eased the Recusancy laws that applied to the attendance of Catholics attending Anglican services.

As the Jacobean years progressed the firm faith of the Queen became more evident, as did the seemingly ambivalent attitude of the King towards Catholicism. Added to which, Gondomar, the Spanish Ambassador, was known to exert a powerful influence upon James. These factors together combined to create a rising tide of anxiety in England that built upon the traditional fear of Spain.

COMEDIES, HISTORIES & TRAGEDIES

CHAPTER TWELVE

The proposed London amphitheatre

On a trip to London from Canada, the late Dr Leslie Hotson, the Shakespearean scholar, and his wife discovered a document in the archives (dated 1620) concerning the proposed building of a vast amphitheatre in Lincoln's Inn Fields, London, to accommodate twelve thousand spectators.

Official approval for the building of a large amphitheatre in London was current during the reigns of James I and Charles I, as uncovered in State papers in 1960 by historian Dr Leslie Hotson and his wife and summarised in his historical document *The projected Amphitheatre*.

Entertaining dignitaries on a grand scale

It appears that attempts were made to establish an amphitheatre for shows of various kinds in or near London; the initiative was set in train in 1620. In order to reduce the expense of entertainment on the royal purse, the project was awarded to private enterprise by means of a license issued from the Privy Seal Office, dated 30th July of that year.

This was confirmed in a letter from King James I to the Privy Council, dated 29th September 1620 wherein, it states that three of the King's servants: John Cotton, John Williams and Thomas Dixon, Sergeants at Arm, had been licensed under his signet to build an amphitheatre. This grant was altered and cancelled before a new one was drawn up, which was to be more specific and give greater monopolistic power over theatrical London.

James I's vision of statecraft and the dignity of the English crown included a notable ambition to lavishly entertain ambassadors and visiting dignitaries to a greater extent than his predecessor.

Confronted in 1603 with the arrival of seven embassies and ten ambassadors, James created the office of Master of the Ceremonies. Until this time court masques, plays and musical fare had been accommodated in court venues. Now the time was ripe, perhaps even necessary, to create a facility for major spectacles and shows. Since most of the foreigners could not understand

English plays the performances also needed to be prepared in Latin, the common language of civilized Christendom.

The proposed Amphitheatre would have solved much of the audience problems posed by the limited staging facility at Court. The license for this structure was found in the archive by the Canadian academic, Dr Leslie Hotson, during one of his vacations to the London Public Records Office.

The document issued an order to *build and prepare an amphitheater upon some convenient peece of ground neere our Citie of London*, which was intended to provide *heroique and majestique recreations*, as well as *to delight and entertain foreign Princes Ambassadors, the Nobility, and Gentry*. The period of the license granted was thirty years and the rent was to be 40 shillings a year. The plays described in the Prospectus of the Amphitheatre as *Comedies, Histories and Tragedies* the same description used of the contents of the First Folio of 1623.

The idea of an arena which could stage gladiatorial combats reflects the desire of the times to emulate the greatness of Classical Rome, while the plan for theatrical tragedies and Olympiad games shows an admiration for ancient Greece.

The order, devised earlier in the year to prepare a *Great readie for his Majestie's Royall Signature* gave the license to build an Amphitheatre and it was signed by four senior officers of State: Lord Pembroke, Lord Arundel, Sir Kenelm Degbye (Digby) and George Calvert, 1st Baron Baltimore. Two of the signatories were Roman Catholic and two were Protestant.

The most significant of the signatories was the Protestant William Herbert, 3rd Earl of Pembroke, Lord Chamberlain and son of Mary Herbert, Countess of Pembroke. William was married to Mary Talbot, heiress of Gilbert Talbot, 7th Earl of Shrewsbury.

Lord Pembroke, William Herbert, 3rd Earl of Pembroke KG, PC, who died in 1630, a Chancellor of the University of Oxford, had Pembroke College named in his honour by King James. An outstanding patron of the arts, the 3rd Earl was a leading Protestant figure who served as Lord Chamberlain from 1615 to 1625. The First Folio publication was dedicated to *"the incomparable Pair"* in 1623: the brothers William and Philip Herbert, 1st Earl of Montgomery.

The second signatory was the Protestant Thomas Howard, the Earl of Arundel. Howard was the 1st Earl of Norfolk, 21st Earl of Arundel KG, Earl Marshal; a prominent courtier during the reign of King James I who made his name as a Grand Tourist and art collector. Howard was married to Lady Alethea Talbot, sole heiress of Gilbert Talbot, 7th Earl of Shrewsbury.

Sir Kenelm Degbye and George Calvert, 1st Baron Baltimore were both Roman Catholics. Degbye was a courtier, diplomat, a highly reputed natural philosopher and known as a leading Roman Catholic intellectual. For his versatility, Anthony à Wood called Degbye the *magazine of all art*.

George Calvert was a politician and coloniser who achieved domestic political success as an MP, and later as Secretary of State under James I, but lost much of his political power after his unpopular support for the failed Spanish Marriage alliance.

The Amphitheatre was planned on a vast scale, accommodating twelve thousand spectators and intended to be constructed in Lincoln's Inn Fields.

The handwritten prospectus proposed:

> *Imprimis Tragedies, Comedies, and Histories acted both in Latine and English full of high State and Royall representmentes with many and variable and delightful properties, with shows of great horse, and rich Caparisons, gracefully prepared to Entertaine Foraigne Princes, and to give content to the most Noble and Worthyest of his Majesties Admired and Happy Kingdomes...*

It was the 30th of July 1620 when the licence was finally granted to John Cotton, John Williams and Thomas Dixon, Serjeants at Arms, for the building of a house and amphitheatre in Lincoln's Inn Fields, London. This was *for baiting or fighting with beasts, fencing, wrestling, tumbling, tumbling on ropes, music and kinds of plays for the entertainment of Ambassadors and persons of honour and quality.*

The scope of the entertainment envisaged for the amphitheatre was extensive. It featured horse riding and horse displays, army and naval battle enactments, wrestling, dancing, music and plays in Latin or English, with other shows *fitt for the more stately and delectable publishing and setting forth of the same.* The gestation of this project is not known, but it is likely that formulation of the plan, presented and approved in 1620 would have commenced much earlier in the reign.

Nevertheless because the applicants seemingly exceeded their original building plan the license was quickly cancelled and not re-applied for until 1626 but the venture did not proceed further. There was opposition both from playing troupes, theatre owners and the Lord Keeper, Thomas Coventry.

It is evident that should the Amphitheatre concept have reached fruition it would have required a large collection of plays to fulfil the prospectus of presenting *Comedies, Histories and Tragedies,* the exact words to be echoed soon after on the title page of the First Folio. Certainly, Pembroke, as Lord Chamberlain, and the official responsible for Court entertainment, was well placed to provide the necessary play texts.

Occupying the position of Lord Chamberlain, superior in rank to the Master of the Revels, the 3rd Earl had the means and authority to determine the collection of plays that formed the First Folio of 1623. The proposed amphitheatre may well indeed have prompted the concept of the First Folio publication. William Herbert was not only in a senior position but represented the tradition of literary patronage held by his family during the reigns of Elizabeth and James.

Typesetting by hand and letterpress printing in the 17th century

CHAPTER THIRTEEN

Preparation and printing of the First Folio

T HE First Folio typesetting and printing by William Jaggard the *Printer to the Honourable City of London* commenced in the spring of 1621 and proceeded through the summer and autumn of that year. There was a considerable break in the book's production thereafter, of some eighteen months, before production continued through the spring, summer and autumn of 1623; the volume was completed by November of that year. The Bodleian Library purchased a copy that was sent for binding in February 1624. The publication was listed by an entry in the Frankfurt Book Fair Catalogue of October 1622, although the book was not printed until the following year.

Jaggard's printshop was one of twenty authorised London printers controlled by The Stationers' Company. Their licensing authority and the trade guild were responsible, in turn, to the Privy Council as England's ultimate censoring authority. Control of printed matter was a matter of primacy for the state throughout the Jacobean age as it had been in Elizabeth's time.

The First Folio volume, unbound, was priced at one pound and at the time a printed play quarto cost sixpence. The only comparable publication of plays printed previously had been Ben Jonson's *Workes*, issued in 1616. The size and format of the First Folio publication shows that it, too, was intended to be a permanent record of literary work and prepared for an educated readership.

Traditionally, the lengthy pause in the production of the volume is explained by the need for negotiating printing rights on the part of Jaggard with other printers or stationers who were in possession of a number of the play texts in quarto.

There are at least two other explanations to be considered however. Firstly, that the work was halted in response to King James' Proclamation of 25th September 1622 promulgating an all-encompassing censorship. This Proclamation posed a threat to writers and publishers who produced material judged seditious by the authorities; punishment of offenders was severe.

Secondly, the task of gathering together source material from the original popular playhouse scripts or printed versions in quartos was somewhat arduous. This work would have required a great deal of editing and rewriting to bring the early texts to the desired literary standard and therefore a timescale of many months, involving many poets. That is not to say that negotiations with various other publishers were not taking place in parallel during this same period of time.

A.W. Pollard analysed the origination of the thirty six plays in the First Folio in 1916 and noted that twenty plays in the First Folio were not printed previously. Sixteen existing quartos were incorporated in the volume and, of these, three were without amendment: *Love's Labour's Lost* 1598, the *Merchant of Venice* 1600, and *Romeo and Juliet* 1599.

Five quartos were used without major additions, corrections or alterations: *Much Ado About Nothing* 1600, *Midsummer Night's Dream* 1619, *Richard II* 1615, *Henry IV* 1613 and *Titus Andronicus* 1611. Eight existing quartos were not used and instead other source material was employed. Most Shakespearean scholars including A.W. Pollard claim these plays were typeset from extant material i.e. prompt books, some quartos and even copies of actor's parts. The first three plays in the volume were set from the scripts of Ralph Crane, the scrivener, and this stage marked a pause in the progress of typesetting.

Much of this material dates from the period of the mid 1590s to early 1600s. After 1611, only three quartos of plays were issued: namely, *Richard III* in 1612, *Henry IV* in 1613 and *Richard II* in 1615. Many of the quartos were copies of playhouse scripts likely to be shortened versions of plays performed either at the indoor theatre, noblemen's houses or at the court.

The publisher Edward Blount had joined the enterprise after April 1622 and played a senior role, alongside Isaac Jaggard, the twenty-six year old son of William and himself a publisher of quality books, including Boccaccio's *Decameron*. By this time the aged and ill Jaggard senior had become blind and William died before the publishing was completed. Two other publishers, John Smethwick and William Aspley, joined the venture, albeit in minor positions. It may be that their participation was due to their ownership of certain quartos.

The final publication, attributed to William Shakespeare, included a number of exceptionally fulsome tributes to the dead author from the literary figures Ben Jonson, Hugh Holland, Leonard Digges and J.M. (John Marston or James Mabbe). Surprisingly to many literary observers such commendatory verses or tributes by these writers were not addressed to Shakespeare during his lifetime.

In addition, Jaggard printed a folio of European chivalric history, *The Theater of Honour and Knighthood...* a translation by an unknown writer of *Le Theatre d'Honneur et de Chevalerie* (1620) by Andre Favyn, a Parisian lawyer. Jaggard dedicated the volume to Henry Montague, Viscount Mandeville. Printed at the same time as the First Folio, published in 1623, The Theatre d'Honneur appears to be a companion piece and was also listed in the Frankfurt Book Fair catalogue.

Shakespeare and multiple authorship publications

Two primary examples of multiple authorship publications that shed some light on the Shakespeare authorship question are the *Passionate Pilgrim* printed in 1599 and the so-called *False Folio* of 1619. Like the First Folio of 1623, these volumes include works by different authors than the claimed William Shakespeare. These publications are accepted as examples of false authorship yet it appears that the First Folio and William Shakespeare are sacrosanct and indissoluble.

The Passionate Pilgrim

The Passionate Pilgrim is an anthology of twenty poems collected and published by printer William Jaggard, and attributed to *W. Shakespeare* on the title page. The anthology, in fact, contains a number of poems that are clearly identifiable as the work of several other authors.

The first edition of *The Passionate Pilgrim* survives only in a single fragmentary copy, but its date cannot be fixed with certainty since its title page is missing. Many scholars judge the volume most likely to be from 1599, the year the second edition appeared.

The title page of this second edition states that the book is to be sold by stationer William Leake, who had obtained the rights to *Venus and Adonis* in 1596 and published five octavo editions of that poem in the 1599–1602 period.

William Jaggard is known as the printer and publisher of Edward Topsell's *The History of Four-Footed Beasts* of 1607 and *The History of Serpents* of 1608, famous for their lush and often-reproduced illustrations. The Topsell books can serve to correct a misapprehension about Jaggard's work: judged by the number of typographical errors and cruxes in the First Folio it is sometimes inferred that Jaggard did poor-quality work. The Topsell printing shows another side of Jaggard's professional accomplishment and his firm was capable of high-quality craftsmanship.

The Merry Wives of Windsor - *"Printed for Arthur Johnson, 1619."* This is a false date and name. Johnson published Quarto 1 of *Merry Wives* in 1602. The authors may be Thomas Nashe and John Danter.

A Midsummer Night's Dream - *"Printed by James Roberts, 1600."* This is misleading in that two quartos of the play were printed in 1600. One version was by Richard Braddock for Thomas Fisher with a correct date, and the other was by Roberts with a false date and name.

Pericles, Prince of Tyre - *"Printed for T. P. 1619,"* date *"corrected"* to 1609 in second state.

Sir John Oldcastle – *"Printed for T. P. 1600."* The play *Sir John Oldcastle* of 1600, printed anonymously with the authorship, ascribed to Anthony Munday, Michael Drayton, Richard Hathwaye, and Robert Wilson.

A Yorkshire Tragedy – *"Printed for T. P. 1619."* The general consensus for authorship is Thomas Middleton, Jacobean playwright and poet. Middleton stands with John Fletcher and Ben Jonson as among the most successful and prolific of playwrights who wrote their best plays during the Jacobean period. This author was one of the few Renaissance dramatists to achieve equal success in comedy and tragedy: a prolific writer of masques and pageants.

The Whole Contention Between the Two Famous Houses, Lancaster and York - *"Printed at London, for T. P."* This was the major innovation of the collection: Jaggard joined together two previously separate texts, *The First Part of the Contention Betwixt the Two Famous Houses of York and Lancaster* (the early version of *Henry VI Part 2*, published by Thomas Millington in 1594 and 1600), and *The True Tragedy of Richard Duke of York* (the early version of *Henry VI, Part 3*, published by Millington in 1595 and 1600). In 1602, Pavier had acquired the rights to both plays from Millington.

Pericles was printed after *The Whole Contention*, since their signatures (the alphanumeric designations of the quires in sequence) run together. However, the nine plays were apparently bound together in no particular order and the few existing collections vary.

The authorship of these early plays has evoked much debate between scholars: traces of Marlowe, Greene, Nashe, Lodge, Kyd and Peele have all been detected in these works.

As Jaggard lacked the rights to Hayes' *Merchant of Venice*, he may also have lacked rights to Butter's *Lear* and Johnson's *Merry Wives of Windsor*.

The scholar, A.W. Pollard, focused much of his attention on the concept of literary *piracy* and his viewpoint coloured much of the scholarly attitude and approach to the False Folio during the twentieth century. By the start of the twenty-first century, some researchers began to take a less melodramatic and more nuanced view of the questions involved – a view that no longer casts Jaggard and Pavier as villainous in a moral context.

Seuerall Comedies, Histories, and Tragedies

Page facsimile from the First Folio

CHAPTER FOURTEEN

Selection of plays for the First Folio

LTHOUGH eighteen of the plays had been printed prior to 1623 the First Folio is the only reliable text for the other plays. The works fall into two categories:

1. Recorded performances or printing of certain plays in the First Folio (Old or published plays)

These comprise plays of which only seventeen or eighteen (according to, respectively, Pollard and Willoughby) were printed and these were of varying quality, some sold by the early playgroups.

These quartos were printed from either the 'foul papers', early scribal versions from the popular theatre, or 'fair copies', which are more sophisticated versions of the early plays.

Four early quartos: *Romeo and Juliet* of 1597, *Henry V* of 1600, *The Merry Wives of Windsor* of 1602 and *Hamlet* of 1603, as well as *The First Part of the Contention Betwixt the Two Famous Houses of York and Lancaster (1594)* and *The True Tragedy of Richard Duke of York* printed in 1595, the earliest versions of *Henry VI, Part 2* and *Henry VI, Part 3,* feature obvious errors, changes in word order, gaps in the sense of the text, jumbled printing of prose as verse and verse as prose, and similar problems when compared with the final plays in the First Folio publication. Although the accepted theory holds that the 'bad' quartos were the result of memorial reconstruction, based on the analysis of errors made by actors, it is more likely that they are renditions of the popular playhouse performances.

These early quartos were sold to printers either because they were surplus copies from defunct play groups, or, more likely, sold to bring in money for the actors and sharers of the playgroup in times of hardship .In the plague years the theatres were closed and one of these closures was from 1592-1594. Significantly, in subsequent years there followed a long list of printed plays. Many of these plays appeared later in a longer, rewritten or edited form in the First Folio almost three decades later.

When times were harsh, Pembroke's Men are reported on at least one such occasion to have sold their possessions. Their valuables included their horse carrying their *Farburden*, a bundle of costumes and effects whilst the players walked on returning from touring: an indication of their desperate need for income.

The early texts referred to may have originated from the commissioning of plays by the Lord Chamberlain for court occasions, or possibly written for performance at the country houses of the nobility. Such plays were then simplified and shortened, perhaps surreptitiously, for the popular stage by the scribe and sometimes assisted by playwrights.

William Shakespeare was in a position as a scribe or part-time member of the playgroup to sell these texts for his own or the company's profit at this time.

Of the plays that had been published prior to the First Folio of 1623, three were printed from their quartos without amendment. An explanation for this is that these were original texts of court productions.

2. Ten previously unpublished plays of which two had been played at court.

Two plays not published previously, and of which there is no record of court performance, may have been commissioned for the First Folio publication to complete the theme of the volume.

The size and content of the book, intended to be read by a well-educated, cultured audience, is likely to have been produced as a presentation gift for the ambassadors, diplomats and other dignitaries visiting the court of James I, having seen possibly a production at the newly planned amphitheatre.

The long pause in the production of the publication, a period of some eighteen months, may be explained by either one of the numerous proclamations issued by James or by the requirement to rewrite parts of the plays from the existing quartos. In this respect it is pertinent that the poets associated with the title pages of the First Folio may have been the editors commissioned to produce the revisions. Leonard Digges, an accomplished Hispanist and minor poet, a fellow Hispanist, James Mabbe, noted for his translations of Cervantes, and Hugh Holland, a much travelled classical scholar who enjoyed the patronage of the Duke of Buckingham, George Villiers, are all worthy candidates. These classicists together with noted poets, John Florio, the outstanding linguist and Ben Jonson,

Poet Laureate could have, over the eighteen month period finalised the texts of the plays.

According to E. K. Chambers and Professor Alvin Kernan, of the thirty-six plays contained in the volume, twenty-two are recorded as having been played before the court and three plays were performed at noblemen's houses. (Ten of the plays not printed previously were performed at court).

Lord Chamberlains and the initiation of some of the plays

Queen Elizabeth's first Lord Chamberlain was her great uncle, Lord William Howard, 1st Baron Howard of Effingham (1558-1572), who succeeded Edward Hastings as Lord Chamberlain and was appointed to the Privy Council on the Queen's accession on 17 November 1558.

Howard's successor was Thomas Radclyffe, third Earl of Sussex, Lord Chamberlain from 1572-1583 and married to Lady Frances Sidney, the daughter of Sir William Sidney. During Radclyffe's period of office, *A Comedy of Error* was staged at Court in 1577. Other versions of the First Folio plays produced during Radcliffe's tenure were *Richard III, Taming of the Shrew, Titus Andronicus* and *Two Gentlemen of Verona. Titus* may have been performed under the earlier title of *Titus Gissipus* by the Children of Paul's at court in 1577according to E. K. Chambers. *Henry VI, Part II, Henry VI, Part III* and *Henry VI, Part I* were written during Radcliffe's tenure, and a version of *Titus Andronicus* originated in Lord Derby's company

Sussex was followed by Charles, second Lord Howard of Effingham for a short period, from Christmas 1583 until 1585.

From July 1585 Elizabeth's half-brother or cousin Henry Carey, 1st Lord Hunsdon, held the office until 1596; the Chamberlainship then passed to William Brooke, seventh Lord Cobham, from July 1596 until March 1597, when the office reverted to George Carey, 2nd Lord Hunsdon, who was Lord Chamberlain until the end of Elizabeth's reign.

Several plays can be connected to George Carey's Chamberlainship: *The Merry Wives of Windsor,* and *Henry IV parts 1 and 2.*

George Carey was replaced by Thomas, Lord Howard of Walden, created Earl of Suffolk by King James in May 1603. This courtier held the post until 1614 when he became Lord Treasurer. The position was then conferred on Robert Carr, Earl of Somerset.

In 1615 when Somerset was implicated in the poisoning of Thomas Overbury, William, third Earl of Pembroke, became Lord Chamberlain and remained in office until 1626.

In Queen Anne's court in 1603 Robert, Baron Sidney of Penshurst, later Ist Earl of Leicester became her Lord Chamberlain. On 4th May 1605 James granted Sidney the title of Viscount Lisle.

Royal entertainment

The royal entertainment during the two decades prior to 1583 sheds light on the question of the discrepancy in actor numbers. The plays at Queen Elizabeth's court during the early years of her reign were performed either by the trained choristers and actors of the Children of the Chapel or the Children of Paul's. The Queen was also entertained by many playgroups such as Ferdinando Strange's Men, who in their early years were acrobats, tumblers and musicians, but who were later to perform in simple plays suitable for the audiences of the expanding popular theatre.

The presence at court of the various troupes of players during Elizabeth's reign requires an explanation. The particular skills of these men traditionally were as touring entertainers providing amusement for the populace. Yet their shows of swordplay, wrestling, song and dance, comic patter and foolery would find a place in court diversions on festive occasions. The players would also have been useful in supplying personnel for the minor cast and crowd scenes of serious drama.

In the twenty years before 1583 a total of eleven adult companies performed at court and the Lord Chamberlain's Men appeared once in the season, immediately preceding the formation of the Queen's Men, who were created at the express command of Queen Elizabeth. The royal troupe then became the dominant acting company at court for the remainder of the decade. Edmund Tilney, Master of the Revels, through Sir Francis Walsingham was ordered to assemble the personnel in March 1583. Tilney selected two or three players from the existing companies: some players were drawn from Leicester's Servants, although James Burbage was not selected. The new Queen's Men totalled twelve in number, allowing for plays of greater complexity, whereas the number of Sussex's Men remained at six cast members. It is relevant to note that at least one of the Queen's Men was noted for his skill in dancing the jig.

From the time when the Queen overcame court rivalry by competing noblemen and insisting upon her own 'Men' the type of plays written changed considerably. As Andrew Gurr states in *The Shakespearean Companies*:

> *In the seventy years from the writing of Skelton's "Magnificence" to Marlowe's "Tamburlaine" the prescription of the cast of a play stageable by an adult travelling company changed substantially.*

As Gurr indicates, it is clear that the plays at court after 1583 reflect the change in the number of actors required for these plays.

John Stow wrote of this period in his Annals (1615):

> Comedians and stage-players of former times were very poor and ignorant...but being now grown very skillful and exquisite actors for all matters, they were entertained into the service of diverse great lords: out of which there were twelve of the best chosen, and...were sworn the Queen's servants and were allowed wages and liveries as Grooms of the Chamber.

By the accession of James I, many of the boy choristers had matured and provided superior acting skills for the King's Men.

The Queen's company was officially authorised to play at two locations in London, the Bel Savage Inn on Ludgate Hill, and the Bell Inn in Gracechurch Street, within the City near Bishopsgate. The former was a large open-air venue, but the latter may have been enclosed. These theatres were suitable for rehearsals for court entertainment. Andrew Gurr suggests the use of these theatres may have been a forerunner of the decision of the King's company in 1608 to use two playhouses, one for the rehearsal of plays for the courtier class and one for the populace.

Performances at court of twenty two of the plays from the First Folio and four recorded at noble houses.

Comedies

The Merry Wives of Windsor - This was prepared from a transcript by Ralph Crane. Probably originally written for the celebration of the Order of the Garter investiture of the Duke of Wurttemberg in 1597, commissioned by the Lord Chamberlain, George, 2nd Baron Hunsdon, patron of Thomas Nashe. The play was also performed by the King's Players during the celebration of the wedding, on 4th November 1604, in the Great Hall at Whitehall, when William, Earl of Pembroke, married Mary Talbot, daughter of Gilbert Talbot, 7th Earl of Shrewsbury.

Much Ado About Nothing - One apparent source of the play could have been one of the Italian *Novelle* ('Tales') by Matteo Bandello in 1554, or by Michelangelo Florio for Herbert entertainment or through the translation by Francois de Belleforest. A version appears in Book V of *Orlando Furioso* by Ludovico Ariosto, in an English translation in 1591. Yet another source may have been

William Painter's *Palace of Pleasure* dedicated to Ambrose Dudley, Earl of Warwick, uncle of Mary, Countess of Pembroke.'

The earliest printed text states that *Much Ado About Nothing* was "sundry times publicly acted" prior to 1600 and it is likely that the play made its debut in the autumn or winter of 1598–1599. The earliest recorded performances are two that were given at court between December and May 1613, during the festivities preceding the marriage of Princess Elizabeth and Frederick V, Elector Palatine, on the 14th February 1613.

Love's Labour's Lost - This play is likely to have been written by Anthony Bacon, poet and scholar, who had resided at the court of Navarre for several years. Unquestionably written for the court of Queen Elizabeth, the work may have marked the planned Order of the Garter investiture of the French King Henri IV, previously King of Navarre. Though first published in quarto in 1598, the play's title page suggests a revision of an earlier version of the play. While there are no obvious sources for the play's plot, the four main characters are loosely based on figures at the Navarre court. The play was performed before Prince Henry in 1603 at Whitehall or Hampton Court and before Queen Anne between 9th-14th January 1605, either at the Earl of Southampton or Viscount Cranborne's residence.

A Midsummer Night's Dream - This is believed to have been written between 1590 and 1596. It is unknown exactly when *A Midsummer Night's Dream* was written or first performed, but on the basis of topical references and an allusion to Edmund Spenser's *Epithalamion*, it is usually dated 1595 or early 1596. Some have theorised that the play might have been written for an aristocratic wedding, for example that of Elizabeth Carey, Lady Berkeley. E. K. Chambers suggests that it may have been performed at the wedding of the Earl of Derby and Lady Elizabeth Vere; others suggest that it was written for the Queen to celebrate the feast day of St. John. The play was performed before Prince Henry at Hampton Court on 1st January 1603.

The Merchant of Venice – This play is believed to have been written between 1596 and 1598. Elements of the 14th-century tale *Pecorone* by Giovanni Fiorentino are present in it, which was published in Milan in 1558. Parts of the trial scene are also found in *The Orator* by Alexandre Sylvane, published in translation in 1596. The play was mentioned by Francis Meres in 1598 in his commonplace book.

The title page of the first edition in 1600 states that it had been performed *"divers times"* by that date. The play was entered in the Register of the Stationers' Company by James Roberts on 22nd July 1598 under the title *The Merchant of Venice*, otherwise called *The Jew of Venice*. The play was printed again in 1619 in the 'False Folio' by William Jaggard. The 1600 edition is generally regarded as being accurate and reliable. It is the basis for the text published in the 1623 First Folio, which adds a number of stage directions, mainly musical cues. *The Merchant of Venice* was performed at Whitehall on 10 February (Shrove Sunday) 1605 and a further performance at court was intended on 12th February 1605, but not played.

The Taming of the Shrew - one of the Italian plays, (see Chapter 10). A version of a play with a similar name, *Taming of a Shrew,* was performed at the wedding of Mary Browne, Countess of Southampton, to Sir Thomas Heneage on 2nd May 1594. Mary Browne was the daughter of Anthony Browne, 1st Viscount Montagu, by his first marriage to Lady Jane Radclyffe, a daughter of Robert Radclyffe, 1st Earl of Sussex, and Lady Margaret Stanley. Thomas Heneage was a patron of the arts; one of his protégés was Sir Philip Sidney.

Efforts to establish the play's date of composition are complicated by its relationship with another Elizabethan play with an almost identical plot, but different wording and character names, *A Pleasant Conceited Historie, called the taming of a Shrew*. The *Shrew's* exact relationship with *A Shrew* is unknown.

Richard II - The First Folio version of the play is not the same as the play that Queen Elizabeth remarked upon after the ill-conceived Essex rebellion, nor does the First Folio version appear to be the play witnessed by Simon Forman at the Globe. There was a performance at court of a play called *Richard II* at court on 30th April 1608 and a further performance before Prince Henry during January 1603.

Henry IV, Part 1 - This is believed to have been written no later than 1597. The primary source for the play was the second edition in 1587 of Raphael Holinshed's *Chronicles,* which in turn drew on Edward Hall's *The Union of the Two Illustrious Families of Lancaster and York.* Scholars have also assumed that the playwright was familiar with Samuel Daniel's poem on the civil wars. Daniel's patron was Mary, Countess of Pembroke, and it was written during the tenure of George, 2nd Lord Hunsdon, as Lord Chamberlain – the patron of Thomas Nashe.

Henry IV, Part 2 - It is believed to have been written sometime between 1596 and 1599. The playwright is most likely to have been Thomas Nashe, who seems to have interrupted his composition of *Henry IV, Part 2* somewhere around Act 3 - 4, so as to concentrate on writing *Merry Wives of Windsor*. This play in Nashe's style may have been commissioned for a meeting of the Order of the Garter, possibly the one due to be held on 23rd April 1597. The recipients were Frederick, Duke of Württemberg, Thomas, 1st Lord Howard de Walden, later 1st Earl of Suffolk, George Carey, 2nd Lord Hunsdon, Charles (Blount), 8th Lord Mountjoy, afterwards Earl of Devonshire, and Sir Henry Lee

The play was entered into the Register of the Stationers' Company in 1600 by the booksellers Andrew Wise and William Aspley and published in quarto the same year. The play was not published again until the First Folio in 1623. Records indicate that the play was performed at court in 1600 before the Flemish Ambassador and records suggest that both parts of *Henry IV* were acted at court in 1612 – the records refer to the plays as *Sir John Falstaff* and *Hotspur*. A record, apparently to the Second part of Falstaff, may indicate a court performance in 1619.

Henry V - This is believed to have been written around 1599. The first Quarto text was entitled *The Chronicle History of Henry the fift*; it was entered into the Register of the Stationers' Company on 14thAugust 1600 and published before the end of the year. The play became *The Life of Henry the Fifth* in the First Folio text.

There is also a bad quarto of *Henry V*. Quarto 1 was a shortened version of the play suitable for performing at the popular theatre. The primary sources for *Henry V* are the same as those referred to in the *Henry IV* plays, and again show a marked familiarity with Samuel Daniel's poem on the civil wars. Daniel was the tutor of William and Philip Herbert and a member of the Wilton circle. An earlier play, the *Famous Victories of Henry V* is also generally believed to have been a model for the work.

The final revised or original superior text was printed in the First Folio in 1623. The play was performed at court on 14th May 1594. It was also performed at the Jacobean court at Whitehall on 7th January 1605 by the King's Men.

Henry VI, Part 2 - This is believed to have been written in 1591. This play has the largest cast of all the First Folio plays, which indicates an important court occasion for its performance. The *Hall and Holinshed Chronicles* were consulted, together with Richard Grafton's *A Chronicle at Large* of 1569 and possibly John Foxe's *Acts and Monuments, Book of Martyrs* of 1563.

On 12th March 1594 a play was entered in the Stationers' Register by the bookseller Thomas Millington and printed in quarto by Thomas Creede later that year as *The First part of the Contention betwixt the two famous Houses of Yorke and Lancaster, with the death of the good Duke Humphrey: And the banishment and death of the Duke of Suffolke, and the Tragicall end of the proud Cardinall of VVinchester, vvith the notable Rebellion of Jacke Cade: And the Duke of Yorkes first claime vnto the Crowne*. It has been theorised that *The Contention* is a reported text of a performance of what is today called *Henry VI, Part II*. If so, the original court play was written no later than 1594.

This play is referred to in Greene's *Groatsworth of Wit*, as discussed in an earlier chapter, confirms the suggestion that the play may have been written several years earlier.

The text of the play that today forms *Henry VI* was not published until the 1623 First Folio, under the title *The second Part of Henry the Sixth, with the death of the Good Duke Humfrey.*

Henry VI, Part 3 - According to some scholars this early play contains indications of the work of Marlowe, Greene, Peele and Nashe.

Apart from Hall and Holinshed the authors were influenced by Sackville and Norton's *Gorboduc,* a play for the court of 1561. Thomas Kyd's *The Spanish Tragedy* may also have served as a minor influence.

Richard III - is believed to have been written around 1592 and the play was entered into the Register of the Stationers' Company on 20th October 1597, and published later that year, Parallels with Christopher Marlowe's *Edward II* may indicate his participation.

The First Folio text is longer than the source play Quarto three, and contains some fifty additional passages, amounting to more than two hundred lines. However, the Quarto contains some twenty-seven passages, amounting to about thirty-seven lines, which are absent from the Folio. The two texts also contain hundreds of other differences.

The earliest certain court performance occurred on 16th or 17th November 1633, when Charles I and Queen Henrietta Maria watched it on the Queen's birthday.

Tragedies

Troilus and Cressida - This was believed to have been written in 1602 and printed after the rest of the Folio was completed. It was published in quarto in two separate editions, both in 1609. The play may have been influenced by Thomas Dekker and Henry Chettle's play of the same name, of which only a fragmentary plot remains. The plotline is sourced from Chaucer's version of the tale, *Troilus and Criseyde,* John Lydgate's *Troy Book* and Caxton's translation of the *Recuyell of the Historyes of Troye.*

Chaucer's source was *Il Filostrato* by Boccaccio, which in turn derives from a 12th century French text, Benoît de Sainte-Maure's *Roman de Troie.* The story is drawn from Homer's *Iliad,* perhaps in the translation by George Chapman, and from various medieval and Renaissance retellings.

It is not known whether the play was ever performed in its own time because the two editions contradict each other: one announces on the title page that the play had been recently performed at the Globe; the other claims in a preface that it is a new play that has never been staged. The play was entered into the Register of the Stationers' Company on 7th February 1603.

One of the first printed quartos still in existence is a good quality script of *Titus Andronicus,* a 'revenge tragedy'. Professor Brian Vickers has, with great skill and an open mind, analysed the content and proved that the main part of the play was written by George Peele, in collaboration with other writers. Peele was writing for Thomas Radclyffe, 3rd Earl of Sussex, patron of Sussex's Men – one of the most powerful aristocrats during the middle years of Queen Elizabeth's reign. Sussex became Lord Chamberlain in 1572.

Titus Andronicus was performed at court on 6th February 1594.

Romeo and Juliet - This Italian play may derive from *Mariotto and Gianozza* by Massucio Salernitano and may have been initiated by Michelangelo Florio. A further source was Arthur Brooke's *The Tragical History of Romeus and Juliet* of 1562. The date of the first performance is unknown. The first Quarto, printed in 1597, says that *"it hath been often (and with great applause) plaid publiquely,"* setting the first performance before that date. The Lord Chamberlain's Men were certainly the first to perform it, the second Quarto actually names one of its actors, Will Kemp, instead of Peter in a line in Act five. The play was performed before Prince Henry during January 1603 at Hampton Court.

Hamlet - The longest play in the First Folio, *Hamlet* was eminently suitable for court performance or reading. Professor Alvin Kernan suggests that the play was probably performed at Oxford or Cambridge before King James on his progress south prior to his coronation as King of England.

Although there is no specific record of the play's performance at court it appears to have been written for the entertainment of the state visit of the royal of Queen Anne's relations from Denmark in 1605.

King Lear - Originally drafted between 1603, its first known performance was in 1607. Thomas Kyd, a protégé of Mary, Countess of Pembroke, wrote a play called *Leir,* based on various accounts of the semi-legendary figure, Leir of Britain.

Edmund Spenser's *The Faerie Queene,* published 1590, also contains a character named Cordelia, who also dies, as in King Lear. Spenser was Sir Henry Sidney's protégé and father of Mary, Countess of Pembroke.

King Lear was performed at court on 26th December, St Stephen's Night, 1606, by the King's Men and again at court in 1594.

Othello - This is believed to have been written in 1603, and based on the short story *Un Capitano Moro* ('A Moorish Captain') by Cinthio, a disciple of Boccaccio, first published in 1565 (see Chapter 10).

Cinthio's tale was part of his *Gli Hecatommithi* (1565), a collection of one hundred tales in the style of Giovanni Boccaccio's *Decameron.* No English translation of Cinthio was available and verbal echoes in *Othello* are closer to the Italian original than to Gabriel Chappuy's 1584 French translation. Cinthio's tale may have been based on an actual incident occurring in Venice about 1508. It also resembles an incident described in the earlier tale of *The Three Apples*, one of the stories narrated in the *One Thousand and One Nights* (Arabian Nights).

The play was performed before Queen Elizabeth in 1602 and a further mention of the play is found in a 1604 Revels Office account, which records that on "*Hallamas Day, being the first of Nouembar ... the Kings Maiesties plaiers*" performed "*A Play in the Banketinghouse at Whit Hall Called The Moor of Venis.*" The work is attributed to "*Shaxberd.*"

The play was entered into the Register of the Stationers' Company on 6th October 1621 by Thomas Walkley, and was first published in quarto format by him in 1622:

"*Tragœdy of Othello, The Moore of Venice. As it hath beene diuerse times acted at the Globe, and at the Black-Friers, by his Maiesties Seruants. Written by William Shakespeare. London. Printed by N. O. [Nicholas Okes] for Thomas Walkley, and are to be sold at his shop, at the Eagle and Child, in Brittans Bursse, 1622.*"

Plays which were not printed prior to 1623, but nevertheless some were performed before the court

The Tempest - This play was set into type from a manuscript prepared by Ralph Crane, a professional scrivener employed by the King's Men. Crane produced a high-quality text, with formal act/scene divisions, frequent use of parentheses and hyphenated forms, and other identifiable features. *The* Tempest is a work generally accepted to be written by Thomas Middleton and performed at court by the King's Men on 1st November 1611, Hallowmas and in the Christmas period in 1612/13.

The Two Gentlemen of Verona - Another transcript by Ralph Crane believed to have been written before 1588, based on the assumption that Launce, the clownish servant of Proteus, and his dog Crab, likely is a reference to Richard Tarlton (who died in 1588) and his dog Crab. The play's author drew on the Spanish prose romance *Los Siete Libros de la Diana* ('The Seven Books of the Diana') by the Portuguese writer Jorge de Montemayor. *Two Gentlemen of Verona* was performed before Prince Henry in January 1603.

Measure for Measure - Probably another Ralph Crane transcript. On 27th December 1604 Philip, Earl of Montgomery, second son of Mary, Countess of Pembroke, married Susan de Vere, daughter of Edward de Vere, 17th Earl of Oxford. The previous evening 26th December, St Stephen's Night, witnessed a performance at court of *Measure for Measure*.

An early moral play now lost called *The Marriage of Mind and Measure was* acted by the Children of Paul's at Court in 1579; this may have been a forerunner of *Measure for Measure*.

The Comedy of Errors - Possibly a later version of an early play the *History of Error*, or possibly a translation by Frances, Countess of Sussex (neé Sidney), for Queen Elizabeth's New Year's Gift Day. A record suggests *The Comedy of Errors* was further performed during the wedding celebrations of Philip Earl of Montgomery and Susan de Vere, daughter of the Earl of Oxford, at Whitehall on 28th December 1604.

As You Like It - This play was said to have been performed at Wilton, one of the country homes of the Earl and Countess of Pembroke to entertain King James and his court on 2nd December 1603.

All's Well That Ends Well - The play is derived from Giovanni Boccaccio's *Giletta of Narbonne* a traditional tale known to Michelangelo Florio, resident in England in 1550-1554, tutor to Lady Jane Grey eldest daughter of the Duke of Suffolk and Henry Herbert, later 2nd Earl of Pembroke. During the 1590's Herbert was patron of Pembroke's Men who performed a version of *Henry V1 part 1*.

Twelfth Night - A performance is described at Queen Elizabeth's court in the research of Dr Leslie Hotson. The play is believed to have been written around 1601–02 as a Twelfth Night's entertainment for the close of the Christmas season. Plot elements drawn from the short story *Of Apollonius and Silla* by Barnabe Rich, based on a story by Matteo Bandello. The first recorded performance at court was on 2nd February 1602, at Candlemas, the formal end of Christmastide in the year's calendar. Barnabe Riche was a member of the Wilton Group under the patronage of Mary, Countess of Pembroke. It was performed before Queen Elizabeth in 1600/1 and at court on 6th April 1618.

The Winter's Tale - Another transcript by Ralph Crane. The main plot of *The Winter's Tale* is taken from Robert Greene's pastoral romance *Pandosto*, published in 1588. The changes to the plot are uncharacteristically slight, especially in light of the romance's undramatic nature, and a fidelity to it gives *The Winter's Tale* is its most distinctive feature: the sixteen-year gap between the third and fourth acts. The style of the play tends to suggest Robert Greene as the originator of the play with later revisions by the editors of the First Folio. Performed before the King on 5th November 1611 at Whitehall and during the wedding celebrations of the King's daughter Princess Elizabeth and Frederick V, Elector Palatine, on 14th February 1613. The play was again performed at court on 18th January 1618.

Histories

King John - The play is written entirely in verse, as is *Richard II. King John* is closely related to an anonymous history play, *The Troublesome Reign of King John*, written about 1589. It has been suggested that *King John* was the earlier play.

The play is derived from Holinshed's *Chronicles* and shows the influence of John Foxe's *Acts and Monuments*. It was mentioned among the plays in the *Palladis Tamia*, the commonplace book of Francis Meres.

Henry VI, Part 1 - This likely derives from an annotated transcript of Thomas Nashe, the main author's, manuscript. Nashe's primary source was Edward Hall's *The Union of the Two Noble and Illustre Families of Lancaster and York* of 1548.

Henslowe's Diary records a performance of a play by Lord Strange's Men called *Harey Vj* (Henry VI) on 3rd March 1592 at the Rose Theatre in Southwark. Henslowe refers to the play as "ne" (which most critics take to mean 'new'). *Harey Vj* is usually accepted as being *Henry VI part 1* for two reasons: firstly, it is unlikely to have been either *2 Henry VI or 3 Henry VI*, as they were published in 1594 and 1595 respectively.

There is a reference in Thomas Nashe's *Piers Penniless his Supplication to the Devil* (entered into the Stationers' Register on 8 August 1592), which supports the theory that *Harey Vj* is *Henry VI part 1*. Nashe praises a play that features Lord Talbot:

> How would it have joyed brave Talbot (the terror of the French), to think that after he had lain two hundred years in his tomb, he should triumph again on the stage, and have his bones new embalmed with the tears of ten thousand spectators (at least), who in the tragedian that represents his person imagine they behold him fresh bleeding.

It is thought that Nashe is here referring to *Harey Vj*, (i.e. *Henry VI part 1*), as there is no other candidate for a play featuring Talbot from this time period (although again, there is the possibility that both Henslowe and Nashe are referring to a now lost play).

The play was not published until the 1623 First Folio, under the title *The first part of Henry the Sixt*.

Henry VIII - Typeset from a fair copy of John Fletcher's manuscript, derived from Raphael Holinshed's *Chronicles*. It is generally agreed by scholars that the play was written for the celebrations of the betrothal or marriage of Princess Elizabeth to the Elector Palatine, although the first recorded performance at court was on 29th June 1613. A version of the play was also performed at the Globe in 1613 when a cannon shot employed for special effects ignited the theatre's thatched roof (and the beams), burning the original building to the ground.

Coriolanus - Set from a high-quality authorial transcript, this is possibly an original play prepared for the First Folio from a play believed to have been written between 1605 and 1608. *Coriolanus* is largely based on the *Life of Coriolanus* in Thomas North's translation of Plutarch's *The Lives of the Noble Grecians and Romans* of 1579. The wording of Menenius's speech about the body politic is derived from William Camden's *Remaines of a Greater Worke Concerning Britaine* of 1605. Coriolanus was performed at court by the King's Men in 1608.

Timon of Athens - This was set from foul papers, or a transcript of them. Largely attributed to Thomas Middleton, who appears to have drawn upon the twenty-eighth novella of William Painter's *Palace of Pleasure*.

The plot of *Romeo and Juliet* – this Italian play may derive from Mariotto and Gianozza by Salernitano and may have been initiated by Michelangelo Florio together with the original of *The Two Gentlemen of Verona* which also echoes Edmund Spenser. Equally, however, the writing has a similarity to Robert Greene, and yet another candidate as the writer is Thomas Sackville, Earl of Dorset, the author of the very popular play *Gorboduc*. Middleton also drew upon Plutarch's *Lives* and perhaps Lucan's *Dialogues,* as well as a lost comedy on the subject of Timon, allusions to which survive from 1584.

Julius Caesar - Set from a prompt-book, or a transcript of a prompt-book believed to have been written in 1599, the main source of the play is Thomas North's translation of Plutarch's *Lives*. A performance was mentioned by Thomas Platter the Younger in his diary in September 1599. A performance of *Julyus Sesar* was performed on February 1st at court in 1562 and now lost. This may be a forerunner of *Julius Caesar,* a play in Latin by Thomas May, performed in 1616 at the Sidney Sussex Cambridge, or an early version of the First Folio play. *'Caesar's tragedy'*, possibly the same play, was performed during the Christmas celebrations of 1612/13.

Macbeth - Probably set from a prompt-book. The play is believed to have been written between 1599 and 1606, and is most commonly dated to 1606. The earliest account of a performance of what was probably this play is the summer of 1606, when Simon Forman recorded seeing a version of the play at the Globe Theatre. It was first published in the Folio of 1623. This is possibly a play prepared for the celebrations surrounding Prince Henry's acceptance into the Order of the Garter. Two songs from Thomas Middleton's play *The*

Witch of 1615 were included and Middleton is conjectured to have inserted an extra scene involving the witches and Hecate. *Macbeth* was performed by the King's men at court in 1606.

Antony and Cleopatra - Possibly taken from foul papers, or a transcript of them. *Antony and Cleopatra* was probably performed first in about 1607 at Blackfriars Theatre by the King's Men. Its first known appearance in print was in the First Folio of 1623. The plot is based on Thomas North's translation of Plutarch's *Lives* Many scholars believe it was written in 1606–07, although the Shakespearean scholar Alfred Bennett Harbage has argued for an earlier dating, around 1603–04. *Antony and Cleopatra* was entered in the Stationers' Register in May 1608, but it does not seem to have been actually printed until the publication of the First Folio in 1623. Fulke Greville, Baron Brooke, a member of the Wilton circle, wrote a play of the same title, which may be the play in the First Folio.

Modern editions divide the play into a conventional five act structure. The play is articulated in forty separate 'scenes', more than were used for any other play. The large number of scenes is necessary because the action frequently switches between Alexandria, Italy, Messina in Sicily, Syria, Athens, and other parts of Egypt and the Roman Republic. The play contains thirty-four speaking characters, which is fairly typical for a play performed at court.

Cymbeline - Possibly another Ralph Crane transcript, or else copied from the official prompt-book. Based on legends that formed part of the *Matter of Britain* concerning the early Celtic British King Cunobeline; the author freely adapts the legend and adds entirely original sub-plots. Iachimo's wager and subsequent hiding-place inside a chest in order to gather details of Innogen / Imogen's room derive from story II.9 of Giovanni Boccaccio's *Decameron*. This play is linked to Mary, Countess of Pembroke, as it describes a Pembroke property and cave. The first recorded production of *Cymbeline,* as noted by Simon Forman, was in April 1611. It was first published in the First Folio in 1623. When *Cymbeline* was actually written cannot be precisely dated. The play was revived at court for Charles I and Henrietta Maria in 1634 and performed by the King's men before the court in 1608.

The Shakespeare Apocrypha

Doubts concerning the genuine authorship of the First Folio and the questionable claim of William Shakespeare are given further credence by the great number of works attributed to Shakespeare for which there is little historical evidence or literary quality. C. F. Tucker Brooke lists forty-two plays conceivably attributable to him in his own lifetime, but dismisses the majority on their face value, leaving only most of those listed below, with some additions. The principal works in question are: *Sir John Oldcastle, A Yorkshire Tragedy, Birth of Merlin, Fair 'Em, Two Noble Kinsman, The London Prodigall, Locrine, Love's Labour Won, Cardenio, Edward III* and others. Several of these plays have been identified as written by collaborations of various playwrights, while others are simple plays that do not bear comparison with the intelligent, thoughtful plays of the First Folio.

Engraving of Ben Jonson

CHAPTER FIFTEEN

Conclusion

This final chapter notes some key conclusions taken from the study of the First Folio. Although ultimately the explanation for gathering the content and publishing the First Folio of 1623 is unlikely to be revealed in its entirety, the crux of this argument is that the evidence points beyond reasonable doubt to many hands being involved in this monumental and seminal publication.

The content of the First Folio was created during a period of some sixty years, broadly from 1560 to 1620. During this time poetry and drama had reached a high point in England's literary advance. The predominant motivation for its production was to preserve, in dangerous times, the glory of the English language that many educated contemporaries thought had become superior to that of the French and Italian.

Sixty years in the making

The recurrent questioning of the true authorship of the First Folio, throughout several centuries, in itself denotes the considerable doubts concerning the literary capability of William Shaksper, or Shakespeare, of Stratford-upon-Avon to be the acclaimed poet and dramatist. The wealth of evidence that challenges the orthodox, or Stratfordian, position (as summarised in this document) should be sufficiently damning to contradict this myth. An impartial observer may indeed draw the conclusion that the attribution of William Shakespeare's authorship of the First Folio plays and other poetry is completely false.

Another explanation is needed in order to comprehend the purpose of the First Folio and why it was thought necessary to falsify its authorship in such an elaborate, sophisticated manner which has deceived so many generations of scholars, researchers and – most importantly – the general public.

Providing an explanation for the production of the First Folio publication and the other works attributed to William Shakespeare does not, however, consist of identifying a single, alternative writer. It is quite clear that this approach is also unsatisfactory in that it produces other anomalies and contradictions for all the writers put forward as candidates, as detailed in Appendix 7.

Quite apart from which, the immense vocabulary employed and the hugely varying styles shown in the thirty-six plays militates against a sole writer. No other author has ever existed who exhibits the facility, learning or creative scope of the presumed author of the First Folio.

Equally, there may be a justifiable argument that one or more of the main alternative, well-qualified literary candidates, such as Edward de Vere, Francis Bacon, Fulke Greville, William Stanley and Edward Dyer have contributed individually, in collaboration, or as influential patrons affecting the composition of some of the works in question.

There is no doubt too that that there were contributions made to the very early plays, the later compositions and the final versions of many of the First Folio plays by a number of writers. They are likely to have included: Michelangelo Florio, Edward Dyer, Thomas Nashe, Anthony Bacon, Thomas Middleton, John Fletcher, Robert Greene, Robert Ayton, George Peele, John Davies of Hereford, Samuel Daniel, Gabriel Harvey, Thomas Dekker, Henry Chettle and, in the finally edited play texts, Ben Jonson and John Florio.

It may well be significant that Ben Jonson, the principal editor of the First Folio, stayed at Penshurst, the country seat of Sir Robert Sidney, poet and scholar. During the lengthy period Jonson had the opportunity to commence editing the texts later published in the First Folio.

The involvement of so many writers and literary figures in the First Folio is not surprising in that the publication stands as a monument to the remarkable progress of the English language that had occurred during the previous six decades of literary striving within England's cultured society.

The evidence that the First Folio works had involved well-educated writers and men of letters lies in the familiarity shown with a literary landscape which would only be known to those with a university education or private tuition, with possibly a literary skill nurtured at the Inns of Court.

Not only do the works in question require widely read, erudite authorship, but the ability to understand both classical texts and, when English translations were not available, French and Italian literature too. The intellectual content of the majority of First Folio plays was not within the mental grasp of anyone with a limited education.

Utilising their appropriate settings, the plays in the 1623 First Folio dramatise the character and actions of royalty, the aristocracy and leading statesmen during many different ages. The common people, in contrast, are portrayed as ignorant buffoons and appear in the plays (with few exceptions) only to provide comic interludes. These characters too usually speak in prose rather than poetry. Questions alluding to the lives, the ambitions or motivations of ordinary people, whether rural or urban, in the First Folio are simply not considered; their humble lives are of no concern to the writer or the presumed audience: readers or viewers of the works.

The subject and content of the dramas and the principal roles portrayed would thus be eminently suited for Court entertainment. Here, the social structure, lifestyle and the interplay of personalities provided an intellectual background for a well-educated audience. In other words, the dramas were written with a cultured audience in mind. These were spectators or readers who could readily appreciate questions of morality and behaviour as well as recognise the classical allusions that graced the sophisticated English writing in use by the 17th century.

There would have been sufficient time for even the longest First Folio plays to have been performed in its entirety at one of the London royal courts or in a nobleman's country house: an impossibility on the existing popular outdoor stage. Sufficient leisure time was also available for the audience to discuss the finer points raised in the play after its performance, or perhaps during an interval of the accompanying formal dinner.

Queen Elizabeth and King James I were highly educated monarchs with notable debating skills on matters of statecraft, theology and philosophy. It is recorded that twenty-six of the First Folio dramas were performed before their play-minded courts, or at noble houses, either on the existing quartos or by direct documentary record. The court setting would have been appropriate for the intellectual challenges that invited debate. A welcome diversion for royalty and their entourage, as well as the well-educated visiting dignitaries and their diplomatic train.

This picture may be contrasted with the popular theatre of the Elizabethan and early Jacobean age, which housed an audience of almost entirely illiterate, ignorant and noisy members of the public. These were viewers accustomed to the spectacle of bear and bull baiting, or cheering onstage sword fights and wrestling, comic turns, clowning, the 'jig' and coarse repartee between the performers and audience. The spectators in the outdoor theatre were served food and ale during the performance and prostitutes plied their trade. Was this the likely gathering to observe and hear the philosophical and existential questions debated in many First Folio plays or listen to sophisticated verse and poetry?

It is scarcely credible that those who made up the popular theatre assembly of apprentices, artisans, boatmen and seafarers would give their rapt attention to the complexities of *Hamlet* or *Measure for Measure*, as found in the First Folio. The later enclosed theatre audiences, on the other hand, included those of a higher level of education and were more likely to comprehend the more thoughtful plays of the time.

In keeping with the staging of plays, most believably written with a court audience in mind, there were included the English history works. These reaffirm the 'Tudor' royal legitimacy and also honour the ancestors of the Earls of Warwick, as well as several other Jacobean Protestant families related to the Herberts and Sidneys. These are subjects for drama that would not be matters for presentation to the masses, but written as dramatised historical record. It is most likely that abbreviated versions of these original plays did, however, provide theatrical fare for the popular theatre, notably the Lancastrian history plays with their dramatic action and the revenge-themed dramas, such as *Titus Andronicus*.

An integral component of the gestation of the First Folio plays involved the essential role of the literary patron. This nurturing of authors embraced members of the monarchy, aristocracy and those Protestant statesmen closely associated with the court, such as the Lord Chamberlain. These senior officials were often major patrons who, with their well-educated writers, occupied a central function with the patron frequently acting as both censor and initiator of court entertainment.

The Lord Chamberlain was best placed to control the quality and production of plays for special occasions. Examples would be Queen Elizabeth's Gift Day, Twelfth Night and notable wedding celebrations, or sometimes to mark an Order of the Garter ceremony. Links may be found with the upper ranks of society and the prestigious Garter celebrations. Two prime examples being *The Merry Wives of Windsor,* written for Frederick, Duke of Württemberg in 1597, and *Love's Labour's Lost,* written for Henry IV, King of France, in 1590.

Ultimately, the explanation for gathering the content and publishing the First Folio of 1623 is unlikely to be revealed in its entirety but certainly the answer does not lie in simply printing the work of one writer: too much of the evidence points to many hands.

What may be glimpsed from information which exists nearly four centuries later is that many contributing factors were present during the fifty years or so preceding publication. Each aspect had a bearing on a final volume that was not only sold in England, but also sent to the Frankfurt Book Fair. This publication was intended to be a permanent and safe record of the English language and a true account of royal Lancastrian history.

The output of numerous writers, an active literary patronage that included the protection of writers, a vigorous court theatre, English aristocrats pride in their ancestry, the development of the English language, the influence of the Italian Renaissance, humanism and not least, censorship and the increasing dread of Roman Catholic control and loss of free expression all had an impact on the creation of this volume.

All of these aspects of English society played their part and intermingled to produce the motivation for the 1623 publication and the cloak of deception that has misled readers for so long.

APPENDICES

Appendix 1

Similarity of First Folio titles to earlier works

There is another aspect concerning the origins of the First Folio dramas which should also be taken into account: a number of plays dating from the mid to late 16th century bear similar titles to those of the later period. The texts of the early plays have unfortunately been lost so it is impossible to compare them, but there remains the possibility that they represent original works from which First Folio plays derive. Examples are:

(Listed in Annals of English Drama 975-1700.)

Romeo and Juliet, dated 1560-62, and a Latin version, *Romeus and Julietta*, was written but not performed in 1615, of which a fragment remains. *Julius Caesar*, dated 1562 was played at court and a Latin play of the same name by Thomas May was also performed.

In 1577 the *History of Error*, and in 1579 *The Marriage of Mind and Measure* were both played by Paul's Boys at court.

In 1589 a play called *Hamlet*, possibly by Thomas Kyd, was performed by the Chamberlain's and the Admiral's companies, and a further play, possibly by Kyd, called *The True Chronicle of King Leir*, was probably performed by the Queen's Men in 1591.

A plot fragment of *Troilus and Cressida* remains of a play that was performed by the Admiral's Men in 1599, written by Chettle and Dekker.

A play called *Richard III*, by Samuel Rowley was performed by Palsgrave's Company in 1623, but unfortunately is also lost.

Appendix 2

Early popular theatre

Research by E. K. Chambers, the theatre historian, records that the first open air theatres in London were the Saracen's Head, Islington and The Boar's Head, Aldgate both in use by 1557. Within a decade or so other play-acting venues were evidently popular: The George Inn, Southwark, The Red Lion Inn, on the Stepney-Whitechapel border, The Theatre, Shoreditch, The Bell Inn and the Cross Keys Inn both in Gracechurch Street, The Bull Inn, Bishopsgate and the Bel Savage Inn, Ludgate Hill.

Other popular places of entertainment included The Swan, Paris Gardens, Bankside, active by 1595 and which housed Pembroke's Men, who staged the infamous play *The Isle of Dogs,* by Thomas Nashe and Ben Jonson. The Swan offered other popular entertainments such as swashbuckling competitions and bull/bear-baiting, but although it was an impressive construction in a popular venue, it was an unsuccessful venture. There were other attractions: The Fortune, Finsbury, assigned to Philip Henslowe and Edward Alleyne, was opened in 1600 and occupied by the Admiral's Men. The Boars Head Inn, Cheapside, may have housed Derby's Men 1599-1601. The Curtain was active by 1601. The Red Bull Inn was referred to in a play of 1607. To the above need to be added the stage venues of The Hope, Bankside, and the Porters Hall.

The indoor auditoriums of The Blackfriars and The Whitefriars were within converted monastery buildings situated outside the jurisdiction of the City of London. These indoor theatres were home to the boy playing troupes: significant contributors to the indoor theatre and court productions during the Elizabethan and Jacobean period.

The Theatre built in 1567 is of particular interest. Proprietors John Brayne and John Reynolds were a grocer and a carpenter, respectively. Brayne, previously constructor of the Red Lion playing-inn, was a brother-in-law of the actor and theatre entrepreneur, James Burbage. Both men were, of necessity, members of their respective Trades Guilds and were thus authorised to construct a building and sell food and alcohol in the same way that a licensed inn would serve their customers. The name Theatre became accepted as a general term for playhouse.

Following a dispute with the landlord the 'sharers' in the playing company in occupation, The Lord Chamberlain's Men dismantled The Theatre building and used the timbers to construct the famous Globe theatre across the river at Bankside 1588-9. The original Globe burnt down in 1613 and was re-built the following year.

Appendices

The conflagration at the Globe occurred during a performance of *"All is True... representing some principal pieces of the reign of Henry VIII,"* according to a letter from Sir Henry Wooton, author and diplomat. Wootton continued,

> *"which was set forth with many extraordinary circumstances of pomp and majesty, even to the matting of the stage; the Knights of the Order with their Georges and garters, the Guards with their embroidered coats etc."*

This description indicates the importance of a colourful, elaborate show on the popular stage for the taste of their mass audience.

Appendix 3

Popular stage entertainment - contemporary comment

Thomas Platter, a native of Basel, visited England in 1599. The following excerpt from his diary, translated from Basel German, describes the many popular amusements and spectacles to be witnessed in Elizabethan London.

> On September 21st after lunch about two o'clock, I and my party crossed the water, and there in the house with the thatched roof witnessed an excellent performance of the tragedy of the first Emperor Julius Caesar with a cast of some fifteen people, when the play was over they danced very marvellously and gracefully together as is their wont, two dressed as men and two as women.
>
> On another occasion not far from our inn, in the suburb at Bishopsgate, if I remember, also after lunch, I beheld a play in which they presented diverse nations and an Englishman struggling together for a maiden; he overcame them all except the German who won the girl in a tussle, and then sat down by her side, when he and his servant drank themselves tipsy, so that they were both fuddled and the servant proceeded to hurl his shoe at his master's head, whereupon they both fell asleep; meanwhile the Englishman stole into the tent and absconded with the German's prize, thus in his turn outwitting the German; in conclusion they danced very charmingly in English and Irish fashion. Thus daily at two in the afternoon, London has two, sometimes three plays running in different places, competing with each other, and those which play best obtain most spectators. The playhouses are so constructed that they play on a raised platform, so that everyone has a good view. There are different galleries and places, however, where the seating is better and more comfortable and therefore more expensive. For whoever cares to stand below only pays one English penny, but if he wishes to sit he enters by another door and pays another penny, while if he desires to sit in the most comfortable seats, which are cushioned, where he not only sees everything well, but can also be seen, then he pays yet another English penny at another door. And during the performance food and drink are carried round the audience, so that for what one cares to pay one may also have refreshment. The actors are most expensively and elaborately costumed; for it is the English usage for eminent lords or knights at their decease to bequeath and leave almost the best of their clothes to their serving men, which it is unseemly for the

latter to wear, so that they offer them then for sale for a small sum to the actors.

How much time then they may merrily spend daily at the play everyone knows who has ever seen them play or act."

Thomas Platter continues…

With these and many more amusements the English pass their time, learning at the play what is happening abroad; indeed men and womenfolk visit such places without scruple, since the English for the most part do not travel much, but prefer to learn foreign matters and take their pleasures at home.

There are a great many inns, taverns, and beer-gardens scattered about the city, where much amusement may be had with eating, drinking, fiddling, and the rest, as for instance in our hostelry, which was visited by players almost daily. And what is particularly curious is that the women as well as the men, in fact more often than they, will frequent the taverns or ale-houses for enjoyment…

This eyewitness account of the nationalistic themed burlesque shown above does not describe the experience of witnessing a play of quality nor, as discussed earlier, does the vulgar, noisy behaviour of the London citizen equate to a ready appreciation of fine verse. There is huge gulf of literary comprehension between the First Folio plays and the fare of the popular theatre that was served to its uneducated audience.

A further comment from John Lyly underlines the atmosphere of the public playhouse. Lyly's prologues, written in the 1580s for 'boy' plays at Blackfriars and Paul's, has the poet more than once express the hope that the gentlemanly audience in the halls would react with *"soft smiling, not loude laughing,"* or at worst would be too courteous to hiss. This behaviour was evidently a common reaction elsewhere by London theatre audiences.

The most prominent feature of the amphitheatres was the physicality of audience responses to the play. The sitters in the galleries matched the reactions of the section standing in the yard. As Gosson said in 1596,

in publike Theaters, when any notable shew passeth over the stage, the people arise in their seates, & stand upright with delight and eagernesse to view it well.

(Stephen Gosson, The Trumpet of Warre, 1598).

Applause, too, was delivered with both cheering and clapping. Michael Drayton has a sonnet, written in about 1600, which refers to his writing plays for Philip Henslowe at the Rose amphitheatre, sitting in the *"thronged Theater"* and listening to the *"Showts and Claps at ev'ry little pawse, / When the proud Round on ev'ry side hath rung."*

Marston, Dekker and many other poets used epilogues to appeal for applause at the end of their plays, but it seems that it was not only at the play's end that applause came. Moreover it was not just *"brawny hands"* which delivered the audience's opinion. In 1616, William Fennor brought to the reader's eyes a performance recently given to a royal audience and offered a pained account of his play's original reception at the Fortune amphitheatre:

> *Yet to the multitude it nothing shewed;*
> *They screwed their scurvy jawes and look't awry,*
> *Like hissing snakes adjudging it to die:*
> *When wits of gentry did applaud the same,*
> *With silver shouts of high lowd sounding fame:*
> *Whil'st understanding grounded men contemn'd it.*
> *And wanting wit (like fooles to judge) condemn'd it.*
> *Clapping, or hissing, is the onely meane*
> *That tries and searches out a well writ Sceane,*
> *So it is thought by Ignoramus crew,*
> *But that good wits acknowledge's untrue;*
> *The stinkards oft will hisse without a cause,*
> *And for a baudy jeast will give applause.*
> *Let one but aske the reason why they roare*
> *They'll answere, cause the rest did so before.*

Tatham's verse confirms the suspicion that when an audience was addressed as *"Gentlemen"* or *"Gentles"* the poet was likely to ask for less riotous behaviour than he had reason to expect.

> *Here Gentlemen our Anchor's fixt; And wee*
> *(Disdaining Fortunes mutability)*
> *Expect your kinde acceptance; then wee'l sing*
> *(Protected by your smiles our ever-spring;)*
> *As pleasant as if wee had still possest*
> *Our lawfull Portion out of Fortunes brest:*

Onely wee would request you to forbeare
Your wonted custome, banding Tyle, or Peare,
Against our cu'taines, to allure us forth.

It may serve as a rough measure of the changes in audience behaviour developed through the 17th century, if we set Jonson's parody of a gallant at Blackfriars in 1616 against what Clitus-Alexandrinus (the Inns of Court poetaster, Richard Brathwait) wrote about an amphitheatre playhouse in the 1620s. Brathwait's Theophrastan character, *"A Ruffian,"* is a belligerent swaggerer who attends plays on his own terms.

> *... To a play they will hazard to go, though with never a rag of money: where after the second Act, when the Doore is weakly guarded, they will make forcible entrie; a knock with a Cudgell is the worst; whereat though they grumble, they rest pacified upon their admittance. Forthwith, by violent assault and assent, they aspire to the two-pennie roome; where being furnished with Tinder, Match, and a portion of decayed Barmoodas, they smoake it most terribly applaud a prophane jeast unmeasurably, and in the end grow distastefully rude to all the Companie. At the conclusion of all, they single out their dainty Doxes, to doze up a fruitlesse day with a sinnefull evening.*

By the end of the second decade of the 17th century the character of entertainment for the masses remained physical 'shows' that did not meet with the approval of their betters. In his capacity as Lord Chamberlain, the Earl of Pembroke, although a great patron of the arts, wrote in 1622 to all mayors, JP's and sheriffs:

> *...that there are many and very great disorders and abuses daily committed by diverse and sundry companies of stage players, tumblers, vaulters, dancers on the ropes, and also by such as go about with motions and shows, and other like kind of persons, who, by virtue of their licenses: do abusively claim to themselves a kind of licentious freedom to travel as well as to show, play, and exercise in the kingdom.*

These players and their 'shows' were to Pembroke *"...full of scandal and offence both against the Church and state."*

Another severe condemnation of the popular theatre was that of Anthony Munday, born in 1560, author and translator, in his 1580 *A second and third blast of retrait from plaies and Theaters,* which describes his experience of plays and the reasons that led him to turn from them:

> *I confess that ere this I haue bene a great affecter of that vaine art of Plaie-making...What I shal speake of the abuse of plaies by my own knowl-edge... Some citizens wius. vpon whom the Lord for ensample to others hath laid his hands, haue euven on their death beds with tears confessed, that they haue receiued at these spectacles such filthie infections, as haue turned their mind from chast cogitations, and made them of honest women light huswiu; by them they haue dishonored the vessels of holiness; and brought their husbandes intocontempt, their children into question, their bodies into sicknes, and their soules to the state of everlasting damnation...When I gaue my selfe first to note the abuse of common plaies...the Theater I found to be an appointed place of Bauderie' mine own eares have heard honest women allured with abominable speeches. Sometime I have seen two knaues at once impor-tunate vpon one light housewife; whereby much quarrel hath growen to the disquieting of many. There servants, as it is manifestlie to be prooued, haue consented to rob their maisters, to supplie the wants of their harlots; there is the practicising with married wius to traine them from their husbands, and places appointed for meeting and conference. When I had taken a note of all these abuses, & sawe that the Theater was become a consulterie house of Satan, I concluded with my selfe, neuer to imploie my pen to so vile a purpose, nor to be an instrument of gathering the wicked together.*

Further contemporary descriptions of plays, ostensibly from the First Folio, by Dr Simon Forman

Simon Forman attended the productions and different versions of four entries in the First Folio plays, and his thorough accounts of the performances and the minor details of Simon Forman's narratives are at odds with the text in the First Folio. However, they nonetheless give modern readers an impres-sion of what it would be like to be an audience member at the time. Reprinted below are the relevant excerpts from Simon's record-books with some of the spelling modernised:

Macbeth at the Globe, 20th April 1610

> *In Macbeth at the Globe, 1610, the 20th of April, Saturday, there was to be observed, first, how Macbeth and Banquo, two noble men of Scotland, riding*

through a wood, there stood before them three women fairies or nymphs, and saluted Macbeth, saying three times unto him, "Hail, Macbeth, King of Codon; for thou shall be a King, but shall beget no kings," etc. Then said Banquo, "what all to Macbeth, and nothing to me?" "Yes", said the nymphs, "hail to thee, Banquo, thou shall beget kings, yet be no king"; and so they departed and came to the country of Scotland to Duncan, King of Scots and it was in the days of Edward the Confessor. And Duncan had them both kindly welcome, and made Macbeth forthwith Prince of Northumberland, and sent him home to his own castle, and appointed Macbeth to provide for him, for he would sup with him the next day at night, and did so.

And Macbeth contrived to kill Duncan and through the persuasion of his wife did that night murder the King in his own castle, being his guest; and there were many prodigies seen that night and the day before. And when Macbeth had murdered the king, the blood on his hands could not be washed off by any means, nor from his wives hands, which handed the bloody daggers in hiding them, which by means they became both much amazed and affronted. The murder being known, Duncan's two sons fled, the one to England, the other to Wales, to save themselves. They being fled, they were supposed guilty of the murder of their father, which was nothing so.

Then was Macbeth crowned kings; and then he, for fear of Banquo, his old companion, that he should beget kings but be no king himself, he contrived the death of Banquo, and caused him to be murdered on his way as he rode. The next night, being at supper with his noble men whom he had to bid to a feast, to the which also Banquo should have come, he began to speak of noble Banquo, and to wish that he were there. And as he did thus, standing up to drink a carouse to him, the ghost of Banquo came and sat down in his chair behind him. And he, turning about to sit down again, saw the ghost of Banquo, which fronted him so, that he fell into a great passion of fear and fury, uttering many words about his murder, by which, when they hardthat Banquo was murdered, they suspected Macbeth. Then MackDove fled to England to the kinges sonn, and soon they raised an army and cam to Scotland, and at Dunstonanse overthrue Macbeth. In the meantime, while MacDove was in England, Macbeth slew MackDove's wife and children, and after in the battle MackDove slewe Macbeth. Observe also how Macbeth's queen did rise in the night in her sleep, and walked and talked and confessed all, and the doctor noted her words.

Simon Forman also witnessed *The Winter's Tale* at the Globe, 15th May 1611:

Observe there how Leontes, the king of Sicilia, was overcome with jealousy of his wife with the king of Bohemia, his friend, that came to see him. How he contrived his death, and would have had his cupbearer to have poisoned him: who have the king of Bohemia waning thereof and fled with him to Bohemia.

Remember also how he sent to the oracle of Apollo, and the answer of Apollo -- that she was guiltless and that the King was jealous, etc.; and how, except the child was found again that was lost, the King should die without issue. For the child was carried into Bohemia and there laid in a forest and brought up by a shepherd. The King of Bohemia's son married that wench. And how they fled into Sicilia to Leontes. The shepherd, having shown the letter of the nobleman by whom Leontes sent away that child and the jewels found about her, she was known to be Leontes' daughter, and was then sixteen years old.

Remember also the rogue that came in all tattered like Coll Pixie; how he feigned him sick and to have been robbed of all that he had. How he cozened the poor man of all his money. And, after, came to the sheep-shearing with a pedlar's pack and there cozened them again of all their money. How he changed apparel with the King of Bohemia's son, and then how he turned courtier, etc. Beware of trusting feigned beggars or fawning fellows.

Simon Forman's observations on *Cymbeline* at the Globe, 1611 (unspecified date)

Remember also the story of Cymbeline, king of England, in Lucius' time. How Lucius came from Octavius Caesar for tribute; and, being denied, sent Lucius with a great army of soldiers, who landed at Milford Haven, and after were vanquished by Cymbeline, and Lucius taken prisioner. All by means of three outlaws: of which two of them were the sons of Cymbeline, stolen from him when they were but two years old by an old man whom Cymbeline banished. He kept them as his own sons twenty years with him in a cave.

And how one of them slewe Cloten, the Queen's son, going to Milford Haven to seek the love of Imogen, the King's daughter, whom he had banished also for loving his daughter. How the Italian that came, from her love [from love of her], conveyed himself into a chest; and said it was a chest of plate sent, from her love and others, to be presented to the King. In the deepest of the night, she being asleep, he opened the chest and came forth of it. And viewed her in bed and the marks on her body; took away her bracelet, and after accused her of adultery to her love.

"n the end, how he came with the Romans into England and was taken prisoner. And after revealed to Imogen, who had turned herself into man's apparel and fled to meet her love at Milford Haven and chanced to fall on the cave in the woods where her two brother were. How by eating a sleeping dram they thought she had been dead, and laid her in the woods, the body of Cloten by her, in her love's apparel that he left behind him. And how she was found by Lucius, etc.

Simon Forman's view of *Richard II* at the Globe, 20 April 1611

Remember therein how Jack Straw by his overmuch boldness, not being politic nor suspecting anything, was suddenly at Smithfield Bars stabbed by Walworth, the mayor of London. So he and his whole army was overthrown. Therefore, in such a case or the like, never admit any party without a bar between; for a man cannot be too wise, nor keep himself too safe.

Also remember how the duke of Gloucester, the earl of Arundel, Oxford and others, crossing the King in his humour about the duke of Ireland and Bushy, were glad to fly and raise an host of men. Being in his castle, how the duke of Ireland came by night to betray him with three hundred men; but having privy warning thereof kept his gates fast and would not suffer the enemy to enter. Which went back again with a flea in his ear, and after was slain by the earl of Arundel in the battle.

Remember also, when the duke (Gloucester) and Arundel came to London with their army, King Richard came forth to them, met them and gave them fair words; and promised them pardon and that all should be well if they would discharge their army. Upon whose promises and fair speeches they did it. And, after, the King bid them all to a banquet and so betrayed them and cut off their heads, etc., because they had not his pardon under his hand and seal before, but his word.

Remember therein also, how the duke of Lancaster privily contrived all villainy to set them together by the ears; and to make the nobility to envy the King, and mislike of him and his government. By which means he made his own son king, which was Henry Bolingbroke.

Remember also how the duke of Lancaster asked a wise man whether himself should ever be king; and he told him No, but his son should be a king. When he had told him, he hanged him up for his labour, because he should not bruit it abroad or speak thereof to others.

"This was a policy in the commonwealth's opinion, but I say it was a villain's part and a Judas kiss to hang the man for telling him the truth. Beware by this example of noblemen of their fair words, and say little to them, lest they do the like by thee for thy goodwill.

Long Meg of Westminster

Another example of the common fare of the popular theatricals of the Elizabethan age was *Lange mege*, presumed to be *Long Meg of Westminster*, performed in March 1595 (although an original text was registered in August 1590). The tales or *"...mad merry pranks"* of this six-foot woman from the North form the basis of the chapbook of 1590 and the play.

Meg is a formidable adversary who attacks the Carrier who brings her to London for overcharging, beats a Catholic clergyman singing Mass, a Spanish Knight, the 'Baily of Westminster' and thieves at St James. Then, the spirited woman travels to *Bulloigne,* where she proceeds to fight the French valiantly before returning to England and engaging in combat with a Waterman and a Miller, among other adventures. After her marriage Meg kept a house at Islington and eventually died having given penance to a Friar.

The storyline provided plenty of action for the popular audience: wrestling, boxing, sword-fighting, quarterstaff contests and the vanquishing of unpopular figures: notably the Catholic clergy and foreigners.

Played by a man on stage the Elizabethan feisty Meg has echoes in modern times of the popular Old Mother Reilly of Music Hall fame, played by the drag artist Arthur Lucan for several decades.

It would be difficult today to describe the performances of the First Folio plays in this manner.

Appendix 4

First Folio plays. Chronology of performances at court or at noble houses

As stated previously, versions of twenty-six of the plays contained in the First Folio were performed before the courts of Queen Elizabeth, King James and Queen Anne, or at noble houses. A number of the plays were performed at both courts.

The plays given royal production were:

The Comedy of Error or *History of Error, Titus Andronicus, Henry VI, The Merry Wives of Windsor, The Taming of a Shrew, King Leir (Lear), Henry V, Twelfth Night, As You Like It, Two Gentlemen of Verona, Love's Labour's Lost, Romeo and Juliet, Richard II, Midsummer Night's Dream, The Merchant of Venice, Othello, Measure for Measure, Macbeth, Antony and Cleopatra, Coriolanus, Cymbeline, The Tempest, The Winter's Tale, Much Ado About Nothing, Henry VIII* and *Henry IV*.

The plays of which there is no note of a performance at the Courts of either Queen Elizabeth or James I and Queen Anne, are the two further parts of *Henry VI* and an additional part of *Henry IV*, as well as *Troilus and Cressida, Timon of Athens, Richard III, Julius Caesar, Hamlet, King John* and *All's Well That Ends Well.* Court productions of these were recorded, but without the title of the play staged so a complete verification is not possible.

First Folio plays and their court performance:

The Elizabethan court:

The Comedy of Error, History of Error by the Chapel Children January 1577.

Titus Andronicus, 6th February 1594, possibly originally connected to a significant royal occasion for Thomas or Henry Radclyffe, 3rd or 4th Earls of Sussex, patrons of the poet, George Peele, who has been identified as the major author of the play.

Henry VI, Part I, performance at Court on 12th March 1594 and influenced by *Contention of York and Lancaster.* The original version for the Court was possibly written by Christopher Marlowe, with a plagiarised version created for the public stage. The 1623 text is likely to have been an edited version of the early manuscript.

The Merry Wives of Windsor was most likely written for the 1597 Order of the Garter investiture of either Frederick, Duke of Württemberg or Thomas, 1st Lord Howard de Walden, George Carey, 2nd Lord Hunsdon, Charles (Blount), 8th Lord Mountjoy and Sir Henry Lee who each received the Order of the Garter in that year.

This play is in the witty style of the playwright Thomas Nashe. George Carey was Lord Chamberlain at the time, and the principal patron of Nashe.

The Taming of the Shrew, performed at a wedding at court before Queen Elizabeth, this play may have been one of Michelangelo Florio's original contributions (see Chapter Ten)

King Lear, played at Court 1594.

Henry V, performed at Court on 14th May 1594.

Twelfth Night, before Queen Elizabeth I 1600/1.

Henry IV; the earliest factually-known performance occurred on the afternoon of 6th March 1600, when the play was acted at Court before the Flemish Ambassador.

Othello, before the Queen in 1602.

There is also a reference to a performance of *Miles Gloriosus* being played before Queen Elizabeth in January 1565. This was by the *Westminster Boys*, who were gradually absorbed by the *Children of the Chapel.*

The Jacobean court:

As You Like It, 2nd December 1603 at Wilton, Pembroke. Possibly written by Gabriel Harvey, Samuel Daniel and John Florio. Philip Massinger is another possible collaborating writer.

Two Gentlemen of Verona, Love's Labour's Lost, Romeo and Juliet, Richard II, Midsummer Night's Dream were all played at Hampton Court before Prince Henry, during January 1603.

(The Moor of Venice) Othello, 1st November 1604, as listed in E. K. Chamber's Court Calendar.

The King's Men performed seven First Folio plays at court between 1st November 1604 and 31st October 1605, including two performances of *The Merchant of Venice.*

The Merry Wives of Windsor, 4th November 1604. The date marked the marriage of William Herbert, Earl of Pembroke to Mary Talbot daughter of Gilbert Talbot, 7th Earl of Shrewsbury. The play was performed as part of the Court celebrations by the King's Players.

Measure for Measure, 26th December 1604. Philip Herbert married Lady Susan

De Vere, daughter of Edward De Vere, 17th Earl of Oxford on 28 December 1604. The play was performed, two nights before their wedding, at the Great Hall at Whitehall. James I played a prominent part in the elaborate wedding ceremony, and gave the bride £500 in land and the bridegroom lands to the value of £1,000 a year.

Four plays in total were performed as part of the Herbert de Vere wedding celebrations, one of which was *A Comedy of Error*, at Whitehall on the 28th December, performed by the King's Players. Philip Herbert's great aunt Frances Sidney, Countess of Sussex, literary and educational patron, may have contributed to the original translation.

Henry V, 7th January 1605, performed by the King's Players.

Measure for Measure was played again at Whitehall Great Hall, 26th December, St Stephen's Night 1605.

On 23rd December 1605, William Knollys, Ist Earl of Banbury, married Lady Elizabeth Howard, the daughter of Thomas Howard, 1st Earl of Suffolk. The performance of *Measure for Measure* may have been part of their wedding celebrations.

Love's Labour's Lost is likely to have been written by Anthony or Francis Bacon. The Earl of Southampton had the play performed before Queen Anne between 1st-14th January 1605.

The Merchant of Venice, performed at Whitehall 10th February (Shrove Sunday) 1605 and scheduled for a further performance on 12th February 1605, but it was not played.

Macbeth, King's Players 1606.

King Lear, 26th December 1606, the King's Players.

Antony and Cleopatra, possibly the play of that name written by Sir Fulke Greville, Baron Brooke. Performed by the King's Players in 1607.

Coriolanus: The King's Players 1608.

Cymbeline: The King's Players. 1608.

Richard II, performed 30th April 1608.

Tempest, 1st November 1611 (Hallowmas). A work generally accepted to be written by Thomas Middleton and performed by The King's Players.

Henry IV, court performance recorded in 1612.

The Winter's Tale was performed in front of the king on 5th November 1611. Chosen again at Whitehall during the wedding celebrations of the king's daughter, Princess Elizabeth to Frederick V, the Elector Palatine, on 14th February 1613. Played again at court on 18th January 1618.

Much Ado about Nothing, played between December and May 1613.

Henry VIII, performed in June 1613.

Julius Caesar, a lost play performed at court in Latin in 1616 (Thomas May).

Twelfth Night, performed at court 6th April 1618.

Extant records suggest that both parts of *Henry IV* were acted at King James court in 1612 although the plays are referred to as *Sir John Falstaff* and *Hotspur* and a further record infers a Court performance of *Henry IV, Part II* in 1619 known then as the *Second part of Falstaff*.

Appendix 5

Mary Herbert, Countess of Pembroke. Lancastrian history plays and family relationships.

Genealogical research presented in *Sweet Swan of Avon* by Professor Robin P. Williams

King John

Character	Relationship to Mary Sidney
King John	11G Grandfather
Queen Eleanor	12G Grandmother
Prince Henry, afterwards Henry III	10G Grandfather
Arthur Plantagenet	1C 12R
Constance of Brittany	12G Aunt
William Marshall, 1st Earl of Pembroke	12G Uncle
Geoffrey FitzPeirs, 4th Earl of Essex	10G Grandfather
William Longsword, 3rd Earl of Salisbury	12G Uncle
Roger Lord Bigot, 2nd Earl of Norfolk	11G Grandfather
Hubert de Burgh	
Philip, King of France	
Lewis, the Dauphin	*married to Mary's* 1C 12R
Blanche of Castile	
Cardinal Pandolf	
Mentioned in the play:	
Richard the Lionheart	12G Uncle
Geoffrey Plantagenet, 3rd son of Henry II	12G Uncle

Richard II, Henry IV parts 1 and 2
and Henry V

King Richard II	1C 7R
Queen Isabel	*(by marriage)*
John of Gaunt, Duke of Lancaster	6G Grandfather
Eleanor de Bohun, Duchess of Gloucester	7G Aunt
Edmund of Langley, 1st Duke of York	7G Uncle
Duchess of York, mother of Aumerle	7G Aunt
Edward of Norwich, Duke of Aumerle	1C 7R
Henry Bolingbroke, Duke of Hereford, afterwards King Henry IV	6G Uncle (half)

Thomas Mowbray, 1st Duke of Norfolk	5G Grandfather
Thomas Holland, Duke of Surrey	2C 5R
John Montacute, 3rd Earl of Salisbury	*his son married Mary's* 2C 5R
Thomas Lord Berkeley	6G Grandfather
Sir Henry Green	4G Uncle
Sir John Bushy	
Sir William (or John) Bagot	
Henry Percy, 1st Earl of Northumberland	7G Uncle
Henry Percy, called Hotspur	1C 7R
William, Lord Ross	married to 1C 7R
William, 5th Baron Willoughby de Ersby	6G Uncle
Walter Lord Fitzwater	*very distantly related*
Thomas Marke Bishop of Carlisle	
William de Colchester, Abbot of Westminster	
Thomas Holland Lord Marshall	2C 5R
Sir Stephen Scroop (Scrope)	*unclear*
Sir Piers of Exton	
Henry Prince of Wales (Prince Hal), afterwards King Henry V	1C6R (half)
Prince John of Lancaster, Duke of Bedford	1C 6R (half)
Ralph Neville, 1st Earl of Westmorland	5G Grandfather
Sir Walter Blunt	7G Grandfather
Lady Percy, wife of Hotspur	2C 6R
Thomas Percy, Earl of Worcester	1C 7R
Edmund Mortimer	2C 6R
Lady Mortimer (Glendower's daughter)	*married to 2C 6R*
Richard Scroop (Scrope), Archbishop of York	*distant relation*
Archibald, 4th Earl of Douglas	
Owen Glendower	*his daughter married Mary's 2C 6R*
King Henry V	1C 6R (half)
Thomas Beaufort, Duke of Exeter	5G Uncle
Edward of Norwich, 2nd Duke of York	1C 7R
Thomas Montacute, 4th Earl of Salisbury	*married to Mary's 2C5R*
Richard Plantagenet, Earl of Cambridge	1C 7R
Henry Chichele, Archbishop of Canterbury	
John Fordham, Bishop of Ely	
Henry of Masham, 3rd Baron Scrope	*married to 2C 5R*

Sir Thomas Grey	1C 6R
Captain Fluellen (Welsh)	*based on Davy Gam ancestor of William Herbert, Earl of Pembroke*
Captain Jamy (Scottish)	*probably a refer ence to King James I of Scotland who went to France with Henry V*
Sir Thomas Erpingham	
Philip the Good, Duke of Burgundy	*distant relation*
Sir Richard Vernon	
Thomas Plantagenet, Duke of Clarence	1C 6 R (half)
Humphrey Plantagenet, Duke of Gloucester	
and Earl of Pembroke	1C 6R (half)
Richard Beauchamp, 13th Earl of Warwick	5G Grandfather
Thomas Fitzalan, 5th Earl of Surrey	
and 11th Earl of Arundel	6G Uncle
Sir Thomas Harcourt (probably)	
Sir John Blunt	6G Uncle
Lord Chief Justice, Sir William Gascoigne	*very distant*
Margaret Neville, Lady Northumberland	7G Aunt
Thomas, Lord Mowbray	4G Uncle
Thomas, Lord Bardolf	
Sir John Coleville	
Sir John Falstaff	

Mentioned in the plays:
Straight out of Holinshed:
    Sir Thomas Blount of Belton
    Sir Bennet Seely
    Sir John Norberry
    Reginald, 2nd Lord Cobham
    Francis Quoint (or Point)

Sir Walter Blunt	7G Grandfather
William le Scrope, Earl of Wiltshire	*unclear*
Thomas of Woodstock, Duke of Gloucester	7G Uncle
Owen Glendower	*his daughter*

Davy Gam	*married* *Mary's 2C 6R* *7G Grandfather of* *Mary's husband.* *His daughter* *became the mother* *of William* *Herbert, 1st Earl of* *Pembroke in the* *Herbert house.*
Michael de la Pole, 3rd Earl of Suffolk	2C 6R
Gilbert Talbot	5G Uncle
Sir Richard Ketley	
John Holland, Earl of Huntingdon	1C 6R (half)

Three parts of Henry VI, plus Richard III

King Henry VI	2C 5R (half)
Queen Margaret of Anjou	*(by marriage)*
Humphrey Plantagenet, Duke of Gloucester and Earl of Pembroke	1C 6R (half)
Prince John of Lancaster, Duke of Bedford	1C 6R (half)
Thomas Beaufort, Duke of Exeter	6G Uncle
Henry Beaufort, Bishop then Cardinal of Winchester	6G Uncle
John Beaufort, 3rd Earl of Somerset	1C 6R
Richard Plantagenet, 3rd Duke of York	5G Uncle
Cecily Neville, Duchess of York	5G Aunt
Edmund Plantagenet, Earl of Rutland	1C 5R
Richard Beauchamp, 13th Earl of Warwick	5G Grandfather
Thomas Montacute, 4th Earl of Salisbury	*married to Mary's* *2C 5R*
William de la Pole, 4th Earl of Suffolk, later 1st Duke of Suffolk	2C 6R
John Lord Talbot, 1st Earl of Shrewsbury	4G Grandfather
John Talbot (son of above), Viscount and 1st Baron Lisle	3G Grandfather
Edmund Mortimer, 5th Earl of March	3C 4R
Edmund Beaufort, 2nd Duke of Somerset	5G Uncle
Edward Plantagenet, 3rd Earl of March	

(to become King Edward IV)	1C 5R
Humphrey Stafford, Duke of Buckingham	5G Grandfather
Richard Neville, 5th Earl of Salisbury	5G Uncle
Richard Neville, 16th Earl of Warwick the Kingmaker	1C 5R
Thomas Lord Clifford	*unclear*
John, Young Clifford, later Lord Clifford	*unclear; there is a John Lord Clifford in her genealogy, but it is a mistake*
Edward, Prince of Wales (son of Henry VI)	3C 4R (half)
(Henry &) Edmund Beaufort	
(3rd &) 4th Dukes of Somerset	1C 5R
Henry Holland, 2nd Duke of Exeter	2C 5R (half)
Henry Percy, 3rd Earl of Northumberland	1C 5R
Ralph Neville, 2nd Earl of Westmorland	1C 5R
George Plantagenet, Duke of Clarence	1C 5R
Richard Plantagenet, Duke of Gloucester (afterwards Richard III)	1C 5R
Elizabeth Woodville, Lady Grey (afterwards Queen to Edward IV)	GG Aunt
John Neville, Marquis of Montague	1C 5R
William Herbert, Earl of Pembroke (non speaking part)	Mary's husband's 5G Grandfather *married to* 1C 5R
William Lord Hastings	*distantly related*
John de Vere, 13th Earl of Oxford	
Edward Plantagenet, Prince of Wales (afterwards King Edward V)	2C 4R
Richard Plantagenet, Duke of York (prince in the Tower)	2C 4R
Margaret, Countess of Salisbury ('Girl')	2C 4R
Edward Plantagenet, Prince of Wales, Earl of Warwick ('Boy')	2C 4R
Lady Anne Neville	2C 4R
Cardinal Thomas Bourchier	2C 6R
Thomas Scott Rotherham, Archbishop of York	
Henry Stafford, 2nd Duke of Buckingham	2C 4R
John Howard, Duke of Norfolk (grandson of Mowbray in Richard II)	1C 5R

Thomas Howard, Earl of Surrey	
(and 2nd Duke of Norfolk, son of above)	2C 4R
John Mowbray, 3rd Duke of Norfolk	1C 5R
Sir Thomas Grey, 1st Marquis of Dorset	1C 3R
Sir Thomas Stanley, 1st Earl of Derby	*married to* 1C 5R
Sir Thomas Vaughan	
Francis, 12th Lord Lovel	2C 4R (his great-grand father was Mary's 5G grandfather)
Sir Richard Radcliffe	*distantly related*
Sir William Catesby	*distantly related*
Sir James Blunt, grandson of Walter Blunt	5G Uncle
Sir Walter Herbert	her husband's 5G Uncle
Sir William Brandon	
Sir Robert Brackenbury, Keeper of the Tower	*he served under Mary's* 2C 4R
Sir Christopher Urswick, priest	*and he was personal agent and messenger for Margaret Beaufort Mary's* IC 5R
Henry Long of Wrexall, Sherrif of Wiltshire	
Humphrey, Lord Stafford (non speaking part)	*distant relation*
Sir John Mortimer	*unclear; there are lots of Mortimers' in her genealogy*
Sir Hugh Mortimer (non speaking)	*unclear*
Henry Tudor, Earl of Richmond	
(afterwards Henry VII)	3C 4R
Anthony Woodville, 2nd Earl Rivers	*brother to Mary's GG Aunt*
William Neville, Lord Falconbridge	
and Earl of Kent	5G Uncle
Sir Thomas Stanley, 1st Earl of Derby	
(non speaking part)	*married to* 1C 5R
Sir John (Thomas) Montgomery	2C 3R

Thomas Lord Scales	3C 5R
James Fiennes, Lord Say	*(there are other Fiennes and a Sir John Say in Mary's Genealogy, but not this one)*

Sir John Stanley
Sir William Vaux
Matthew Goffe (Gough)
Alexander Iden of Kent

Mentioned in the plays:

Sir Walter Blunt	7G Grandfather
Sir John Blunt	7G Uncle
Lord Walter Hungerford	5G Grandfather
Thomas de Scales, Lord Scales	3C 5R
Lionel of Antwerp, Duke of Clarence	7G Uncle
James Butler, Earl of Wiltshire and 5th Earl of Ormonde	2C 5R
Lord Clifford	*unclear*
Roger Mortimer, 4th earl of March	2C 6R
Edmund (Edward Brooke, Lord Cobham of Kent)	2C 4R
Lord Richard Grey, 8th Baron Ferrers of Groby	4C 3R *(error for Sir John Grey, first husband of (Elizabeth Woodville) Sir John Grey first husband of Elizabeth Woodville who later married King Edward 1V (Woodville)*
George Stanley	2C 4R
Sir John Guilford	3G Grandfather
Sir Richard Guilford	2G Grandfather
Sir Gilbert Talbot	1C 4R (half)
Sir William Stanley (brother to Thomas)	4C 2R
Jasper Tudor, Earl of Pembroke, "redoubted Pembroke"	
Rhys ap Thomas	
Henry Percy (melancholy) Lord Northumberland	1C 5R
Walter Devereaux, Lord Ferrers	

Sir John Fastolf
Philip the Good, Duke of Burgundy — *distant relation*
Richard Woodville, Lieutenant of the Tower — *distant relation*
Sir Edward Courtenay
Bishop of Exeter
Sir William Lucy — *distant relation*
Sir William Glansdale
Sir Thomas Gargrave
Sir Richard Vernon

Henry VIII

Henry VIII	3C 3R
Queen Catharine of Aragon	
Anne Boleyn, Marchioness of Pembroke	4C 2R
Thomas Howard, 2nd Duke of Norfolk	2C 4R
Charles Brandon, Duke of Suffolk	
Edward Stafford, 3rd Duke of Buckingham	3C 3R
Charles Somerset, Lord Chamberlain	Great Grandfather
Sir Thomas More, Lord Chancellor	
Stephen Gardiner, Bishop of Winchester	
John Longland, Bishop of Lincoln	
George Neville, Lord Abergavenny	1C 4R
Lord Sandys, Sir William Sandys	*distantly related*
Sir Henry Guildford	Great Uncle (half)
Sir Thomas Lovel	
Sir Anthony Denny	
Sir Nicholas Vaux	*his sister is Mary's 2G Grandmother*

Cardinal Wolsey
Cardinal Campeius
Thomas Cranmer, Archbishop of Canterbury
Thomas Cromwell

From "Memoirs of the Sidney family"

Held in the library of the University of California, Los Angeles

> *...Sir William de Sidenie, who accompanied Henry II to England on his accession to the throne in 1154 and received the office of Chamberlain to the monarch, with a grant of land in the counties of Surrey and Sussex. This knight was descended from an ancestry possessed of much wealth and influence in Normandy and Anjou, where its pedigree can be proved to extend back upwards of some two centuries before the coming of the Conqueror into England.*
>
> *From the time of this Sir William (who was buried in the Lady Chapel of Lewes Priory, 1188) until the reign of Henry V., his posterity, although sending representatives to the Crusades and Agincourt, lived for the most part the lives of country squires, intermarrying with some of the best families among the nobility and gentry, and frequently obtaining the honour of knighthood. But it was reserved for Nicholas Sidney... Edward IV., to found the fortunes of his descendants by an alliance contracted with Anne Brandon, aunt of Charles, Duke of Suffolk, the husband of Mary, sister to Henry VIII., and widow of Louis XII of France. By this marriage of Nicholas, his descendants became enabled, through the Brandons, to deduce their descent from William I. and from the ancient Kings of Scotland...*

Ancestors of William Herbert, Earl of Pembroke and holders of the title run as a thread through the tapestry of England's history:

> *King John, Queen Eleanor, Prince Henry afterward Henry III, Arthur Plantagenet, Constance of Brittany, Geoffrey FitzPeirs, 4th Earl of Essex, William Longsword, 3rd Earl of Salisbury, Roger, Lord Bigot, 2nd earl of Norfolk.*

...including titles held by the Neville family who appear as characters in the Lancastrian plays of the First Folio: Beauchamp, the Duke of Bedford, Marquess of Montagu, Marquess of Abergavenny, Earl of Westmorland, Earl of Salisbury, Earl of Warwick, Earl of Kent, Earl of Northumberland, Earl of Abergavenny, Earl of Lewes, Baron Neville de Raby, Baron Fauconberg, Baron Latimer, Baron Bergavenny, Baron Montagu.

William and Philip Herbert's ancestors, the Yorkist supporters, brothers William and Walter Herbert, fought for Edward IV. William Herbert, on the attainder of Jasper Tudor in 1468, was made Earl of Pembroke and he became the guardian of Henry, Earl of Richmond, later Henry VII.

A year later, however, Pembroke was executed alongside his brother Sir Richard Herbert after the Yorkist army was defeated by the Lancastrians at Edgcote Moor. The rebel army was led by Richard Neville, earl of Warwick. Sir William Herbert is a character in the play *Henry VI Part III* and Sir Walter Herbert, the son of the earl, is named in *Richard III*.

The Dudley family does not appear in the plays which chronicle the Lancastrian cause. Although the powerful Dudleys did play a significant role in the reigns of two monarchs (Henry VII and Edward IV) during a momentous period of English history, the family have not been the subject of any dramatic works. Conversely, the Neville's are featured frequently.

The Herbert family: direct ancestry

William Herbert, 3rd Earl of Pembroke, and his brother Philip, Earl of Montgomery, were descended from an illustrious English ancestry. In addition to the noble Pembrokes, which included the Beauforts, Earls and Dukes of Somerset descended from John of Gaunt, their forebears also included the Beauchamps, Earls of Warwick.

Other members of the extensive inter-related branches of the Herbert family included the Earls of Worcester and several noble families.

For more than two centuries the extended family of Herbert also included Talbot, Barclay, Devereaux, Woodville, Neville, Boleyn, Blunt, de Vere, Radcliffe, Grey and Sidney etc., all of whom were to occupy a distinctive place in English history. For a comprehensive listing see Dr Williams' analysis above.

Appendix 6

The Spanish Marriage negotiations

The Lords of the Privy Council swore an oath concerning the proposed marriage of Charles, Prince of Wales and Maria, Donna Infanta of Spain, before the ambassadors don Carlos de Colonna and don Juan de Mendoza marquis of Inojosa at Whitehall on 20th July 1623. The oath seems to have related only to the acceptance of the treaty (although the text is not recorded), and was contingent on the marriage actually taking place Although James I was still keen on the match, the Spanish had lost interest by July 1623 and although the Pope agreed to the marriage, the conditions he applied were so stringent that it was hoped the English would also be deterred. The following councilors were present:

George Abbot, archbishop of Canterbury (signed under duress), John Williams, Bishop of Lincoln and keeper of the Great Seal, Lionel Cranfield, Earl of Middlesex and Lord Treasurer, Henry Montague, Viscount Mandeville and Lord President of the Privy Council, Edward Somerset, Earl of Worcester and Keeper of the Privy Seal, Ludovick Stuart, Duke of Richmond and Lennox, Lord Steward of the Household, James, Marquis Hamilton, James Hay, Earl of Carlisle, Oliver St John, Viscount Grandison, Lancelot Andrews, Bishop of Winchester, Sir Thomas Edmonds, Treasurer of the Household, Sir George Calvert, Secretary of State, Sir Richard Weston, Chancellor of the Exchequer, Thomas Fenton, Earl of Kelly, George, Lord Carewe of Clapton, Lord Arthur Chichester, Baron of Belfast, Sir John Suckling, Comptroller of the Household, Sir Edward Conway, Secretary of State, Sir Julius Caesar, Master of the Rolls.

Both William, Earl of Pembroke and Fulke Greville, Baron Brooke, were absent and did not sign the document.

William Herbert, 3rd Earl of Pembroke was the leader of the anti-Spanish faction at court.. This was a coalition of patriots led by Pembroke, Southampton and George Abbot, Archbishop of Canterbury.

Prince Charles who, with the duke of Buckingham, was negotiating directly in Madrid until his return in October 1623, omitted many of James I's political requirements from the discussions. The chief imperative was to secure Spanish help to restore to the Palatinate of the Rhine to Frederick V. The marriage of Prince Charles was only likely if he converted to Catholicism, but Charles was disinclined to take this momentous step.

Appendix 7

First Folio alternative authorship

There have been literally dozens of candidates put forward as the writer of the First Folio of 1623 and the volume of Sonnets written between 1597-9: both attributed to William Shakespeare. The quest to uncover the 'true' writer is not surprising in view of the overwhelming evidence that suggests the claimed authorship by Shakespeare is fraudulent. Of the many claimants proposed during the last two centuries it would be fair to suggest that only four of these possible authors bear a truly critical scrutiny, namely; Edward de Vere, 17th Earl of Oxford, Sir Francis Bacon, Christopher Marlowe, and William Stanley, 6th Earl of Derby.

The likelihood of **Edward de Vere, 17th Earl of Oxford,** being the incomparable writer of the age and the leading candidate is supported by the facts surrounding his life. The Oxfordian premise incorporates the view that a conspiracy took place during the period when the plays were written in that the relevant documents were falsified. The purpose of this deception was to protect the identity of the real author when at the time an aristocrat publishing a written composition was unacceptable. As an example, Sir Philip Sidney desired that his poetry and prose compositions should be destroyed after his death but they were preserved fortunately by Mary Sidney.

As a royal ward of Sir William Cecil, Lord Burleigh, senior statesman to Queen Elizabeth, the young nobleman de Vere studied with learned men of the age and enjoyed access to Cecil's extensive library of books and manuscripts. Cecil was a Cambridge scholar and Cecil's wife Mildred [neé Cooke] was an exceptionally learned. Subsequently Edward de Vere gained degrees at the universities of Cambridge and Oxford and studied law at Grays Inn. The plays in the First Folio frequently show the writer was trained in English law.

The Earl of Oxford as a senior nobleman maintained a lifestyle that meant de Vere was familiar with the sporting and cultural activities of court. Many of the First Folio plays demonstrate an ease with the world of the English aristocrat.

The earl travelled extensively on the Continent including eighteen months spent in Italy where de Vere visited the major cities of Florence, Venice, Verona, Milan, Padua as well as Sicily and there is a remarkable knowledge of Italy in many First Folio works.

The Oxfordian argument rests also upon biographical evidence which relates incidents and experiences in the life of de Vere being echoed in several of the plays and sonnets. Additionally, numerous markings in a copy of the English translation of the Geneva Bible owned by the earl can also be linked to words and passages in the plays and poetry attributed to Shakespeare.

Textual analysis of the writings of Shakespeare and de Vere which compare vocabulary, idiom and thought indicate to some academics that Oxford provides the best match of the leading contenders for a Shakespeare alternative. The data available for study of de Vere's work however is rather limited since only twenty six poems of the earl survive.

Oxfordians emphasise the literary connections of the earl. A maternal uncle of de Vere was Arthur Golding, scholar and translator of Ovid's *Metamorphoses* and a paternal uncle was Henry Howard, 5th Earl of Surrey the originator of the English sonnet. Oxford arranged theatrical events for the Queen at Whitehall, acquired the lease of the Blackfriars theatre and was the patron of the Oxford's Men and Oxford's Boys playing companies.

The Earl of Oxford received dedications from John Lyly and Edmund Spenser among other poets and George Puttenham in *The Arte of English Poesy*, 1589, suggests that Oxford, among other courtiers, was masking his identity as a writer...

> *And in her Majesty's time that now is are sprung up another crew of Courtly makers [poets], noblemen and gentlemen of her Majesty's own servants, who have written excellently well as it would appear if their doings could be found out and made public with the rest, of which number is first that noble gentleman, Edward earl of Oxford.*

Edward de Vere is also mentioned in Francis Mere's *Pallas Tamia, Wits Treasury, 1598*, a literary common-place book as *..best for comedy...and interludes.*

The principal argument against the Earl of Oxford's claim of his authorship is that de Vere died in 1604 whereas several of the First Folio plays were written after that date. It seems most unlikely, as Oxfordians claim, that the thirty-six plays were all written before the earl's demise and further that some were subsequently revised by other writers.

There is sufficient evidence nevertheless to suggest that the earl may well have contributed to large degree in the creation of some of the Italian plays.

As with all single candidates a strong negative is that the huge variety of work encompassed in the First Folio and the two long poems militates against there being one writer.

Sir Francis Bacon who became Queen Elizabeth's Lord Chancellor was first suggested as the hidden author of *Venus and Adonis* and *The Rape of Lucrece* by the lawyer-poets Joseph Hall and John Marston in satirical poems 1597/8. Following the death of Bacon in 1626 his executor William Rowley published a collection of eulogies in which Bacon is referred to as a concealed poet..*the greatest of his age...* who had re-presented all philosophy by means of comedy and tragedy.

Baconians point to the description of the author carved on the Shakespeare monument in the Stratford church which likens Shakespeare to the wise counsellor Nestor, the philosopher Socrates and the scholar poet Virgil. Francis Bacon supporters claim this description of a man who united philosophy and drama is apt for Sir Francis Bacon but is manifestly untrue of William Shakespeare.

The intellectual calibre of Bacon jurist, philosopher, scientist and statesman was in contrast to his claim as a man of letters. Sir Francis avidly penned sonnets and was involved in the theatrical entertainment at Grays Inn.

Baconians also point to the Northumberland manuscript discovered in 1867 at Northumberland House in the Strand, London. York House was next door in which Francis Bacon lived during the years he was Lord Keeper and remained there until 1621.

The fire-damaged folder contained several manuscripts stitched together and six of the nine manuscripts listed are by Bacon but much of the contents were missing. On the cover amidst many scribbles of words and phrases are written the names of Francis Bacon and William Shakespeare; the latter name shown in various calligraphic styles. It seems probable that the scribbles are written by a scribe whiling away his time waiting for instructions or perhaps a further item to deliver. On the back of the folder are the words " Put in type" so it seems printing was planned.

The folder material included letters, speeches, *Leicester's Commonwealth* and Orations. Some of these writings were of a sensitive nature for which Bacon may have been acting as censor in his judicial role. The copying work may have been carried out in the scriptorium operated by Francis Bacon and his brother Anthony. Ben Jonson and John Davies of Hereford are known to have been "pens" for Bacon.

The plays *Richard II* and *Richard III* are listed in the folder and these were the first two plays published under Shakespeare's name in 1597 and 1598.

Counter arguments against Bacon's authorship of Shakespeare's works include the dissimilarities in writing style and the lack of time available for this senior Minister to compose such a vast creative output. There is no direct contemporary comment either of Sir Francis writing plays on a grand scale.

The **Marlovian theory** holds that the major Elizabethan poet and playwright

Christopher Marlowe did not die in 1593, as the historical records state, but his demise was faked and he continued to write while abroad hidden as the William Shakespeare alias. All of which appears an astonishing deception to persist for so many years.

There are many similarities between Marlowe's works and some of the verse in the First Folio however some textual scholars claim that the style, vocabulary, imagery and his apparent weakness in the writing of comedy, are judged to be too different for Marlowe's claim to be credible.

William Stanley, 6th Earl of Derby 1561-1642 inherited the title from his elder brother Ferdinando, Lord Strange a notable patron of poets, playwrights and the playing company Derby's Men, previously Strange's Men.

The 6th earl was known for his extensive European travels and cultural interests including writing plays. Correspondence dated 1599 mentions him ...*penning letters for the common players.* Another clue to Stanley's authorship is the comic scene *in Love's Labour's Lost* caricaturing the pageant of the *Nine Worthies* that was performed traditionally in Stanley's home town of Chester. The earl is believed to have resided at the court of Navarre.

BIBLIOGRAPHY

Wikipedia and the Oxford Dictionary of National Biography

In addition to consulting the books which follow we have obtained invaluable information from the above on-line sources for which we are immensely grateful.

A

Adams, Joseph Quincy, *Shakespearean Playhouses*, The Riverside Press 1917

Akrigg, C. P. V. *Jacobean Pageant: Or, The Court of King James.* Harvard University Press 1963

A'Dair, Mike, *Four Essays on the Shakespeare Authorship Question.* Verisimilitude Press, California. 2011

Alford, Stephen, *The Watchers*, Penguin Books 2012

Allardyce, Nicoll, *Stuart Masques,* Harcourt, Brace & Co N.Y. 1970, *Shakespeare Survey 1 & 2 Cambridge University Press 1948/9*

Anderson, Mark, *"Shakespeare" by Another Name: The Life of Edward de Vere, Earl of Oxford, The Man Who Was Shakespeare.* Gotham Books 2005

Archer, Peter, *The Queen's Courts,* Penguin 1963

Armstrong Jane, *The Arden Shakespeare Miscellany,* Methuen Drama 2011

Ashdown-Hill, J, *Richard III's "Beloved Cousyn,"* The History Press 2009

B

Bakeless, John, *Christopher Marlowe, the Man in His Time.* New York: W. Morrow and Company, 1937. *The Tragicall History of Christopher Marlowe,* MA: Harvard University Press, 1942

Baldwin E.C. *Rosalynde By T. Lodge,* Ginn & Co USA 1910

Baldwin, T. W. *On Act and Scene Divisions,* S. Illinois University Press 1965

Barker, Juliet, *Agincourt,* Abacus 2007

Barrell, Charles Wisner (1942). *"Shake-speare's' Unknown Home On the River Avon Discovered Edward De Vere's Ownership of a Famous Warwickshire Literary Retreat Indicates Him As the True 'Sweet Swan of Avon'".* The Shakespeare Fellowship News-Letter (Shakespeare Fellowship)

Barroll, J. Leeds, *Anna of Denmark*, University of Pennsylvania 2001

Barroll J. Leeds, J. Leggatt A. Hosley, Richard, Kernan, Alvin *The Revels History of Drama in English Vol. 3 1576-1613*, Methuen & Co 1975

Baugh, Albert, *A History of the English Language*, Routledge & Keegan Paul

Bate, Jonathan, *Shakespeare and the English Romantic Imagination*. Oxford University Press. 1986. *Shakespearean Constitutions: Politics, Theatre, Criticism 1730–1830*. Oxford University Press. 1989. *Shakespeare and Ovid*. Oxford University Press. 1993. Co-editor, *Shakespeare: An Illustrated Stage History*. Oxford University Press. 1996. *The Genius of Shakespeare*. Picador / Oxford University Press. 1997. *Soul of the Age: the Life, Mind and World of William Shakespeare*. Viking. 2008

Bate, John, *How to find out about Shakespeare*, Pergamon Press 1968

Beauclerk, Charles, *Shakespeare's Lost Kingdom: The True History of Shakespeare and Elizabeth*. Grove Press

Beltz, George, *Noble Order of the Garter* (1841) Forgotten Books, reprint-Amazon

Bennett, Michael, *The Battle of Bosworth,* Sutton Publishing 1993

Bentley, G.E. *The Jacobean and Caroline Stage*. London. 1941 5 vols. *The Kings playwright Shakespeare and Jonson: Their Reputations in the Seventeenth Century Compared* (1945)

Shakespeare: *A Biographical Handbook* (1961) *Shakespeare and His Theatre* (1964) *The Profession of Dramatist in Shakespeare's Time, 1590–1642* (1971)

Benarz, James P. *Shakespeare and the Poet's War,* Columbia University Press 2001

Bergeron, David M. *Shakespeare- research guide,* Macmillan Press 1976. Textual Patronage in English Drama, Ashgate Publishing 2006

Bevington, David Martin, *Shakespeare: The Seven Ages of Human Experience.* Wiley-Blackwell. *Henry IV, Part I: The Oxford Shakespeare* (Oxford World's Classics) 2008. *Shakespeare's Ideas* (Blackwell Great Minds) 2008. Shakespeare: *The Seven Ages of Human Experience* Blackwell Publishing 2005

Bevan, Bryan, *King James I of England,* The Rubicon Press 1996 *Henry VII: The First Tudor King* 1 Jan 2000

Bindoff, T. S. *Tudor England,* Penguin 1980

Bingham, Caroline, *James VI of Scotland,* Weidenfeld and Nicholson 1979. *The making of James I,* Collins 1968

Bowen, Catherine, *Francis Bacon,* Little Brown & Co 1963

Booth, Stephen, *Shakespeare's Sonnets,* Yale University, 1977

Brennan, Michael G. *The Sidneys of Penshurst And the Monarchy, 1500 1700.*Burlington, VT: Ashgate Publishing, 2006

Bradbrook, M. C. *Beaumont and Fletcher Select Plays,* Dent & Sons 1970

Brazil, Robert Sean, *Edward de Vere and the Shakespeare Printers.* Seattle, WA not known

Brooks, Alden, *Will Shakspere: Factotum and Agent,* 1937, *Will Shakspere and the Dyer's Hand,* Charles Scribner's Sons 1943

Brooke-Little J.B. *Boutell's Heraldry,* Warne & Co 1970

Brooks Richard, *The Knight Who Saved England: William Marshal and the French Invasion* Osprey Publishing 2014

Boas F.S. *Shakespeare and His Predecessors* (1896). *The Works of Thomas Kyd* (1901) editor. *Shakespeare and the Universities: And Other Studies in Elizabethan Drama* (1923). *Marlowe And His Circle: A Biographical Survey* (1929). *Elizabethan and Other Essays by Sidney Lee* (1929) editor. *An Introduction to the Reading of Shakespeare* (1930). (1932) editor. *An Introduction to Tudor Drama* (1933) editor. *Christopher Marlowe: A Biographical and Critical Study* (1940). *Songs & Lyrics from the English Playbooks* (1945) editor. *An Introduction to Stuart Drama* Oxford University Press 1945. *Ovid And The Elizabethans* (1947). *Thomas Heywood* (1950). *Queen Elizabeth in Drama and Related Studies* Allen & Unwin (1950) *Sir Philip Sidney, Representative Elizabethan; his life and writings* (1955)

Butcher, S.H. *Aristotle's Theory of Poetry,* Macmillan & Co 1923

Buxton J. *Sir Philip Sidney and the English Renaissance* 3rd ed. London. Macmillan & Co 1954, 1987

Britannica Concise Encyclopaedia, 2007, de Vere, Edward

C

Campbell, Gordon, *The Alchemist and other plays,* Oxford University Press

Caputi, Anthony, *John Marston, Satirist,* Cornell University Press, 1961

Carson, Annette, *Richard III. The Maligned King,* The History Press 2009

Carson, Neil, *A Companion to Henslowe's Diary,* Cambridge University Press 1988

Caso, Adolf, *Romeo and Juliet : Original texts,* Dante University of America 1992

Chambers, E.K. *The Elizabethan Stage.* London: 1928 4 volumes. *Medieval stage* 2 Vols. 1903 *The History and Motives of Literary Forgeries* (1891). *Shakespeare: A Survey* (1925) *William Shakespeare: A Study of Facts and Problems* (2 volumes; 1930) *Vol. I The Oxford Book of Sixteenth Century Verse* (1932, editor) *The English Folk-play* (1933). *Shakespearean Gleanings* (1940) Oxford University Press 1944. *English Literature at the Close of the Middle Ages* (1945) *Aurelian Townsend's Poems and Masques* Henry Frowd undated re-print

Chapman, G. & Acheson, A. *Shakespeare and the Rival Poet,* BiblioLife 1903

Cheney, Patrick; Hadfield, Andrew; Sullivan, Jr., Garrett A. *Early Modern English Poetry: A Critical Companion.* Oxford University Press 2006

Childs, Jesse, *Henry VIII's Last Victim,* Vintage 2008

Chrimes, S.B., *Henry VII,* Methuen 1977

Chute, Marchette, *Ben Jonson of Westminster,* Souvenir Press 1978

Clarke, P.D. & Zutski P.N. *Apostolic Penitentiary: Supplications 1410, 1464,* Boydell Press 2012

Clare, Janet, *Shakespeare's Stage Traffic: Imitation, Borrowing and Competition in Renaissance Theatre* (Cambridge University Press, 2014). *Revenge Tragedies of the Renaissance* (Plymouth, 2006) *Drama of the English Republic, 1649-1660* (Manchester, 2002).*'Art Made Tongue-tied by Authority': Elizabethan and Jacobean Dramatic Censorship* (Manchester University Press, 1991; second edition, 1999)

Clegg, C. S. *Press Censorship in Elizabethan England,* Cambridge University Press 1986

Cockburn, N. B. *The Bacon Shakespeare Question,* Biddles Ltd 1998

Cook, Judith, *Dr Simon Forman,* Chatto & Windus 2011

Cooper, John, *The Queen's Agent, Walsingham,* Faber & Faber 2011

Cormac, Nussbaum, and Strier, *Shakespeare and the Law* University of Chicago Press 2013

Collins, J.G. *Robert Greene. Plays and Poems.* Oxford Clarendon Press 1905 MDCCCCV

Cousins, A. D. *Shakespeare's Sonnets, The Cambridge Companion to the Sonnet,* Cambridge University Press, 2011

Coward, Barry, *The Stuart Age,* Longman Group 1994

Craik T.W. *Philip Massinger: A new way to pay old debts,* A & C Black 1993

Cressy, David, *Dangerous Talk,* Oxford University Press 2010

Cressy & Ferrell, *Religion in Society in Early Modern England,* Routledge 1996

Crinkley, Richmond (1985). *New Perspectives on the Authorship Question.* Shakespeare Quarterly (Folger Shakespeare Library)

Croft, P. J., ed. *The Poems of Robert Sidney.* Oxford: Oxford University Press, 1984

D

Davenport, Arnold, *The Poems of John Marston.* Liverpool University Press 1961

Dawson, G. & Skipton L. K. *Elizabethan Handwriting,* Faber & Faber 1981

Deane Jones I. *The English Revolution,* William Heinemann 1952

Deats S. M., Logan, Robert A. *Placing the plays of Christopher Marlowe.* Ashgate Publishing 2008

Desens, Marliss C. *The Bed-Trick in English Renaissance Drama: Explorations of Gender, Sexuality, and Power.* Associated University Presses 1994

de Lisle, Leanda, *After Elizabeth*, Harper Perennial 2004. *The Sisters Who Would Be Queen: The tragedy of Mary, Katherine and Lady Jane Grey*, Harper Press 2008. *Tudor: The Family Story*

du Maurier, Daphne, *Golden Lads,* Virago Press 2007. *The Winding Stair,* Virago 2006

Dickson, Andrew, *The Rough Guide to Shakespeare*, Rough Guides 2005

Dover Wilson, John, *Life in Shakespeare's England,* Cambridge University Press 1945

Duffy, Eamon, *Fires of Faith,* Yale University Press 2009, *The Stripping of the Altars,* Yale University Press 1992

Duncan Jones, Katherine, Arden Shakespeare 2011 *Shakespeare: Upstart Crow to Sweet Swan of Avon. Shakespeare. An ungentle Life.* London 2010. *Shakespeare's sonnets*, The Arden Shakespeare 1997

Durrant David N. *Bess of Hardwick*, Weidenfeld and Nicolson 1977.

E

Edmondson, Paul, & Wells, Stanley, eds. *Shakespeare Beyond Doubt: Evidence, Argument, Controversy.* Cambridge University Press

Elam, Kier (2007). *'At the cubiculo': Shakespeare's Problems with Italian Language and Culture.*

Marrapodi, Michele, *Italian Culture in the Drama of Shakespeare & his Contemporaries: Rewriting, Remaking, Refashioning.* Ashgate Publishing. **(2008)**

Elliott, Ward E. Y. & Valenza, Robert J. (2004). *"Oxford by the Numbers: What Are the Odds That the Earl of Oxford Could Have Written Shakespeare's Poems and Plays?"* Tennessee Law Review

F

Farina, William, *De Vere as Shakespeare: An Oxfordian Reading of the Canon,* Jefferson, North Carolina: McFarland & Company 2006

Farley-Hills, David, *Jacobean Drama 1600-25* Macmillan 1988

Feuillerat, Albert, *Sir Philip Sidney: Poems,* Cambridge University Press 1922

Fields, Bertram, *The Mysterious Identity of William Shakespeare*, Sutton Publishing 2006

Finklepearl, P. J. *John Marston of the Middle Temple*, Harvard University Press 1969

Fleay, Frederick Gard, *A Biographical Chronicle of the English Drama, 2vols 1559-1642* (Reeves and Turner, London,1891 *Shakespeare's Manual*, Macmillan and Co 1878. *A Chronicle History of the London Stage 159-1642.* New York 1909

Ford, Boris, *The Age of Shakespeare,* Pelican Guide 1962

Forrest, H.T. *The Five Authors of "Shakespeare's Sonnets,"* Chapman & Dodd 1923

Foster, Don, (1987), *Master W.H., R.I.P, PMLA* : Remove

Fowler, William Plumer, *Shakespeare Revealed in Oxford's Letters,* Portsmouth, New Hampshire: Peter E. Randall 1986

Foxe, John, *Foxe's Book of Martyrs,* Ambassador Productions 1995

Fraunce, Abraham, *The Arcadian Rhetorike,* Oxford 1950

Froude, J. A. The Reign of Mary Tudor, Continuum 2009

G

Gaw, Alison, *The Origin and Development of I Henry VI,* University of Southern California 1926

Gibson, H.N. *The Shakespeare Claimants,* Routledge Library Editions—Shakespeare. Routledge 1962

Gill, Louise, *Richard III and Buckingham's Rebellion,* Sutton Publishing 1999

Gollancz, Israel, *The Inferno of Dante,* University of California 1903

Goss, Anthony, *Dissolution of the Lancastrian Kingships,* Paul Watkins 1996

Granville-Barker, Harley, *A Companion to Shakespeare Studies,* Cambridge University Press 1955

Greg, Walter W., *Henslowe's Diary,* A. H. Bullen, 1904 *The Editorial Problem in Shakespeare,* Oxford at the Clarendon Press 1954

Green, Dominic, *The Double Life of Doctor Lopez,* Arrow Books 2004

Greenwood, Granville George, *Shakespeare Problem Restated,* 1908

Grosart, Alexander, *Works of Gabriel Harvey,* Oxford University Press 1979 *The Poems of John Marston,* Reprint 1869

Griffin, Benjamin. *Playing the Past: Approaches to English Historical Drama; 1385 - 1600.* Boydell & Brewer 2001 *William Shakespeare: The Extraordinary Life of the Most Successful Writer of All Time,* HarperCollins 1996. *The Shakespearean Playing Companies,* Oxford University Press, 1999. *Rebuilding Shakespeare's Globe,* Weidenfeld & Nicolson 1988. *Studying Shakespeare: an Introduction,* Arnold 1987. *Playgoing in Shakespeare's London,* Cambridge University Press 1984. *Hamlet and the Distracted Globe,* Scottish Academic Press for Sussex University Press 1974. *The Shakespearean Stage, 1574-1642,* Cambridge University Press 1969

Greenblatt, Stephen, *Will in the World: How Shakespeare Became Shakespeare* W. W. Norton, New York 2004

Greenwood, Sir Granville George, *The Shakespeare Problem Restated* 1908. *The*

Vindicators of Shakespeare 1911. *Is There a Shakespeare Problem?* 1916. *Shakespeare's Law and Latin* 1916.*Shakespeare's Law* 1920. *Shakspere's Handwriting* 1920. *Ben Johnson and Shakespeare* 1921.*Baconian Essays* (Introduction and two essays) 1922. Lee, *Shakespeare and a Tertium Quid* 1923. *Shakespeare's Signature and "Sir Thomas More"* 1924. *The Stratford Bust and the Droeshout Engraving* 1925

Gunn, Thomas, *Selected Poems of Fulke Greville*, University of Chicago 1908

Gurr, Andrew, *Shakespeare's Opposites: The Admiral's Company 1594 - 1625*, Cambridge University Press 2004. *The Shakespeare Company*, Cambridge University Press 2000 *Staging in Shakespeare's Theatres*, with **Mariko Ichikawa**, Oxford University Press 1996, *The Shakespearean Stage* , Cambridge University Press 2009. *Playgoing in Shakespeare's London* Cambridge University Press 2004. *Rebuilding Shakespeare's Globe*, with John Orrell Weidenfeld and Nicolson 1989.

H

Hall's Chronicles, *History of England*, Henry II to Henry VIII Reprint 1809

Hamilton, Charles, *In search of Shakespeare*, Robert Hale 1986

Hamilton, Donna B. *Anthony Munday and the Catholics.* Surrey, England 2005 University Press of Kentucky, *Shakespeare and the Politics of Protestant England.* University of Kentucky 1992

Hannay, M. P., et al. *Domestic Politics And Family Absence: The Correspondence (1588-1621) of Robert Sidney, First Earl of Leicester, and Barbara Gamage Sidney, Countess of Leicester.* Burlington, VT: Ashgate Publishing, 2005. *Mary Sidney, Lady Wroth,* Louisiana State University 1992

Hanspeter, Born, *"Why Greene was Angry at Shakespeare"*, Medieval and Renaissance Drama 2012 Routledge

Harbage, Alfred, *Annals of English Drama, 975-1700*

Harman, E.G. *Gabriel Harvey and Thomas Nashe*, Ouseley and Son 1923

Harrison, G.B. *Introducing Shakespeare*, Penguin Books 1950. *Dekker's Shoemaker's Holiday* Robert Holden 1927. *Gabriel Harvey: Letters and Sonnets* Barnes & Noble NY

Hay, Millicent V. *The Life of Robert Sidney, Earl of Leicester.* Associated University Press 1984

Haynes, Alan, *Invisible Power Secret Services: 1570-1603*, Alan Sutton 1994

Hazlitt, W. *Elizabethan Literature: Shakespeare's Characters.* George Bell & Sons 1884

Hibbert, Christopher, *Charles I*, Palgrave Macmillan 1967

Hicks, Michael, *Richard III*, Tempus Publishing, 2003

Hill, Christopher, *The Century of Revolution 1603-1570* Sphere Books 1972

Hogge, Alice, *God's Secret Agents*, Harper Perennial 2006

Hohnen, David, *Hamlet's Castle Shakespeare's Elsinore*, Vine House Distribution 2004

Honan, Park, *Christopher Marlowe*, Oxford University Press, 2005

Hoeniger, F. D. *Review of Studies in the Shakespeare Apocrypha by Baldwin Maxwell*. Shakespeare Quarterly 1957

Hoenselaars, Ton, *Shakespeare and Contemporary Dramatists*, Cambridge University Press 2012

Holland, P. & Orgell, S. *From Performance to Print : Shakespeare* Palgrave Macmillan 2008

Honigman, EA. J. *Shakespeare's Impact on his contemporaries* Macmillan Press 1982

Hope, Warren, & Kim Holston. *The Shakespeare Controversy: An Analysis of the Authorship Theories* (2nd Edition) (Jefferson, N.C. and London: McFarland and Co., 2009 [first pub. 1992])

Hotson, L. *The Death of Christopher Marlowe, 1925. The Commonwealth and Restoration Stage, 1929*

Shakespeare versus Shallow, Nonsuch Press 1931 *The Adventure of a Single Rapier* 1931. *I, William Shakespeare. Shakespeare's Sonnets Dated*, Rupert Hart -Davis 1949. *Shakespeare's Motley. The First Night of Twelfth Night*, Mercury Books, 1954. *Shakespeare's Wooden O*, 1959. *Mr WH*, 1964. *Shakespeare by Hilliard*, 1977

Hulme, Hilda, *Explorations in Shakespeare's Language*, Baines & Noble N.Y.

Humphries, Rolfe, *Ovid, The Art of Love*, John Calder 1958

Hunt, William, *The Puritan Movement*, Harvard University Press 1983

Hunter, G. K. *"Introduction." All's Well That Ends Well*. The Arden Shakespeare, Second Series 1959

J

Jackson, Macdonald P., *Shakespeare's Richard II and the Anonymous Thomas of Woodstock, in Medieval and Renaissance Drama in England* (2001)

Janko, Richard, *Aristotle Poetics*, Hackette Publishing USA 1987

Jardine, L., Stewart, A. *Hostage to Fortune, Francis Bacon*, Hill & Wang N.Y. 1998

Jenkins, Harold, ed. *Hamlet, Prince of Denmark*. The Arden Shakespeare. London, England: Methuen 1982

Jones, Michael, Underwood, Malcolm G, *The King's Mother*, Cambridge University Press 1992. *Bosworth 1485*, Tempus Publishing 2002

K

Kay, David W. *Ben Jonson. A literary life,* Macmillan Press 1995

Keeton, George W. *Shakespeare's Legal and Political Background,* Sir Isaac Pitman & Sons

Kendall, Paul, *Richard II1,* Allan & Unwin 1973

Kernan, Alan, *Shakespeare, the King's Playwright, Theater in the Stuart Court, 1603-1613 Yale* University 1995

Kirkpatrick, Robin, *English and Italian Literature,* Longman Group 1995

Kreiler, Kurt. *Anonymous Shake-Speare. The Man Behind.* Munich: Dölling und Galitz, 2011

L

Lawrence, Jason (2005). *Who the Devil Taught Thee So Much Italian?* Italian Language Learning and Literary Imitation in Early Modern England. Manchester University Press.

Lee, Maurice, Jr. *Jacobean Letters 1603-1624*

Lee, Sidney, *A life of William Shakespeare, Shakespeare,* 1898 and the *Modern Stage* 1906

Leech C. & Craik T.W. *The Revels. History of Drama in English.* Methuen 1925

Lever, J.W. *The Elizabethan Love Sonnets,* University Paperbacks 1968

Lewalski, Barbara, *Writing Women in Jacobean Court,* Harvard University Press, 1994

Lewis, C. S. (1990) [1944]. *Poetry and Prose in the Sixteenth Century.* Oxford: Clarendon Press

Limon, Jerzy, *Dangerous Matters 1623-1624* Cambridge University Press 1986

Loades, David, *The Cecils,* National Archives 2007

Loewenstein, J. *Ben Jonson & Possessive Authorship,* Cambridge University Press

Looney, J. Thomas. *Shakespeare Identified in Edward De Vere,* the Seventeenth Earl of Oxford. New York: Frederick A. Stokes 1920

Love, Harold. *Attributing Authorship: An Introduction.* Cambridge University Press. 2002

Lovell, Mary S. *Bess of Hardwick,* Little Brown 2005

Lyly, J. *Euphues. The Anatomy of Wit* Constable & Co reprint 1919

Lubbock, Peter, *The Halls of the Livery Companies of the City of London,* Morrison and Gibb 1981

M

Maclean, Hugh *Ben Jonson and the Cavalier Poets* Norton & Co 1974

MacMillin S. S.B. MacLean, *The Queen's Men and their Plays*, Cambridge University Press 2008

Malim, Richard, ed. Great Oxford: *Essays on the Life and Work of Edward de Vere, 17th Earl of Oxford, 1550–1604*.London: Parapress, 2004.

Malone, Edmund, *Life of Shakespeare. In Works of Shakespeare* (1821), Volume II

Massie, Allan, *The Royal Stuarts*, Jonathan Cape 2010

May, Steven W. *Tudor Aristocrats and the Mythical "Stigma of Print"* Renaissance Papers, 1980

The Poems of Edward De Vere, Seventeenth Earl of Oxford and of Robert Devereux, Second Earl of Essex. Studies in Philology University of North Carolina Press 1980. *The Elizabethan Courtier Poets: The Poems and Their Contexts.* University of Missouri Press. 2004. *Early Courtier Verse: Oxford, Dyer, and Gascoigne* 2007

Mazzola, Elizabeth. *Favorite Sons: The Politics and Poetics of the Sidney Family.* New York: Palgrave Macmillan, 2003

McCrea, Scott, *The Case for Shakespeare: The End of the Authorship Question.* Greenwood Publishing Group 2005

McFarlane K.B. *The Nobility of the later Medieval England* Oxford University Press 1973

Mc Grath, Patrick, *Papists and Puritans under Elizabeth I*, Blandford Press, 1967

McMichael, George L.; Glenn, Edgar M. (1962). *Shakespeare and His Rivals: A Casebook on the Authorship Controversy.* Odyssey Press

Michell, John, *Who wrote Shakespeare?* Thames and Hudson 1996

Milford, Humphrey *Brooke's Romeo and Juliet* Chatto and Windus 1957

Milward, Peter, *Religious Controversies of the Elizabethan Age,* University of Nebraska Press 1977 *Religious Controversies of the Jacobean Age.* The Scholar Press. 1978

Mortimer, Ian, *The Fears of Henry IV*, Jonathan Cape 2007

Muchow Towers, S. *Control of Religious Printing, early Stuart England*, Boydell Press 2003

Muir, Kenneth, *The Sources of Shakespeare's Plays.* London: Methuen & Co. 1977

Mulryne, J.R., *Shakespeare, Marlowe, Jonson: new directions in biography*, Ashgate Publishing, *Thomas Kyd - The Spanish Tragedy* A & C Black

Munro, Lucy, *Children of the Queen's Revels*, Cambridge University Press, 2011

Myers R. & Harris M. *Censorship and the Control of Print*, St Paul's Biographies 1992

N

Nelson, Alan H. *Monstrous Adversary: The Life of Edward de Vere, 17th Earl of Oxford*. Liverpool University Press 2004

Neile, J.E. *Elizabeth I and her Parliaments 1509-1660* Jonathan Cape 1957

Nicholl, Charles, *The Lodger on Silver Street*, Allen Lane 2007. *The Reckoning: The Murder of Christopher Marlowe*. Jonathan Cape 1992 *A Cup of News. Life of Thomas Nashe*, Routledge Keegan Paul 1984

Nicoll, A. & J. *Holinshed's Chronicle in Shakespeare's plays*, Dent 1975

Niederkorn, William S. *A Historic Whodunit: If Shakespeare Didn't, Who Did?* The New York Times 2001

Nicholls, John, *Progresses, Processions and Festivities of James I* (reprint) Lightening Source UK

Nicholson, Brinsley, *Ben Jonson: Three plays*, Fisher Unwin X1X

Nicolson, Adam, *Earls of Paradise: England & the Dream of Perfection*. Harper Press 2008

O

O'Connor, E.M. *An Index to the works of Shaksper*, Keegan Paul Trench 1887

O'Farrell, Brian, *Shakespeare's Patron*, Continuum International Publishing Group 2011

Ogburn, Charlton and Dorothy *This Star of England*. New York: Coward-McCann 1952. *The Mysterious William Shakespeare: The Man Behind the Mask*. New York: Dodd, Mead & Co. 1984

Orgel, Stephen *Christopher Marlowe: Complete Poems*, Penguin Books 1971

P

Painter, Sidney, *William Marshal*, Baltimore John Hopkins Press 1933

Painter, William, *The Palace of Pleasure,* reprint

Parfitt, George, *Ben Jonson*, J. M. Dent 1976, *Ben Jonson, Complete Poems*, Penguin Books 1988

Patterson, Annabelle, *Censorship and Interpretation*, University of Wisconsin 1984

Peck, Linda Levy *The Mental World of the Jacobean Court*, Cambridge University Press 1991 *Court Patronage and Corruption in Early Stuart England,* Unwin Hyman, 1990 Northampton, *Patronage and Policy at the Court of James I*. Allen & Unwin, 1982. Pollard, A.J. *Warwick the Kingmaker*, Continuum, 2007

Pembry, E.D. *Christopher Marlowe, Complete Plays and Poems* J. M. Dent 1976

Percy, Lord Eustace, *Privy Council under the Tudors*, Blackwell 1907

Petter C.G. *Eastward Ho: Jonson, Chapman and Marston*, A & C Black 1993

Pickard, Eliza, *Elizabeth's London*, Weidenfeld & Nicholson 2004

Plowden, Alison, *Tudor Women - Queens and Commoners*, Weidenfeld and Nicholson 2007. *Young Elizabeth* 1971. *Danger to Elizabeth* 1973. *The House of Tudor* 1976. *Marriage with My Kingdom: The Courtships of Queen Elizabeth I* 1977. *Two Queens in One Isle: The Deadly Relationship of Elizabeth I and Mary Queen of Scots* 1984. *Lady Jane Grey: Nine Days Queen* 1985. *The Elizabethan Secret Service* 1991

Pointon, A.J. *The Man who was never Shakespeare*, Parapress 2011

Pollard, Alfred W. *Shakespeare's Folios and Quartos*, Cooper Square Publishing N.Y. 1970

Porter, Stephen, *Shakespeare's London*, Amberley Publishing 2009

Powell, Neil, *Fulke Greville Selected Poems*, Carcanet Press 1990

Pressly, William L. *The Ashbourne Portrait of Shakespeare: Through the Looking Glass.* Shakespeare Quarterly (Folger Shakespeare Library) (1993) 54–72, 54.

Preston J. Yeandle L. *English Handwriting 1400-1650*, Pegasus 1999

Price, Diana *Shakespeare's Unorthodox Biography*, Greenwood Press 2001

Pritchard R.B. *Lady Mary Wroth, Poems*, Keele University Press 1996

Prothero, G. W. *Constitutional Documents Elizabeth and James I, 1913* Oxford University Press

R

Rebholz, Ronald, *The Life of Fulke Greville*, Oxford University Press 1971

Rendall, Gerald H. *Shakespeare Sonnets and Edward de Vere.* London: John Murray 1930

Riggs, David, *Ben Jonson: a life.* Harvard University Press 1989. *The World of Christopher Marlowe*, Faber and Faber 2004

Roberts, Josephine, *The poems of Lady Wroth*, Louisiana State University 1992

Robertson Davies, W. *Shakespeare's Boy Actors* 1939

Robertson, J.M. *Shakespeare and Chapman* T. Fisher Unwin 1917. *Study of the Shakespeare Canon*, Greenwood Press 1970 *Elizabethan Literature*, Williams and Norgate 1914

Roe, John, *The Poems*, University Press Cambridge 1992

Roe, Richard Paul, *Shakespeare's Guide to Italy*, Harpers Perennial 2011

Rose, H. J. *A Handbook of Latin Literature* 1996 Methuen & Co

Rostenberg, Leona, *The Minority Press & English Crown 1558*, Niewkoop Hague, 1971

Rosenberg, Eleanor, *Leicester Patron of Letters,* Columbia University Press 1955

Rothery, Guy, *Concise Encyclopaedia of Heraldry,* Studio Editions 1915

Rowse A.L. *Queen Elizabeth and Her Subjects (*with **G. B. Harrison***), London:* Allen & Unwin, 1935. *The England of Elizabeth: the Structure of Society.* London: Macmillan, 1950. *An Elizabethan Garland,* London: Macmillan, 1953. *The Expansion of Elizabethan England,* London: Macmillan, 1955. *William Shakespeare: a Biography,* London: Macmillan, 1963. *Christopher Marlowe: a biography,* London: Macmillan, 1964. *Shakespeare's Sonnets,* London: Macmillan, 1964. *Shakespeare's Southampton: Patron of Virginia,* London: Macmillan, 1965. *The Elizabethan Renaissance: the Life of Society,* London: Macmillan, 1971Shakespeare The Man,* London: Macmillan, 1973. *Simon Forman: Sex and Society in Shakespeare's Age,* London: Weidenfeld & Nicolson, 1974. *Shakespeare the Elizabethan,* London: Weidenfeld & Nicholson, 1977. *Shakespeare's Globe: his Intellectual and Moral Outlook,* London: Weidenfeld & Nicolson, 1981. *Shakespeare's Characters: a Complete Guide,* London: Methuen, 1984. *Reflections on the Puritan Revolution,* London: Methuen, 1986

Royle, Trevor, *The Road to Bosworth Field,* Little Brown 2009

Rubinstein, William D., *Who wrote Shakespeare's plays,* Amberley Publishing 2012

Russell, Conrad, *The Crisis of Parliaments 1509-*1660 Oxford University Press 1992

S

Shakespeare's England various contributors Volumes 1 & 2 Oxford University Press 192)

Saccio, Peter, *Shakespeare's English Kings,* Oxford University Press 1977

Saintsbury, George, *Shorter Elizabethan Novels,* J. M. Dent& Sons 1953. *A History of Elizabethan Literature* Macmillan & Co 1893

Scard, Margaret, *Tudor Survivor: William Paulet,* History Press 2011

Schelling, Felix, *Ben Jonson's Plays,* J. M. Dent 1967

Schoenbaum, S. (1991). *Shakespeare's Lives* (2nd ed.). Oxford University Press 1991. *Internal Evidence and Elizabethan Dramatic Authorship,* Edward Arnold Publishers Ltd 1966

Schoone-Jongen, Terence G. (2008). *Shakespeare's Companies: William Shakespeare's Early Career and the Acting Companies, 1577–1594.* Ashgate Publishing 2008. *Studies in Performance and Early Modern Drama.* Ashgate Publishing.

Schrickx, Dr W. *Shakespeare's Early Contemporaries,* AMS Press Inc NY 1972

Scott, A.F. *The Stuart Age Commentaries,* Scott & Finlay 1974

Seward, Desmond, *The Wars of the Roses,* Constable & Co 1995

Shahan, John M. and Waugh, Alexander, *Shakespeare Beyond Doubt? -- Exposing an Industry in Denial* – Llumina Press 2013

Shapiro, James, *Contested Will: Who Wrote Shakespeare?* UK edition: Faber and Faber 2010

Sheavyn, Phoebe, *The Literary Profession in the Elizabethan Age, Manchester University Press 1067*

Shepherd, Geoffrey, *Sir Philip Sidney,* Manchester University Press 1973

Sidney, Philip, *The Sidneys of Penshurst* (1901) S. H. Bousfield & Co Ltd

Smeaton, Oliphant, *Francis Bacon's Essays,* J.M. Dent 1975

Smith, Emma, *The Shakespeare Authorship Debate Revisited.* Literature Compass Blackwell Publishing 2008

Sobran, Joseph, *Alias Shakespeare: Solving the Greatest Literary Mystery of All Time.* New York: Simon and Schuster 1997

Somerset, Anne, *Elizabeth I,* St. Martin's Press 1992, *Unnatural Murder: Poison at the Court of James I,* Weidenfeld & Nicolson 1997, *Ladies in Waiting: From the Tudors to the Present Day,* Sterling Publishing 2005

Southern, Richard. *The Staging of Plays Before Shakespeare.* London: Faber. 1973

Southworth, John, *Fools and Jesters at the English Court,* Sutton Publishing 1998

Spark Notes, *No Fear Shakespeare's Sonnets,* Spark Notes, 2004

Steane, J. B. *Thomas Nashe: The Unfortunate Traveller,* Penguin 1985

Stern, Virginia F., *Gabriel Harvey,* Oxford University Press 1979

Stewart, Alan, *The Cradle King, A life of James VI & I,* Chatto & Windus, 2003. *Philip Sidney. A Double Life,* Chatto & Windus 2000

Stokes, F.G. *A Shakespeare Dictionary,* George G. Harrap & Co 1924

Stone, Lawrence, *The Crisis of the Aristocracy 1558-1641,* Oxford University Press 1985

T

Tanner, J.R. *Tudor Constitutional Documents 14-85-1603* Cambridge University Press 1951

Tames, Richard, *Shakespeare's London,* Thames and Hudson 2009

Taylor, Walt, *English Sonnets,* Longman Green & Co 1947

Theobald, B. G. *Enter Francis Bacon,* Cecil Palmer 1932

Thomas, David, *Shakespeare in the Public Records,* HMSO 1985

Thomson, Peter, *Shakespeare's Professional Career,* Cambridge University Press, 1992. *Shakespeare's Theatre,* Routledge & Keegan Paul 1992

Thomson, Elizabeth, *The Chamberlain's Letters.* G.P. Putnam's Sons 1965

Tillyard, E. M, *Shakespeare's History Plays* 1944

Traversi, Derek, *Shakespeare, The Roman Plays,* Hollis & Carter 1964

Trevelyan, G. M., *England Under the Stuarts,* Methuen & Co 1954

Trussler, Simon, *The Spanish Tragedy by T. Kyd* , Nick Hern Books 1997

Tucker, Brooke, *Authorship of King Henry VI,* Yale University Press, 1912 *The Apocryphal Shakespeare* (1908), *English Drama 1580-1642* D.C. Heath & Co, Boston 1933 *The Tudor Drama: A History of English National Drama to the Retirement of Shakespeare,* Houghton Mifflin Company 1911 *The Authorship of the Second and Third Parts of King Henry VI, Shakespeare's Plutarch,* 1909 *The Life of Marlowe and the Tragedy of Dido,* Queen of Carthage 1930.*Essays on Shakespeare* Oxford University Press 1948

Tweedie, David, *David Rizzio and Mary Queen of Scots* Sutton Publishing 2007

V

Varlow, Sally, *The Lady Penelope (Devereaux),* Andre Deutsch 2007

Vaughan, Alden T. 2008 *"William Strachey's "True Reportory" and Shakespeare: A Closer Look at the Evidence".* Shakespeare Quarterly 2008, The Johns Hopkins University Press.

Velz, John W. (2006), "Shakespeare and the Geneva Bible: The Circumstances", Edited by **Kozuka, Takashi; Mulryne, J. R.** University of Warwick, UK (Burlington, VT: Ashgate, 2006)

Vickers, Brian, (2004). *Shakespeare, Co-Author: A Historical Study of Five Collaborative Plays.* Oxford University Press.

W

Wadsworth, Frank (1958). *The Poacher from Stratford: A Partial Account of the Controversy over the Authorship of Shakespeare's Plays.* Berkeley: University of California Press

Wait R.J.C. *The Background to Shakespeare's Sonnets,* Chatto and Windus 1972

Warton, Thomas, *Warton's History of English Poetry, 11th - 117th C,* Ward, Lock & Co. Reprint 1798

Waugh, Arthur, *The Poems of George Herbert,* Henry Frowde, Oxford University Press 1907

Weir, Alison, *Britain's Royal Families* The Bodley Head UK 1989, Pimlico, 1989, *The Princes in the Tower 1992, Lancaster and York – The Wars of the Roses 1995, Children of England: The Heirs of King Henry VIII 1996, Elizabeth the Queen 1998 Mary, Queen of Scots and the Murder of Lord Darnley 2003 Katherine Swynford: The Story of John of Gaunt and his Scandalous Duchess 2007, Mary Boleyn: The Mistress of Kings 2011 Elizabeth of York – A Tudor Queen and Her World 2013*

Bibliography

Wells, Robin, Headlam, *Shakespeare's humanism,* Cambridge University Press, 2005

Wells, Stanley, *English Drama,* Oxford University Press, 1975 *Re-Editing Shakespeare for the Modern Reader* (1984). *The Oxford Dictionary of Shakespeare* 1998 *Shakespeare in the Theatre: An Anthology of Criticism* (2000). *Shakespeare: The Poet and his Plays* 2001.The Oxford Shakespeare: *King Lear* 2001. *Shakespeare For All Time* 2002. *Shakespeare & Co.* 2006.

Westfall, Suzanne R. *Patrons and Performance,* Clarendon Press Oxford, 1990

Whalen, Richard, *Shakespeare: Who Was He? The Oxford Challenge to the Bard of Avon.* Westport, Ct.

Whittemore, Hank, *The Monument: "Shake-Speares Sonnets" by Edward de Vere, 17th Earl of Oxford.* Meadow Geese Press. *Shakespeare's Son and His Sonnets.* Martin and Lawrence Press

Wilders, John, *The Lost Garden: Shakespeare's History Plays* Macmillan 1982

Williams C. H. *The Tudor Despotism,* Thomas Nelson & Sons 1928

Williams, Robin P. *Sweet Swan of Avon: Did a Woman Write Shakespeare?* Wilton Circle Press U.S.A. 2002

Williamson, Aubrey, *The Mystery of the Princes,* Amberley Publishing 2010

Willoughby, E. B. *A Printer of the First Folio,* Philip Allan & Co. *The Printing of the First Folio,* Oxford University Press 1932

Wilson, A.N. *The Elizabethans,* Hutchinson 2011

Wilson, David, H. *King James VI & I,* Jonathan Cape, 1963

Wingfield -Strafford, E. *Charles, King of England,* Hollis & Carter 1949

Wilson, Ian, *Shakespeare: The Evidence,* St. Martin's Press 1999. (Headline Book Publishing 1993)

Woudhuysen, H.R. *The Penguin Verse of the Renaissance,* Penguin Books 1993

Wraight, A.D., *In Search of Christopher Marlowe* 1965 *The Real Christopher Marlowe, an open letter to Charles Nicholl* 1992 *Christopher Marlowe and Edward Alleyn* 1993 *The Story that the Sonnets Tell* Adam Hart 1994 *Shakespeare: New Evidence* Adam Hart 1993

Y

Yates, Frances A. *John Florio* Cambridge University Press 1934. *Giordano Bruno: Hermetic Tradition,* Routledge & Keegan Paul 1971. *The Rosicrucian Enlightenment* Routledge Keegan Paul 1972

Yeowell, James, *The Poetical works of Sir Thomas Wyatt,* George Bell 1894

Z

Zurcher, Andrew, *Shakespeare and the Law,* The Arden Shakespeare Methuen 2010
The Arden Second Series edited by Una Ellis-Fermor (1946–58); Harold F.
  Brooks (1952–82), Harold Jenkins (1958–82) and Brian Morris (1975–82).
Macbeth, ed. by **Kenneth Muir** (1951) *King John,* ed. by **E. A. J. Honigsmann**
  (1954) *Cymbeline,* ed. by **J. M. Nosworthy** (1955) *All's Well That Ends Well,*
  ed. by **G. K. Hunter** (1959) *The Comedy of Errors,* ed. by **R. A. Foakes** (1962)
  Measure for Measure, ed. by **J. W. Lever** (1965) *A Midsummer Night's Dream,*
  ed. by **Harold F. Brooks** (1979) *King Henry IV, Part 2,* ed. by **A. R.
  Humphreys** (1981)
Arden series of Plays *King Henry V,* ed. by **T. W. Craik** (1995) *Antony and
  Cleopatra,* ed. by **John Wilders** (1995) *Titus Andronicus,* ed. by **Jonathan Bate**
  (1995) *Othello,* ed. by **E. A. J. Honigmann** (1996) *King Lear,* ed. by **R. A.
  Foakes** (1997) *Troilus and Cressida,* ed. by **David Bevington** (1998) *Love's
  Labour's Lost,* ed. by **H. R. Woudhuysen** (1998) *Julius Caesar,* ed. by **David
  Daniell** (1998) *King Henry VI,* Part 2, ed. by **Ronald Knowles** (1999) *The
  Merry Wives of Windsor,* ed. by **Giorgio Melchiori** (1999) *The Tempest,* ed. by
  Virginia Mason Vaughan and **Alden T. Vaughan** (1999) *King Henry VI, Part
  1,* ed. by **Edward Burns** (2000) *King Henry VIII,* ed. by **Gordon McMullan**
  (2000) *King Henry VI, Part 3,* ed. by **John D. Cox** and **Eric Rasmussen** (2001)
  King Richard II, ed. by **Charles R. Forker** (2002) *King Henry IV, Part 1,* ed. by
  David Scott Kastan (2002) *The Two Gentlemen of Verona,* ed. by **William C.
  Carroll** (2004) *Much Ado About Nothing,* ed. by **Claire McEachern** (2005)
  Hamlet: The Text of 1604, ed. by **Ann Thompson** and **Neil Taylor** (2006)
  As You Like It, ed. by **Juliet Dusinberre** (2006) *Hamlet: The Texts of 1603 and
  1623,* ed. by **Ann Thompson** and **Neil Taylor** (2007) *Shakespeare's Poems,*
  ed. by **Katherine Duncan-Jones** and **H. R. Woudhuysen** (2007) *Twelfth
  Night, ed.* by **Keir Elam** (2008) *Timon of Athens,* ed. by **Anthony B. Dawson**
  and **Gretchen E. Minton** (2008) *King Richard III,* ed. by **James R. Siemon**
  (2009) *The Taming of the Shrew,* ed. by **Barbara Hodgdon** (2010) *The Winter's
  Tale,* ed. by **John Pitcher** (2010) *The Merchant of Venice,* ed. by **John Drakakis**
  (2011) *The Tempest,* revised edition, ed. by **Virginia Mason Vaughan** and
  Alden T. Vaughan (2011) *Romeo and Juliet,* ed. by **René Weis** (2012)
  Coriolanus, ed. by **Peter Holland** (2013)

INDEX

Index

Notes

Made in the USA
Lexington, KY
17 April 2016